USER'S GUIDE

Lotus 1·2·3

RELEASE 4

Spreadsheet for Windows

Contents

How to Use This Book

The *User's Guide* describes how to use Lotus® 1-2-3® Release 4 for Windows™. It includes basic concepts for most 1-2-3 features and step-by-step procedures for using 1-2-3. It also contains examples, tips, shortcuts using SmartIcons™, and illustrations of dialog boxes and worksheets.

Who should read this book

The *User's Guide* is for both new and experienced spreadsheet users. It contains basic and advanced information about using 1-2-3. If you're already familiar with a previous release of 1-2-3, reading the *User's Guide* is a good way to review 1-2-3 basics and learn how to use new commands and features specific to 1-2-3 Release 4.

Before reading the *User's Guide*, you should be familiar with basic Windows concepts and techniques. Chapter 3 in this book describes some common tasks, such as using the mouse and working with windows. Chapter 4 describes how to use menus and dialog boxes. For more information, refer to your Windows documentation. If you have Windows 3.1, you can also use the Windows 3.1 online tutorial.

Using this book with Help

The *User's Guide* and online Help complement each other. Help documents every 1-2-3 feature, @function, and macro. It provides step-by-step descriptions, examples, and some conceptual information.

The *User's Guide* has step-by-step descriptions of most 1-2-3 tasks along with illustrations, examples, and basic concepts. For example, though the *User's Guide* doesn't describe individual @functions or macros, it's your primary source of information about how to enter and work with @functions and macros. Throughout the *User's Guide* and in the index, cross-references to Help tell you where to look for information about commands or features not described in the book.

Organization

The *User's Guide* has eight parts.

- Part I "Getting Started" contains information about 1-2-3 system requirements and describes how to install, start, and end 1-2-3. It explains how to work with 1-2-3 windows, commands, and dialog boxes, and lists keyboard shortcuts and function keys.

- Part II "Using Worksheets" describes how to use worksheets to enter, edit, style, print, and protect data. It also describes how to calculate with formulas and @functions.

- Part III "Using Charts" describes how to create, work with, and customize charts. It includes pictures and descriptions of all 1-2-3 chart types.

- Part IV "Using Graphics" tells you how to create and work with drawn objects, such as arrows, shapes, text blocks, and pictures you paste into a 1-2-3 worksheet.

- Part V "Analyzing Data" describes how to analyze the formulas and links in your worksheets; and how to perform statistical analysis, such as a frequency distribution. It also describes several ways to do what-if analysis, including using the Version Manager to create and share scenarios.

- Part VI "Working with Databases" describes working with 1-2-3 database tables and external database tables, and how to use criteria and query tables.

- Part VII "Automating and Customizing 1-2-3" describes how to customize SmartIcons and automate your work with macros. It also describes ways to transfer data between 1-2-3 and other Windows applications via electronic mail, DDE, and OLE.

- Part VIII "Appendixes" contains three appendixes. The first appendix describes how to use the Lotus Multibyte Character Set (LMBCS) and lists the LMBCS codes. The second explains how to use memory efficiently with 1-2-3. The third lists the formulas 1-2-3 uses for certain @functions.

Conventions used in this book

The *User's Guide* uses the following conventions:

? Help   introduces a cross-reference to Help along with a topic you can search for in Help to find additional information. Look on the inside front cover of this book for a description of how to use Help.

This is an example of a tip.   Tips with additional information appear in italic in the margin.

SmartIcons next to a step in a procedure indicate that you can click the icon in place of the command in that step. If an icon in the documentation doesn't appear in your set of SmartIcons, you can add it using Tools SmartIcons. For more information, see Chapter 25.

 Shortcut   introduces additional ways of using SmartIcons to simplify your work.

Note   introduces additional technical information about a command or procedure.

Caution   introduces information essential to the safety of your data and software.

The following conventions indicate mouse and keyboard instructions in a procedure:

Mouse   introduces a procedure using the mouse. When a procedure says to press a mouse button, use the left mouse button unless you specified left-handed use of the mouse in the Windows Control Panel. For more information, see your Windows documentation.

Keyboard   introduces a procedure using the keyboard.

The following are conventions for function keys, key names, and information you type:

- Function keys appear in small capitals and are identified by the 1-2-3 key name. For example, F1 (HELP).

- Key names separated by a + (plus sign) indicate that you hold down the first key, press the second key, and then release both keys. For example, CTRL+Z.

- Key names separated by a space indicate that you press the first key and release it, and then press the second key and release it. For example, END HOME.

- Information that you type appears in a different typeface. For example, Operating Expenses.

- Variables you must supply are in an italic font. For example, *filename*.

- [ ] (brackets) enclose optional arguments in @functions and macro commands; for example, [*password*]. When you type an optional argument, don't include the brackets.

- Words in **bold** are followed by a definition. For example, the **cell pointer** is the highlight indicating the current cell.

Roadmap for using the documentation

How you use the 1-2-3 documentation depends on your level of experience with 1-2-3. The roadmap below suggests reading paths for new and experienced 1-2-3 users.

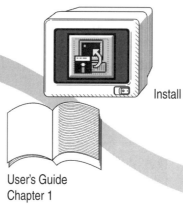

Install

User's Guide
Chapter 1

Guided Tour

New
1-2-3 User

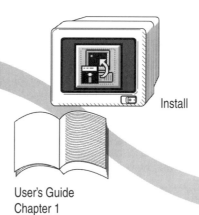

Install

User's Guide
Chapter 1

Guided Tour

Experienced
1-2-3 User

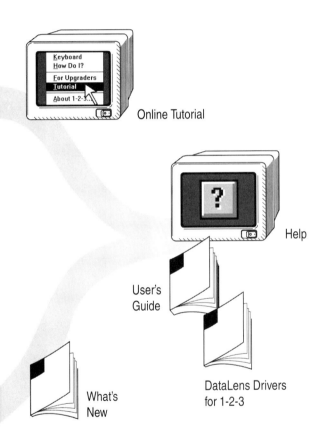

Online Tutorial

Help

User's
Guide

DataLens Drivers
for 1-2-3

What's
New

- The *User's Guide* provides basic concepts and step-by-step procedures for the most common 1-2-3 tasks, and directs you to Help for information not in the *User's Guide*.

- *What's New* tells experienced 1-2-3 users what's new or different in 1-2-3. *What's New* also discusses sharing files and how to use macros created in previous 1-2-3 releases.

- Online Help documents every 1-2-3 feature, menu command, and dialog box. Help is the primary source for detailed information about @functions and macros.

- The online Guided Tour gives you a quick overview of the work area including using the mouse, status bar, and SmartIcons. The Guided Tour also introduces hot features, such as charting, drawing, databases, and macros.

- The online Tutorial provides interactive lessons that teach you how to use the major features of 1-2-3.

- *DataLens Drivers for 1-2-3* describes the drivers included with 1-2-3 that let you work with external databases without leaving 1-2-3.

Part I
Getting Started

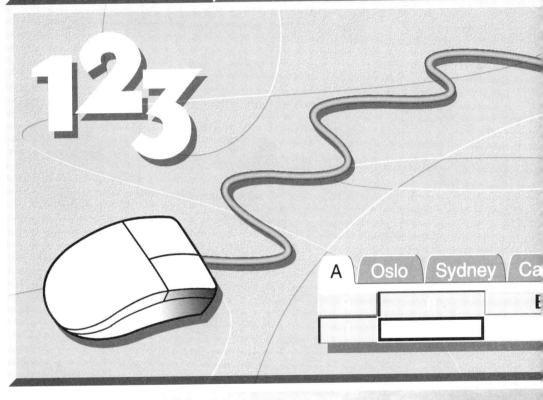

1 Before You Begin

Welcome to Lotus 1-2-3 Release 4 for Windows. This chapter lists what's in your 1-2-3 package and the system requirements for using 1-2-3. It also describes how to install 1-2-3 for the first time, and how to return to Install later to add optional features or Help files you didn't install the first time.

Checking your package

This section lists the disks and documentation in your package. Check the contents of your package against these lists. If your package isn't complete, contact your computer dealer or supplier.

Disks

Your package contains either one set of high-density 5.25" disks or one set of high-density 3.5" disks.

Documentation

The following list describes the 1-2-3 documentation.

- The *User's Guide* is a task-oriented book that explains basic concepts, gives you step-by-step procedures for the most common 1-2-3 tasks, and tells you where to look in online Help for information not in the *User's Guide*.

- *What's New* tells experienced 1-2-3 users what's new or different in 1-2-3 Release 4 for Windows. It also explains how to share files and use macros created in previous releases of 1-2-3.

- *DataLens Drivers for 1-2-3* describes how to use 1-2-3 with the DataLens® drivers available for Paradox®, dBASE IV®, SQL Server, Informix®, and IBM® Database Manager.

- The *Network Administrator's Guide* describes how to install 1-2-3 on a network. You can also look in Install Help for information about installing 1-2-3 on a server and setting up user directories.

- Online Help documents every 1-2-3 feature, menu command, and dialog box. Help is the primary source for detailed information about @functions and macros. See the inside front cover of this book to find out how to get Help, and choose Help Using Help from the 1-2-3 menu to learn more about Help's features.

- The online Tutorial provides hands-on lessons for using 1-2-3. If you choose to install the Tutorial, it appears in the Help pull-down menu. To start the Tutorial, choose Help Tutorial.

- The online Guided Tour explores basic concepts and new or enhanced features, such as charting, drawing, macros, working with databases, auditing your worksheets, and managing scenarios. The Tour takes about 30 minutes to complete. To start the tour, double-click the Guided Tour icon in the Lotus Applications window, or the group window that contains 1-2-3. The Guided Tour requires Windows 3.1.

  Note   You must use a mouse and a VGA monitor or higher to view the Tour.

- The READ.ME file contains information received after the documentation was printed. For more information, see "Reading product updates" on page 7.

- The Adobe Type Manager® (ATM®) *Quick Installation Card* describes how to install ATM version 2.5.

Other contents

Other contents of your 1-2-3 package are the Customer Assurance Plan, the Software Agreement, the Warranty Registration Card, and your Lotus PROMPT® ID number.

System requirements

This section describes what you need to use 1-2-3 on a stand-alone computer or network node. To run 1-2-3, you need

- An 80286, 80386, or 80486-based computer certified for use with Microsoft® Windows 3.0 or later

- A color or grayscale EGA, VGA, or IBM 8514 monitor

  If your computer displays VGA colors in grayscales, use Windows Setup to choose the appropriate color driver.

- A mouse (not required but strongly recommended)

  You must use the mouse to select individual chart elements, collections, or multiple drawn objects. You also need the mouse to begin drawing, moving, or sizing a drawn object; and to use SmartIcons, the status bar, and worksheet tabs.

- Microsoft Windows 3.0 or later; the Guided Tour requires Windows 3.1

- DOS Version 3.30 or later

- 4 megabytes (MB) of random access memory (RAM); use on an 80286-based computer may require more RAM

  A 2MB or more swap file is recommended in 386 enhanced mode.

- A maximum of 13MB of available disk space on a stand-alone computer; 7.5MB or more on a laptop; 16MB on a network server; and 150K (kilobytes) on a network node

  The Guided Tour requires Windows 3.1 and 3.3MB of additional disk space.

Installing 1-2-3

If you're installing 1-2-3 on

- A stand-alone computer or a laptop computer, read "Installing 1-2-3 on a stand-alone computer" on the next page.

- A network node, read "Installing 1-2-3 on a network node," on page 5.

- A network server, read the *Network Administrator's Guide*.

  Note   For more information about installing when you're upgrading to 1-2-3 Release 4, see Chapter 1 of *What's New*.

Installing 1-2-3 on a stand-alone computer

Before you can use 1-2-3, you must use the 1-2-3 Install program to transfer the program files to your hard disk. To install 1-2-3 for the first time or to return to Install later to add optional features or Help files you didn't install the first time, you must use the installation disks in your 1-2-3 package.

The directions that follow assume you're starting Install from a high-density A drive. If you start Install from a different drive, substitute the letter of that drive in the installation procedure. You must start Install from Windows 3.0 or later running with DOS version 3.30 or later.

To install on a stand-alone computer

1. Insert the Install disk in drive A and close the drive door.
2. Open the Windows Program Manager.
3. Choose File Run.
4. Type a:install in the Command Line text box.
5. Choose OK.

   Install displays an introductory screen.

6. Choose OK to start Install.

The Install program displays a series of dialog boxes that prompt you for information about what to install and how to install it. For example, an Install dialog box asks you to select the type of installation you want: Default Install, Customized Install, or Install for laptops.

To get Help while installing 1-2-3

While you're installing 1-2-3, you can get Help about the options in each Install dialog box.

1. Choose Help:

   Mouse   Click the Help button.

   Keyboard   Press TAB to move the highlight to the Help button and press ENTER.

Install displays information about the options in the dialog box you're currently using.

Backing up your disks

After installing 1-2-3, you may want to back up your 1-2-3 program disks. The disks you use for the backup must be the same size as your install disks; you can't back up 5.25" disks on 3.5" disks, or 3.5" disks on 5.25" disks. Also, if you're backing up on 5.25" disks, the backup disks must be high density.

To back up your disks, use the Disk Copy Disk command (Windows 3.1) or the Disk Copy Diskette command (Windows 3.0) in the Windows File Manager. See your Windows documentation for information.

Installing 1-2-3 on a network node

Before you can use 1-2-3, you must use the 1-2-3 Install program. To install 1-2-3 for the first time or to return to Install later to add optional features or Help files you didn't install the first time, you must connect to the 1-2-3 directory on your server. If you don't know how to connect to the 1-2-3 directory, ask your network administrator. You must start Install from Windows 3.0 or later running with DOS version 3.30 or later.

To install on a network node

1. Open the Windows Program Manager.
2. Choose File Run.
3. Type *x*:*path*\install in the Command Line text box.

    x:*path* is the drive letter and path for the 1-2-3 directory on your server. For example, type n:\123r4w\install to start Install from a 1-2-3 directory named \123R4W on drive N.
4. Choose OK.

    Install displays an introductory screen.
5. Choose OK to start Install.

The Install program displays a series of dialog boxes that prompt you for information about what to install and how to install it. For example, an Install dialog box asks you to select the type of installation you want: Default Install or Customized Install.

To get Help while installing 1-2-3

While you're installing 1-2-3, you can get Help about the options in each Install dialog box.

1. Choose Help:

   Mouse   Click the Help button.

   Keyboard   Press TAB to move the highlight to the Help button and press ENTER.

   Install displays information about the options in the dialog box you're currently using.

Returning to Install

When you install 1-2-3, you have the option of not installing optional features and Help files. You can install them later by running Customized Install. To install optional features and Help files, you must use the Install disks that came in your 1-2-3 package.

You can also use Install to install a different country driver or sort order. For more information, start Install as described below and choose Help in the Install main menu.

To return to Install

1. Start Windows and open the Windows Program Manager.

2. Open the Lotus Applications window (or the group window that contains 1-2-3).

3. Select the 1-2-3 Install program icon:

1-2-3 Install

   Mouse   Double-click the icon.

   Keyboard   Move the highlight to the icon with ↑, ↓, →, ←; and press ENTER.

   Install displays an introductory screen.

4. Choose OK to start Install.

5. Choose Install 1-2-3.

6. Choose Customized Install.

   The Install Program displays the Customized Install dialog box.

Choose Help for information about the options in any Install dialog box.

7. Choose the Select button for the type of options you want to install.

   The Install Program displays a dialog box with check boxes for optional features. For example, if you choose the Select button for Help and Sample Files, you see a dialog box that allows you to select the Help and sample files you want to install.

8. Select the check boxes for the options you want, then choose OK.

9. When you finish installing optional features, exit Install.

Reading product updates

The Install program copies the 1-2-3 READ.ME file to your 1-2-3 directory. This file contains notes for upgraders and network administrators, and information received after the documentation was printed.

You can open the READ.ME file from inside the Install program by choosing the View Product Updates button in the Install main menu. You can also open the READ.ME file at any time after installation by clicking the View Product Updates icon in the Lotus Applications window (or the group window that contains 1-2-3).

2 Starting and Ending 1-2-3

1-2-3 combines powerful spreadsheet and presentation features in an easy-to-use graphical environment. This chapter introduces 1-2-3 and describes how to start 1-2-3, what you see when you start, and how to end a 1-2-3 session.

[?] **Help**   Use online Help for quick answers to your questions about 1-2-3. Help provides information about all menu commands, dialog boxes, procedures, and messages. See the inside front cover of this book to find out how to get Help. Choose Help Using Help from the 1-2-3 menu to learn more about Help's features.

What is 1-2-3?

1-2-3 Release 4 is an electronic spreadsheet for managing and presenting data in the Microsoft Windows environment. 1-2-3 offers advanced spreadsheet, charting, drawing, scenario, and database features. It uses the Windows graphical interface, while maintaining compatibility with other releases of 1-2-3.

1-2-3 provides an easy-to-use interface including customizable SmartIcons, an @Function menu, a worksheet navigator, tabs for named worksheets, and an interactive status bar. It also includes drag-and-drop moving and copying of data, improved database querying, a spelling checker, scenario and auditing tools, and more than 200 @functions and macro commands.

Starting 1-2-3

Before starting 1-2-3, you must install it as described in Chapter 1.

To start 1-2-3

1. Start Windows.

2. Open the Windows Program Manager.

3. Open the Lotus Applications window (or the group window that contains 1-2-3).

4. Select the 1-2-3 for Windows application icon (or the name assigned):

   Mouse   Double-click the icon.

   Keyboard   Move the highlight to the icon with ↑, ↓, →, ←, and press ENTER.

1-2-3 displays the program title screen briefly and then opens the 1-2-3 window, containing a full-size Worksheet window and a blank worksheet named Untitled, as shown below.

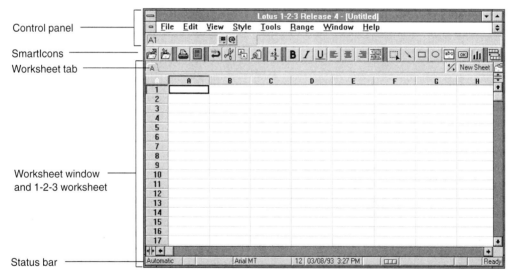

Help   For more information about each part of the Worksheet window, search on "Parts of the 1-2-3 window" in Help. In the picture of the Worksheet window, you can pop up a description of any part of the window by pointing to the part and clicking it.

The control panel

The **control panel** displays information about 1-2-3 and about the active window. It contains the title bar, the main menu, and the edit line.

Title bar

Main menu

Edit line

The title bar

The **title bar** of the 1-2-3 window contains the Control menu box, the program name, the file name, the Minimize button, and the Maximize or Restore button, as shown below.

Program name   File name   Minimize button   Maximize or Restore button

Control menu box

When you highlight a command in the menu or point to one of the SmartIcons while pressing the right mouse button, the title bar displays a description of the command or icon. Sometimes when you choose a command, the title bar displays instructions to help you complete the command. For example, look in the title bar when you're drawing an arrow or creating a chart.

The main menu

The **main menu** contains the commands that you use with 1-2-3. One command on the main menu changes, depending on the current selection. For example, when you select a range, the main menu displays the Range command, as shown below.

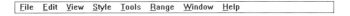

When you select a chart, the Chart command replaces the Range command. See Chapter 4 for more information about using 1-2-3 commands.

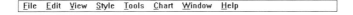

The edit line

The edit line contains the selection indicator, the navigator, the @function selector, the Cancel and Confirm buttons, and the contents box.

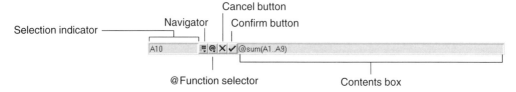

Selection indicator

Navigator

Cancel button

Confirm button

@Function selector

Contents box

The **selection indicator** displays the address or name of the current selection, such as a range, chart, query table, or embedded object. Click the **navigator** to display a list of named ranges in the current file. In Ready mode, you can go to and select a named range by selecting its name from the list. In Value or Edit mode, you can select a named range from the navigator list to put in a formula or dialog box.

Click the **@function selector** to display the @Function menu. You can select an @function and enter it in formulas. You can customize the @Function menu by adding and removing @functions. For more information on using the @Function menu, see page 110. For information about customizing the @Function menu, see page 112.

When you enter data, such as @functions, formulas, numbers, and labels, 1-2-3 displays the data in the **contents box**, and the Cancel and Confirm buttons appear. Click **Confirm** to enter the data or **Cancel** to cancel the entry.

SmartIcons

SmartIcons are shortcuts for many 1-2-3 tasks. For example, you can make an entry bold by clicking an icon instead of choosing the Style Font & Attributes command and selecting the bold option in the dialog box.

To find out what an icon does, point to the icon and hold down the right mouse button. A description appears in the 1-2-3 title bar.

1-2-3 displays a set of SmartIcons that you can move, hide, and customize to contain only the icons you want. You can also assign a macro to an icon and customize the appearance of an icon. For detailed information about customizing SmartIcons, see Chapter 25.

1-2-3 displays a different set of SmartIcons depending on the current selection. The next illustration shows the default sets of SmartIcons.

Set of SmartIcons when a range is selected

Set of SmartIcons when a chart is selected

Set of SmartIcons when a drawn object is selected

Set of SmartIcons when a query table is selected

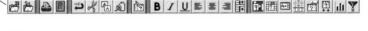

 Help   For a SmartIcons reference organized by function, with a picture and description of each icon, search on "SmartIcons" in Help.

To use SmartIcons

1. If the icon acts on a range, select the range.

    For example, to sum a column of numbers, select the blank cell below the numbers.

2. Click the icon.

    For example, click the SmartSum icon to add the column of numbers and enter the sum in the blank cell.

    Note   You can't select SmartIcons with the keyboard.

    If the icon acts on a range, 1-2-3 performs the command without displaying a dialog box. Other SmartIcons display a dialog box or perform some other action.

The Worksheet window

When you start 1-2-3, you see the 1-2-3 **Worksheet window** containing a blank file named Untitled. The file contains a single **1-2-3 worksheet**, an electronic spreadsheet consisting of a grid of 256 columns and 8,192 rows. Each time you create a new file or open an existing file, 1-2-3 opens an additional Worksheet window with its own worksheet.

Column letters for each column appear above the worksheet. Columns are lettered A to IV (A to Z, AA to AZ, BA to BZ, and so on to IV). Row numbers for each row appear to the left of the worksheet. Rows are numbered 1 to 8192. The next illustration shows the basic parts of a worksheet. The title bar appears when you reduce the worksheet, as shown in the next illustration.

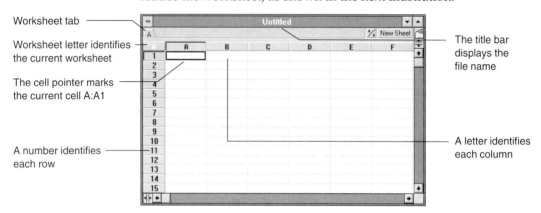

Worksheet tab

Worksheet letter identifies the current worksheet

The cell pointer marks the current cell A:A1

A number identifies each row

The title bar displays the file name

A letter identifies each column

Initially, a 1-2-3 file has only one worksheet. You can insert additional worksheets and create a **multiple-sheet file** with up to 256 worksheets. Each worksheet is identified by a letter from A to IV. The worksheet letter appears in the top left corner of the worksheet.

The intersection of a column and a row is called a **cell**. Each cell has an **address** consisting of a worksheet letter followed by a : (colon), a column letter, and a row number. For example, cell A:A1 is in worksheet A at the intersection of column A and row 1.

The rectangular highlight in the worksheet is the **cell pointer**. The cell pointer identifies the **current cell**. When a cell is current, you can enter data into the cell, edit the contents of the cell, and choose commands that affect the cell. You change the current cell by moving the cell pointer.

The worksheet containing the current cell is the **current worksheet**. You can display any worksheet in a multiple-sheet file, and you can also display more than one worksheet at a time in the Worksheet window.

Worksheet tabs

Worksheet tabs show you if a file contains more than one worksheet. 1-2-3 automatically names each tab A, B, C, and so on. You can use the tab to change the name for the worksheet. You can use worksheet names when referring to ranges in formulas.

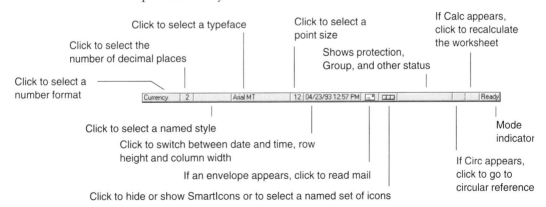

Click to insert a new worksheet after the current worksheet

Click to scroll tabs right or left

To change the worksheet name, double-click the tab and type a new name

Click to hide or show tabs

You can click a worksheet's tab to move to that worksheet. You can also use tabs to select a range across two or more adjacent worksheets, a 3D range. To select a 3D range, select a range on the first worksheet, and then SHIFT+click the tab of the last worksheet in your 3D range.

When you have more tabs than you can see in the Worksheet window, you can click the tab-scroll arrows to scroll the tabs left or right without changing the current selection. SHIFT+click the tab-scroll arrows to scroll the tabs to the first or last worksheet in the file.

The status bar

The status bar gives you information about the current selection and tells you what 1-2-3 is doing. You can also use the status bar to perform many tasks with the mouse.

Click to select a typeface

Click to select a point size

If Calc appears, click to recalculate the worksheet

Click to select the number of decimal places

Shows protection, Group, and other status

Click to select a number format

Mode indicator

Click to select a named style

Click to switch between date and time, row height and column width

If an envelope appears, click to read mail

If Circ appears, click to go to circular reference

Click to hide or show SmartIcons or to select a named set of icons

Ending 1-2-3

When you end a 1-2-3 session, 1-2-3 closes all active files and redisplays the Windows Program Manager window. When 1-2-3 closes a file, it removes the file from memory but not from disk.

To end a 1-2-3 session

1. Choose File Exit or press ALT+F4.

   If you saved all changes to the active files, the 1-2-3 window closes. If you changed an active file without saving the changes, you see this dialog box for each modified file:

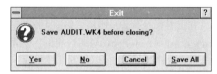

2. If a dialog box appears, choose an option:

   - Yes saves the changes to the file listed in the dialog box, and then ends the session or displays another dialog box if there are more modified files.

     If the file doesn't exist on disk, the Save As dialog box appears and lets you enter a file name.

   - No ends the session without saving changes.

   - Cancel returns you to 1-2-3 without saving changes.

   - Save All saves changes to all modified files and ends the session.

     If a file is untitled, the Save As dialog box appears and lets you enter a file name.

3

Managing the 1-2-3 Windows

This chapter describes the different types of windows in 1-2-3. It also describes how to use the mouse and how to work with windows.

What are the 1-2-3 windows?

You use the following windows when you work in 1-2-3:

- The **1-2-3 window** contains 1-2-3. All 1-2-3 windows, except the Help window, open within the 1-2-3 window.

- A **Worksheet window** always opens when you start 1-2-3 or open a file. It contains a **worksheet file**, the 1-2-3 electronic spreadsheet. You enter and work with numbers, formulas, text, and graphics in a worksheet file.

- The **Help window** displays Help about 1-2-3. For more information about Help, see the inside front cover of this book, or choose Help Using Help.

- The **1-2-3 Classic**® **window** displays the 1-2-3 Release 3.1 menu or the Wysiwyg menu. You can use 1-2-3 Classic as an alternative to using the 1-2-3 main menu. For more information, see "Using 1-2-3 Classic" on page 39.

- The **Transcript window** is where you can record keystrokes, menu choices, and mouse actions as a series of macro commands. You can create a macro by copying or cutting recorded commands from the Transcript window and pasting them into a worksheet, icon, or macro button. For more information, see "Recording a macro" on page 313.

- The **Macro Trace window** helps you debug macros by showing the current macro command as it runs. For more information about using the Macro Trace window, see "Debugging a macro" on page 322.

- The **Print Preview window** shows you how your printed output will appear. For more information, see "Print previewing" on page 134.
- The **Version Manager window** helps you create, maintain, and track versions and scenarios. For more information, see Chapter 22.

Using the mouse

You can use the mouse, like the keyboard, to choose commands, highlight ranges, and manipulate charts and other drawn objects. There are some actions that you can do only with the mouse, such as using SmartIcons.

Press the right mouse button to display a menu of useful commands for working with the current selection. For more information about using the right mouse button, see "Using 1-2-3 quick menus" on page 29.

Note   When a procedure says to press a mouse button, use the left mouse button unless you specified left-handed use of the mouse in the Windows Control Panel. For more information, see your Windows documentation.

The table below lists the terms for mouse actions.

Term	Action
Click	Quickly press and release the mouse button
Double-click	Quickly press and release the mouse button twice
Drag	Press and hold down the mouse button while moving the mouse
Point	Position the mouse pointer

The mouse pointer

The **mouse pointer** tells you what part of the screen your next mouse action will affect. For example, when you move the mouse pointer to a window border, your next mouse action will affect that border. To move the mouse pointer, you move the mouse.

The shape of the mouse pointer changes depending on the current pointer location and the task you can perform at that location. For example, when you move the mouse pointer to a window border, the pointer changes to a white two-headed arrow. This pointer shape indicates that you can use the mouse to size the window.

The table below shows some different mouse pointer shapes and describes the tasks you can perform when each pointer shape appears.

Mouse pointer shape	*Tasks*
	Move the cell pointer and select cells and ranges; make a window active; move a window; scroll a window; open a Control menu; choose commands; move around in a dialog box; select dialog box options
	Reminds you to wait until 1-2-3 finishes performing a task
	Size a window with the keyboard
	Size a window with the mouse
	Enter and edit data
	Size a row; create or size a horizontal pane
	Size a column; create or size a vertical pane
	Select a range
	Indicates that you're ready to move or copy the current selection by dragging
	Drag the current selection to a new location
	Drag a copy of the current selection to a new location
	Position a new chart
	Position a drawn object
	Select one or more drawn objects
	Create a freehand drawing
	Display a definition in Help or go to a Help cross-reference; or click a macro button

Working with 1-2-3 windows

Within the 1-2-3 window, you can size and move windows, arrange windows in a cascade or tile pattern, and close a window. Using the mouse is the simplest and most efficient way to size, move, and close 1-2-3 windows. You can also use the Window commands and the commands in each window's Control menu.

To make a window active

To work with any window, you must first make it active.

Mouse

1. Click anywhere in the window.

Keyboard

Press **CTRL+F6** *to make the next Worksheet window or Transcript window active.*

1. Press **ALT+W** to display the Window pull-down menu.
2. Press the number next to the window name; or press ↓ to highlight the window name, and press **ENTER**.

    Note   Only one window can be active at a time. When a window is active, its title bar is highlighted.

To display a Control menu

You can use the Control menu commands to size, move, and close 1-2-3 windows. You can also switch to another open Windows application by choosing the Switch To command in the Control menu of the 1-2-3 window. See Appendix A in *What's New* for a description of the Control menu commands.

Mouse

1. Click the Control menu box in the top left corner of the window.

Keyboard

1. Press **ALT+ SPACEBAR** to display the Control menu for the 1-2-3 window or a dialog box; press **ALT+ -** (hyphen) to display the Control menu for a window that's open in the 1-2-3 window.

1-2-3 window
Control menu

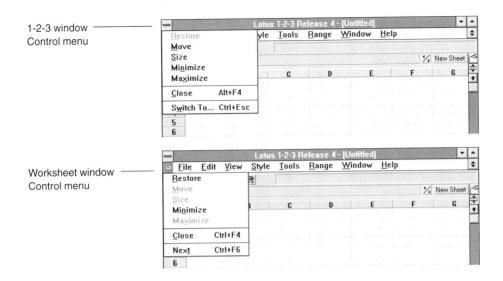

Worksheet window
Control menu

To restore a maximized window

By default the Worksheet window first appears maximized, as shown below.

Restore button

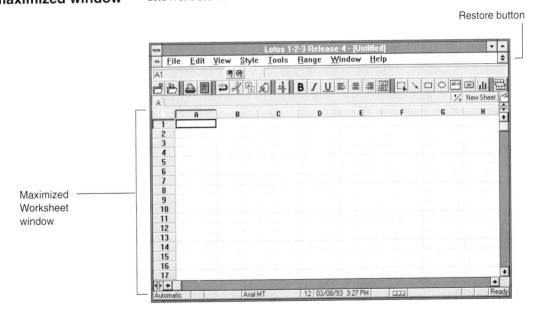

Maximized
Worksheet
window

You can restore the Worksheet window so it doesn't fill the 1-2-3 window and lets you see more than one window at a time.

Mouse

1. Click the Restore button.

Keyboard

1. Press ALT+ - (hyphen) to display the Control menu.

2. Choose Restore.

After you restore a window, 1-2-3 displays the Minimize and Maximize buttons, which you can click to minimize or maximize the window. 1-2-3 also displays the Control menu box and the file name in the Worksheet window's title bar, as shown below.

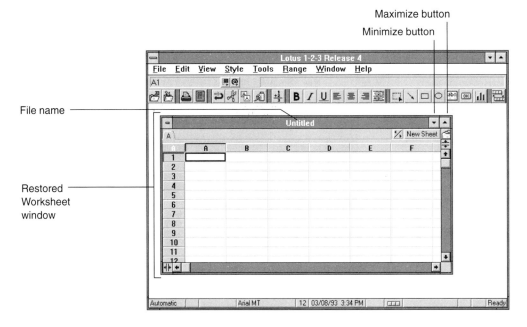

To maximize a window

Mouse

1. Click the Maximize button.

Keyboard

1. Make the window active.

2. Press ALT+ - (hyphen) to display the Control menu.

3. Choose Maximize.

To minimize a window to an icon

Mouse

1. Click the Minimize button.

Keyboard

1. Make the window active.

2. Press ALT+ - (hyphen) to display the Control menu.

3. Choose Minimize.

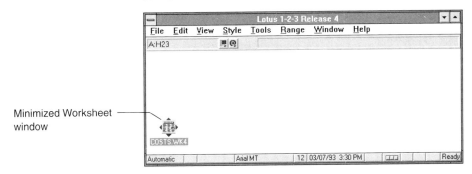

Minimized Worksheet window

To restore a minimized window

Mouse

1. Double-click the minimized window.

Keyboard

1. Make the window active.

2. Press ALT+ - (hyphen) to display the Control menu.

3. Choose Restore.

1-2-3 restores the window to its original position and size.

To size a window

Mouse

1. Move the mouse pointer to a border or corner of the window.

   The mouse pointer changes to a white two-headed arrow.

2. Drag the window border or corner.

   Dragging a border expands or contracts the window vertically or horizontally. Dragging a corner expands or contracts both dimensions of the window simultaneously.

3. Release the mouse button when the window is the size you want.

Keyboard

1. Make the window active.

2. Press ALT+ - (hyphen) to display the Control menu.

3. Choose Size.

4. Size the window:

   Press → or ← to select the right or left border, and then use → and ← to move the border.

   Press ↓ or ↑ to select the bottom or top border, and then use ↑ and ↓ to move the border.

5. Press ENTER when the window is the size you want.

To move a window

Mouse

1. Point to the title bar.

2. Drag the window to the position you want, and release the mouse button.

Keyboard

1. Make the window active.

2. Press ALT+ - (hyphen) to display the Control menu.

3. Choose Move.

4. Use ↑, ↓, →, ← to move the window.

5. Press ENTER when the window is at the position you want.

To cascade windows

When you **cascade** windows, 1-2-3 arranges them on top of one another with the active window on top of the cascade and only the title bars of each underlying window visible.

1. Choose Window Cascade.

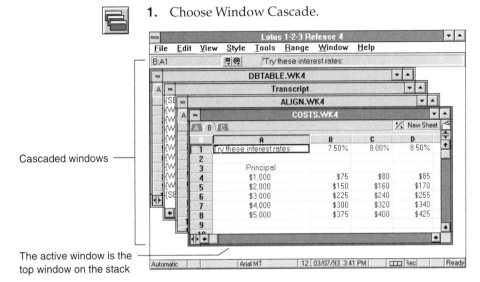

Cascaded windows ———

The active window is the —— top window on the stack

To tile windows

When you **tile** windows, 1-2-3 arranges them side-by-side like floor tiles with the active window in the top left corner.

1. Choose Window Tile.

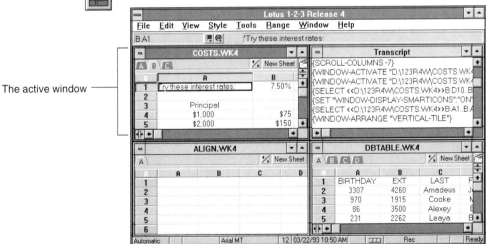

The active window ———

To close a window

Mouse

1. Double-click the Control menu box in the top left corner of the window.

Keyboard

1. Make the window active.

2. Press CTRL+F4.

If you close a Worksheet window and don't save changes to the file, 1-2-3 displays a message asking if you want to save the changes.

4 Using 1-2-3 Commands

This chapter describes different ways to perform a command in 1-2-3 for Windows. You can use the menus, the keyboard, or the 1-2-3 Classic. This chapter also describes how to cancel a command and undo a command or other action.

> **Note** You can also perform a command by clicking SmartIcons and by using the status bar. For information about using SmartIcons, see page 12. For information about what you can do with the status bar, see page 15.

Using main menu commands

Commands appear in the **main menu**, directly below the title bar. You choose **commands** from the menu to perform actions in 1-2-3. The commands in the main menu change depending on your current selection, as shown below.

When you select a range, the menu displays the Range command

When you select a chart, the menu displays the Chart command

When you select a query table, the menu displays the Query command

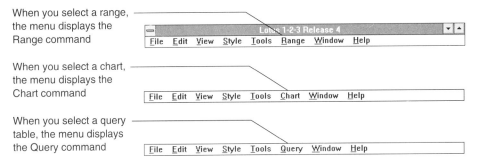

When you choose a command in the main menu, a **pull-down menu** appears listing additional commands you can choose. For example, when you choose Tools from the main menu, you see the Tools pull-down menu, as shown on the next page.

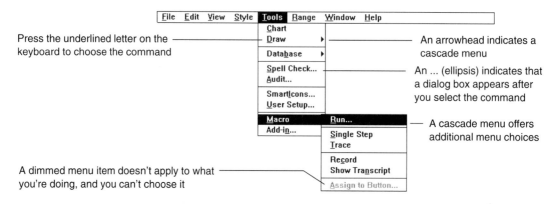

Press the underlined letter on the keyboard to choose the command

An arrowhead indicates a cascade menu

An ... (ellipsis) indicates that a dialog box appears after you select the command

A cascade menu offers additional menu choices

A dimmed menu item doesn't apply to what you're doing, and you can't choose it

When you choose a command not followed by an ... (ellipsis) or an arrowhead, 1-2-3 performs the command immediately. For example, when you select a range and choose Tools Chart, 1-2-3 creates a chart without displaying any additional commands or a dialog box.

To choose a main menu command

1. Highlight the top-level command in the menu:

   Mouse   Click the command to make the pull-down menu appear.

   Keyboard   Press ALT and the underlined letter of the command (usually the first letter); or press F10 (MENU), use → and ← to move the menu pointer, and press ENTER when the command is highlighted.

   The pull-down menu appears. For example, to choose File from the 1-2-3 main menu, click File or press ALT and press f. The File pull-down menu appears.

2. Choose the command from the pull-down menu:

   Mouse   Click the command.

   Keyboard   Press the underlined letter of the command or use ↑ and ↓ to move up and down in the pull-down menu, and press ENTER when the command is highlighted.

   For example, to choose Open from the File pull-down menu, click Open or press o. The Open File dialog box appears.

3. If a dialog box appears, use the dialog box as described on page 30. If there's a cascade menu, choose a command from the cascade menu:

Mouse   Click the command.

Keyboard   Press the underlined letter of the command or use ↑ and ↓ to move up and down in the cascade menu, and press **ENTER** when the command is highlighted.

The rest of this book condenses these three steps into one. For example, instead of separately listing each menu choice for opening a file (Choose File, then choose Open), a single step says Choose File Open.

Using 1-2-3 quick menus

Pressing the right mouse button is a convenient and quick way to display a menu containing useful commands for working with the current selection. For example, if you select a range and then press the right mouse button, you see a menu containing commands appropriate for working with ranges, as shown in the illustration below.

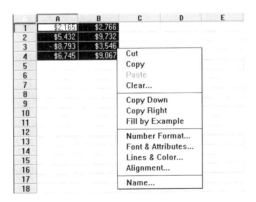

If you select a drawn object and then press the right mouse button, you see a menu containing commands appropriate for working with drawn objects, as shown in the illustration below.

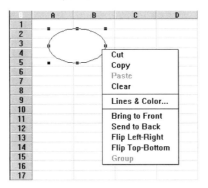

You can press the right mouse button to display a menu for many different worksheet items, such as query tables, charts, chart elements, and embedded objects.

Using a dialog box

You can move a dialog box like any other window if it blocks data you want to see.

You use a **dialog box** to select options and identify data you want a command to work on. In a dialog box, you can select an option, select check boxes, enter text in a text box, and select an item from a list or drop-down box. You may need to do all these actions or only one of them. When you're done, you either complete the command or cancel it. The next illustrations show what you can do with the various parts of a dialog box.

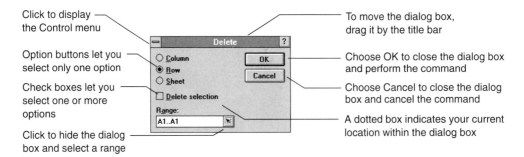

Click to display the Control menu

Option buttons let you select only one option

Check boxes let you select one or more options

Click to hide the dialog box and select a range

To move the dialog box, drag it by the title bar

Choose OK to close the dialog box and perform the command

Choose Cancel to close the dialog box and cancel the command

A dotted box indicates your current location within the dialog box

A text box lets you enter and edit text

The highlight indicates the current selection in a list box

A list box displays available choices

The information box displays information on an item in a list box

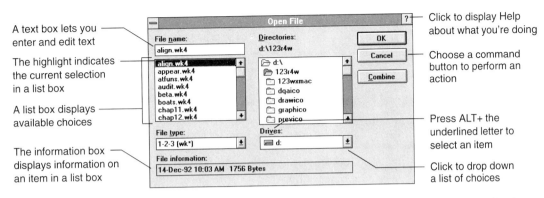

Click to display Help about what you're doing

Choose a command button to perform an action

Press ALT+ the underlined letter to select an item

Click to drop down a list of choices

Some dialog box options change depending on the current selection. For example, if you select a range and then choose Style Lines & Color, the dialog box displays options appropriate to working with ranges. If you select a chart and then choose Style Lines & Color, you see different options appropriate for working with charts.

To select an option button

You can only select one option button in a group of option buttons. A selected option button contains a black dot.

Mouse

1. Click the button of the option you want.

Keyboard

1. Hold down **ALT** and press the underlined letter in the option button name; or press **TAB** or **SHIFT+TAB** to move the dotted box to a group of option buttons and use ↑, ↓, →, ← to select the button of the option.

To select a check box

You can select as many check boxes as you want. A selected check box contains an X.

Mouse

1. Click the check box.

Keyboard

1. Hold down **ALT** and press the underlined letter in the check box name; or press **TAB** or **SHIFT+TAB** to move the dotted box to a check box and press **SPACEBAR**.

To enter text in a text box

File name:

Mouse

1. Click the text box and type the text.

Keyboard

1. Hold down ALT and press the underlined letter in the text box name; or press TAB or SHIFT+TAB to move to the text box. Then type the text.

To enter a range in a text box

Range selector

The easiest way to make a command work on a range is to select the range before choosing a command. You can also enter the range in a text box after you've chosen the command. Some commands, such as Tools Chart, require you to select the range before choosing the command.

Mouse

1. Click the text box.

2. Select the range in the worksheet.

If you want, click the range selector to remove the dialog box temporarily while you're selecting the range. The dialog box reappears when you release the mouse button. The address of the selected range appears in the text box. To specify a collection, CTRL+click the range selector after you specify the first range.

Keyboard

1. Hold down ALT and press the underlined letter in the text box name; or press TAB or SHIFT+TAB to move to the text box.

2. Type the range name or address; or select the range in the worksheet using ↑, ↓, →, ← and then press ENTER.

The dialog box disappears while you're selecting the range and reappears when you press ENTER. The address of the selected range appears in the text box. To specify a collection, type a ; (semicolon) between each range address.

For more information about selecting ranges, see page 60. For more information about entering range names in a dialog box, see page 88.

To select an item from a list box

Mouse

1. Click the item.

   If you don't see the item you want in the list box, click the scroll arrows or drag the scroll box until your choice appears.

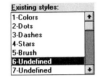

Keyboard

1. Hold down ALT and press the underlined letter in the list box name; or press TAB or SHIFT+TAB to move to the list box.

2. Press the first letter of the item you want, or use ↑, ↓, →, ← to scroll to the item.

3. Press ENTER.

To select an item from a drop-down box

Mouse

1. Click the arrow to drop down the list.

2. Click the item you want.

Keyboard

1. Hold down ALT and press the underlined letter in the drop-down box name; or press TAB or SHIFT+TAB to move to the drop-down box.

2. Press ALT+↓ to drop down the list.

3. Press the first letter of the item you want, or press ↑ or ↓ to move to the item.

4. Press ALT+↑ to choose the item you want and close the drop-down box.

To complete a dialog box command

Mouse

1. Click OK.

Keyboard

1. Press ENTER.

1-2-3 performs the command using the options and data you specified in the dialog box.

Canceling a command

At any point, while you're making a menu choice or using a dialog box, you can cancel the command. When you cancel a command, 1-2-3 closes the dialog box or menu without completing the command and returns the worksheet to the condition it was in before you chose the command.

Note   If a dialog box has a Close button instead of a Cancel button, you can't cancel commands that you perform with the dialog box. For example, once you name a range, you can't cancel the command.

To cancel a command

Mouse

1.   Click anywhere outside the menu, or click the Cancel button in the dialog box.

Keyboard

1.   Press ESC or CTRL+BREAK.

Undoing an action

You can often undo a command or other action by performing Undo immediately before doing anything else. For example, you can undo the effects of editing a cell or moving data.

You can't undo the effects of Print commands, File commands that write to disk, cell-pointer movements, pressing F5 (GOTO), F6 (PANE), or F9 (CALC). You also can't use Undo to reverse a previous use of Undo.

Note   If you chose to turn off Undo when you installed 1-2-3, you can turn it on by choosing Tools User Setup and selecting the Undo option. If Undo is turned off, you can't undo a command or other action.

To undo an action

1.   Choose Edit Undo or press CTRL+Z.

Using 1-2-3 keys

You can use the keyboard to perform some 1-2-3 commands and other actions. Keyboard shortcuts perform tasks you can also perform with a menu command. Function keys perform different actions depending on whether you press only the function key or hold down **ALT** or **CTRL** while pressing the function key.

? **Help**   For information about Control menu keys, dialog box keys, editing keys, Help keys, and special keys, choose Help Keyboard.

Using keyboard shortcuts

The table below lists each keyboard shortcut and the function you can perform with it. Many keyboard shortcuts appear on the menu next to the equivalent command.

Key	Function
ALT+F4	Ends the 1-2-3 session; equivalent to File Exit.
CTRL+ *a letter*	Runs a macro, if the macro's name consists of a \ (backslash) and a letter; equivalent to Tools Macro Run.
CTRL+B	Makes the current selection bold; or, if the current selection is already bold, removes bold.
CTRL+C or CTRL+INS	Copies selected data and styles from the worksheet to the Clipboard; equivalent to Edit Copy.
CTRL+DEL	Deletes both styles and contents in the current selection.
CTRL+E	Center-aligns the current selection.
CTRL+F4	Closes the current file; equivalent to File Close.
CTRL+GRAY MINUS	This key on the numeric keypad deletes columns, rows, or worksheets; equivalent to Edit Delete.
CTRL+GRAY PLUS	This key on the numeric keypad inserts columns, rows, or worksheets; equivalent to Edit Insert.
CTRL+I	Makes the current selection italic; or, if the current selection is already italic, removes italic.
CTRL+L	Left-aligns the current selection.
CTRL+N	Removes bold, italic, and underlining from the current selection.

Continued

Key	Function
CTRL+O	Displays the dialog box for opening an existing file; equivalent to File Open.
CTRL+P	Displays the Print dialog box; equivalent to File Print.
CTRL+R	Right-aligns the current selection.
CTRL+S	Saves the current file; equivalent to File Save.
CTRL+U	Underlines the current selection; or, if the current selection is already underlined, removes the underline.
CTRL+V or **SHIFT+INS**	Pastes styles from the Clipboard to the selected location in the worksheet; equivalent to Edit Paste.
CTRL+X or **SHIFT+DEL**	Cuts selected data and styles from the worksheet to the Clipboard; equivalent to Edit Cut.
CTRL+Z or **ALT+BACKSPACE**	Reverses the effect of the most recently executed command or action that you can undo; equivalent to Edit Undo.
DEL	Deletes the contents of selected cells without using the Clipboard; equivalent to choosing Edit Clear cell contents only; also deletes selected charts, drawn objects, and query tables.

Caution   DEL permanently deletes data. However, you can restore the data you deleted if you use Edit Undo before performing another action.

Note   If you use CTRL+ *a letter* to run a macro and this combination is the same as a keyboard shortcut using CTRL+ *a letter*, the macro overrides the keyboard shortcut. For example, if you run a macro named \e by pressing CTRL+E, this macro overrides the keyboard shortcut for center-aligning the current selection, CTRL+E.

Using function keys   You can use the 1-2-3 function keys to perform special actions. The table below describes the 1-2-3 function keys.

Key	Function
F1 (HELP)	Opens the Help window and displays context-sensitive Help.
F2 (EDIT)	Puts 1-2-3 in Edit mode so that you can edit cells.
F3 (NAME)	Displays a list of names related to the command you chose or the formula you're creating.
F4	In Ready mode, anchors the cell pointer so you can specify a range.
F4 (ABS)	In Edit, Point, and Value modes, changes the cell or range reference in formulas from relative to absolute to mixed.
F5 (GOTO)	Goes to and selects a specific cell, named range, or named object in the current worksheet, the current file, or in another active file.
F6 (PANE)	Moves the cell pointer between horizontal, vertical, or perspective panes.
F7 (QUERY)	Updates the data in a query table; equivalent to Query Refresh Now.
F8 (TABLE)	Repeats the most recent Range Analyze What-if Table command.
F9 (CALC)	In Ready mode, updates all formulas in all active files; in Edit mode, converts a formula to its value.
F10 (MENU)	Makes the menu bar active; equivalent to pressing **ALT**.
ALT+F1 (COMPOSE)	Creates characters in 1-2-3 that aren't on your keyboard; see Appendix A for details.
ALT+F2 (STEP)	Switches Step mode on and off for debugging macros.
ALT+F3 (RUN)	Displays a list of macros to run.

Continued

Key	Function
ALT+F6 (ZOOM PANE)	Enlarges the current horizontal, vertical, or perspective pane to the full size of the window or shrinks it to its original size; *not* equivalent to View Zoom In or View Zoom Out.
ALT+F7 (ADD-IN 1), *ALT+F8 (ADD-IN 2),* *ALT+F9 (ADD-IN 3)*	Starts an available 1-2-3 add-in assigned to the key.

You can use F3 (NAME) at the following times:

- When specifying a range in a text box, press F3 (NAME) to display a list of range names in the current worksheet file and the names of other active files.

- When entering a formula, press F3 (NAME) after specifying a cell or range address to replace the address with the corresponding range name. If the specified cell or range has no range name, or if it has more than one name, 1-2-3 displays a complete list of range names when you press F3 (NAME).

- When entering a formula, press F3 (NAME) after typing any operator (for example, +, &, ^, or #AND#) to display a list of range names in the current file and names of other active files.

- When entering an @function, press F3 (NAME) after typing @ (at sign) to display the list of @functions.

- When entering a macro command, press F3 (NAME) after typing { (open brace) to display the list of macro commands.

- When you want information about an @function or macro, after typing @ (at sign) or { (open brace), press F3 (NAME) to display the list of @functions or macros; then select an @function or macro from the list, and press F1 (HELP) to display a Help topic about the @function or macro.

Using 1-2-3 Classic

You can drag the 1-2-3 Classic window to a different location in the 1-2-3 window.

1-2-3 Classic lets you use the 1-2-3 Release 3.1 menu or the Wysiwyg menu. When you press / (slash) or < (less-than symbol) in Ready mode, the 1-2-3 Classic window appears at the top of the 1-2-3 window. The 1-2-3 Release 3.1 main menu appears in the 1-2-3 Classic window, as shown below.

To use the Wysiwyg menu, press : (colon) in Ready mode. 1-2-3 displays the Wysiwyg menu in the 1-2-3 Classic window, as shown below.

You can work with the 1-2-3 Release 3.1 main menu or Wysiwyg menu just as you do in 1-2-3 Release 3.1. When you complete a command or press ESC, the 1-2-3 Classic window disappears.

Note   You can't use the mouse to choose commands in the 1-2-3 Classic window.

? **Help**   For more information on using 1-2-3 Release 3.1 commands in 1-2-3 Release 4 for Windows, choose Help For Upgraders and select the topic "1-2-3 Classic." Also, if you highlight a command in 1-2-3 Classic and press F1 (HELP), Help points you to the equivalent 1-2-3 Release 4 for Windows command.

Part II
Using Worksheets

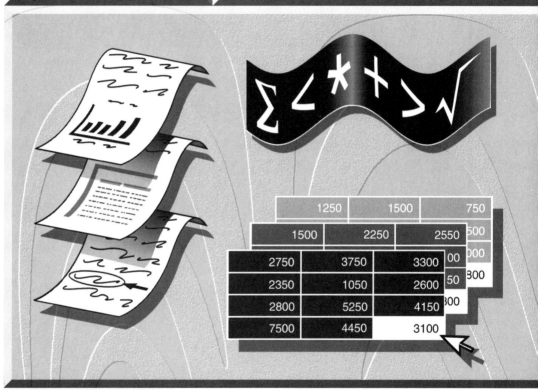

5

Worksheet Basics

This chapter describes how to perform basic worksheet and file tasks, such as opening and saving a file, inserting and deleting worksheets, naming worksheets, and moving around in worksheets and files.

Opening a file

To work in a file, you must open it. You use File New to open a new file and File Open to open an existing file. You can have several files open at a time. Open files are called **active files**, and the file containing the cell pointer is the **current file**.

The 1-2-3 Release 4 for Windows default file type is .WK4. You can also open files from other releases of 1-2-3 and Symphony®, and Microsoft Excel. For details about opening other types of files, see Chapter 5 in *What's New*.

To open a new file

1. Choose File New.

1-2-3 opens a new file, gives it a default file name, and displays it in a Worksheet window. The first default file name is FILE0001.WK4, the next default name is FILE0002.WK4, and so on. 1-2-3 increases the number in the file name by one for each new file that uses the default name.

After opening a new file and working in it, you may want to save your work and name the file. For more information, see "Saving a file" on page 56.

To open an existing file

1. Choose File Open or press CTRL+O.

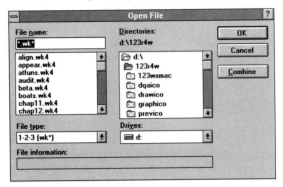

2. To see a list of files of a particular type, select the type of file you want from the File type drop-down box.

3. Specify the file you want to open by doing one of the following:

   • Enter the file name in the File name text box.

   • Use the File name and Directories list boxes, and the Drives drop-down box to select the file you want.

4. Choose OK.

Windows 3.1 users can also open a 1-2-3 file by double-clicking it in the File Manager or dragging one or more 1-2-3 files into the 1-2-3 window.

1-2-3 opens the file in a Worksheet window and makes it the active window. Other windows remain open.

Note   If the file you want to open is password-protected, 1-2-3 asks you to enter the password. If someone else is using the file and has the file reservation, 1-2-3 asks whether you want to open the file with read-only access. For more information about file passwords, see page 147.

? Help   For information about file reservations, search on "Reservation" in Help. For information about how to combine data from a file on disk with data in the current file, search on "Combining files" in Help.

To open a recently used file

1.   Select the file from the bottom of the File menu.

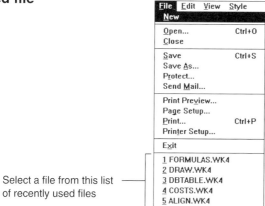

Select a file from this list of recently used files

Inserting and deleting worksheets

You can insert worksheets before or after the current worksheet. You can insert up to 255 worksheets, depending upon available memory and the number of worksheets in other active files.

> **Note**   You can insert and delete columns, rows, and ranges as well as worksheets. For information, see page 81.

To insert one worksheet at a time

Using the New Sheet button is the quickest way to insert one worksheet at a time. A click of this button inserts one worksheet immediately after the current worksheet.

1.   Click the New Sheet button shown at left.

To insert a specified number of worksheets

Using Edit Insert, you can insert a specified number of worksheets immediately before or after the current worksheet. This method is convenient when you want to insert many worksheets and don't want to click the New Sheet button over and over. It's also the only way to insert worksheets before the current worksheet.

1. Choose Edit Insert.

2. Select Sheet.

3. Select Before or After.

4. In the Quantity text box, click the arrows or enter the number of worksheets you want to insert.

5. Choose OK.

 Shortcut   Select a range that includes cells in the same number of worksheets that you want to insert. Then, click the icon shown at left to insert the worksheets after the last worksheet in the selection.

To delete a worksheet

1. Select at least one cell in each worksheet you want to delete.

   For example, to delete worksheets B, C, and D, select cells B:A1..D:A1. If you're not sure how to select a range across worksheets (a 3D range), see page 61.

2. Choose Edit Delete.

3. Select Sheet.

To delete a single worksheet, click the worksheet letter and choose Edit Delete.

4. Choose OK.

When you delete worksheets, 1-2-3 automatically changes the letters of the remaining worksheets and adjusts formulas. For example, if you have four worksheets in a file, and you delete worksheet A, 1-2-3 changes the remaining three worksheets to A, B, and C. For more information about how 1-2-3 adjusts formulas, see "How inserting and deleting affects formulas" on page 83.

 Shortcut   Select at least one cell in each worksheet you want to delete, and click the icon shown at left.

? **Help**   For information about deleting an entire file, search on "Deleting files" in Help.

Naming worksheets

You can name a worksheet using its worksheet tab. Initially these tabs display the worksheet letter, such as A, B, C and so on. You can enter names in worksheet tabs, as shown below.

Use the following guidelines when you name worksheets:

- Worksheet names can be up to 15 characters long.
- Don't use a worksheet name that's the same as the worksheet letters; for example, don't name a worksheet A or BB.
- You can enter names in uppercase letters, lowercase letters, or a combination.
- You can use letters, numbers, and _ (underscores) in worksheet names, but don't start a worksheet name with a number.
- Don't start a worksheet name with ! (exclamation point) and don't include , (comma), ; (semicolon), . (period), or the characters +, −, *, /, &, >, <, @, #, or {.
- Don't use spaces in worksheet names. Use underscores instead.
- Don't use @function names, macro command keywords such as BEEP, or the names of keys, such as HOME.
- Don't create names that look like cell addresses, such as Q2 for Quarter 2, or FY93 for Fiscal Year 1993.
- You can't enter duplicate worksheet names in the same file. If you try to enter a worksheet name that's the same as another in the file, 1-2-3 beeps and displays a message.

When referring to a range in a formula or @function, you can use a worksheet name in place of a worksheet letter. For example, if the name of worksheet B is Tokyo, you can refer to cell B5 in that worksheet as Tokyo:B5.

If a worksheet has a name, 1-2-3 converts worksheet letters in formula references to the corresponding worksheet names. For example, if the name of worksheet A is Chicago, 1-2-3 converts +A:A5−B:A3 to +Chicago:A5−B:A3.

To name a worksheet

1. Double-click the worksheet tab.
2. Enter the name.
3. Press ENTER.

The name appears in the worksheet tab.

To delete a worksheet name

1. Double-click the worksheet tab.
2. Press DEL or BACKSPACE.
3. Press ENTER.

The worksheet letter appears in the worksheet tab.

To hide or show worksheet tabs

1. Do one of the following:
   - Click the Tab button, shown at left.
   - Choose View Set View Preferences; under "Show in current file," select or deselect the Worksheet tabs check box, and choose OK.

Moving around a file

You can use the mouse or keyboard to move the cell pointer around in a single worksheet, or from one worksheet to another. To move the cell pointer in a single worksheet, click the cell you want to move to; or use ↑, ↓, →, ←, or other pointer-movement keys. You can also use scroll bars to see data not currently in view without moving the cell pointer.

To move from one worksheet to another, click the tab of the worksheet you want to move to, or use the worksheet navigation keys. Also, you can use the navigator to go to named ranges in the current file; see page 88 for more information.

Using the pointer-movement keys

The table below describes using the pointer-movement keys to move around a worksheet.

Press	To move the cell pointer
↑ or ↓	Up or down one row
← or →	Left or right one column
CTRL+← or **SHIFT+TAB**	One full screen to the left
CTRL+→ or **TAB**	One full screen to the right
END ↑ or **END** ↓	Up or down the current column, to the next cell in the column that contains data and adjoins a cell above or below that doesn't contain data
END ← or **END** →	Left or right in the current row, to the next cell in the row that contains data and adjoins a cell on either side that doesn't contain data
END HOME	To the bottom right corner of the worksheet's active area (the rectangular area between cell A1 and the lowest and rightmost cells that contain data in the worksheet)
HOME	To cell A1, if column A isn't hidden and worksheet titles aren't set
PG UP or **PG DN**	Up or down one full screen

Using the scroll bars

Dragging the scroll boxes in the horizontal and vertical scroll bars, or clicking the scroll arrows, lets you see data not currently in view without changing the current selection. As you drag the vertical or horizontal scroll box, the selection indicator shows the row number or column letter so you can tell how far you've scrolled.

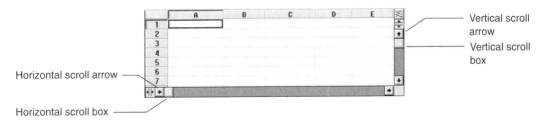

Vertical scroll arrow

Vertical scroll box

Horizontal scroll arrow

Horizontal scroll box

The table below describes how to move around the current worksheet using the mouse and scroll bars.

Do this	To scroll the worksheet
Click the up or down scroll arrow	Up or down one row
Click the left or right scroll arrow	Left or right one column
Click the horizontal scroll bar to the left or right of the scroll box	One full screen to the left or right
Click the vertical scroll bar above or below the scroll box	One full screen up or down
Drag the scroll box in the horizontal scroll bar	To any position left or right
Drag the scroll box in the vertical scroll bar	To any position up or down
Drag the scroll boxes to the far left of the horizontal scroll bar and to the top of the vertical scroll bar	To cell A1, if column A isn't hidden and worksheet titles aren't set

Moving from one worksheet to another

You can move the cell pointer from one worksheet to another using the mouse or the keyboard. To move from one worksheet to another using the mouse, click the tab of the worksheet you want to move to.

The table below describes the worksheet navigation keys, which move the cell pointer between worksheets in the current file.

Press	To move the cell pointer
CTRL+HOME	To cell A1 in the current file, if worksheet A and column A aren't hidden and worksheet titles aren't set.
CTRL+PG DN	To the previous worksheet; for example, from worksheet B to worksheet A.
CTRL+PG UP	To the next worksheet; for example, from worksheet A to worksheet B.
END CTRL+HOME	To the bottom right corner of the file's active area (the three-dimensional area between cell A1, the lowest and rightmost cells that contain data in the file, and the last worksheet that contains data in the file).

Continued

Press	To move the cell pointer
	For example, in a file that contains five worksheets, suppose B:D200 is the lowest, nonblank cell; C:AK200 is the rightmost, nonblank cell; worksheet D contains data; and worksheet E is blank. In that file, **END CTRL+HOME** moves the cell pointer to D:AK200.
END CTRL+PG DN	Back through worksheets in the current file. Staying in the same row and column, the cell pointer moves back to the next cell that contains data and is in front of or behind a blank cell. The cell pointer stops at the first worksheet in the current file.
	For example, **END CTRL+PG DN** moves the cell pointer from F:A1 to D:A1 if E:A1 is blank and D:A1 contains data.
END CTRL+PG UP	Forward through worksheets in the current file. Staying in the same row and column, the cell pointer moves forward to the next cell that contains data and is in front of or behind a blank cell. The cell pointer stops at the last worksheet in the current file.
	For example, **END CTRL+PG UP** moves the cell pointer from A:F5 to D:F5 if B:F5 and C:F5 are blank and D:F5 contains data.

Moving to another file

To move among active files, click a cell in the file you want to move to, or choose Window and select the file name. You can also use the keyboard to move the cell pointer from one active file to another. The table below describes the keys that move the cell pointer from one file to another.

Press	To move the cell pointer
CTRL+END HOME	To the cell you last highlighted in the first active file.
CTRL+END END	To the cell you last highlighted in the last active file.
CTRL+END CTRL+PG DN	To the cell you last highlighted in the previous active file.

Continued

Press	To move the cell pointer
CTRL+END CTRL+PG UP or **CTRL+F6**	To the cell you last highlighted in the next active file.
CTRL+PG DN	To the cell you last highlighted in the previous active file if the cell pointer is in the first worksheet of a file.
CTRL+PG UP	To the cell you last highlighted in the next active file, if the cell pointer is in the last worksheet of a file.

Viewing worksheets

In a multiple-sheet file, you can view three worksheets at the same time by splitting the worksheet window into perspective view. You can also split a worksheet into vertical or horizontal panes, and zoom a worksheet to magnify or shrink the display.

? Help   For more information about splitting a worksheet into panes, search on "Panes" in Help.

To view worksheets in perspective

1. Choose View Split.

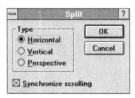

2. Under Type, select Perspective.

3. Choose OK.

   Shortcut   Click the icon shown at left to switch to perspective view.

The illustration below shows a Worksheet window in perspective view with worksheets A, B, and C displayed simultaneously. Worksheet tabs aren't available in perspective view.

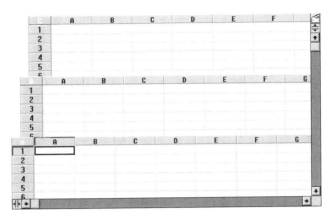

    To move from one worksheet to another, use the icons shown at left, or press **CTRL+PG UP** or **CTRL+PG DN**. You can also press **F6 (PANE)**. To return to single-sheet view from perspective, choose View Clear Split.

To zoom a worksheet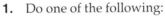

1. Do one of the following:
   - To magnify the worksheet display, choose View Zoom In.
   - To decrease the worksheet display, choose View Zoom Out.

   Each time you choose View Zoom In or View Zoom Out, 1-2-3 magnifies or shrinks the display of the worksheet by 10%.

   Choose View Custom to return to the default display size specified in View Set View Preferences.

Freezing rows and columns as titles

You can freeze rows or columns so they remain visible as you scroll through the worksheet. Rows and columns that you freeze this way are called **frozen titles**.

Freezing titles is convenient when you're scrolling through a large worksheet because you can always see the headings that describe the data. For example, you can freeze a column of student names along the left column and a row of months along the top row, as shown below.

Freeze this row...

... and this column...

... to keep them in view as you scroll

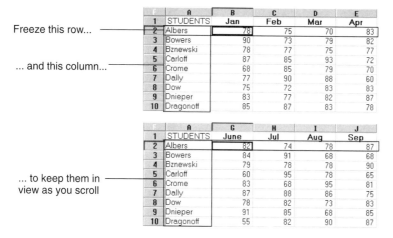

You can freeze rows or columns as titles, or both. Although you can set as many rows and as many columns as you want as titles, it's a good idea to set only a few, so you can still see all the data you want to work with.

To freeze rows and columns as titles

1. Do any of the following:
   - To freeze rows, move the cell pointer one cell below the rows you want to freeze.
   - To freeze columns, move the cell pointer one cell to the right of the columns you want to freeze.
   - To freeze both rows and columns, move the cell pointer to the cell immediately below the rows and to right of the columns you want to freeze.

2. Choose View Freeze Titles.

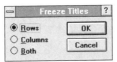

3. Select Rows, Columns, or Both.

4. Choose OK.

To clear frozen titles, choose View Clear Titles.

? **Help**   For information about editing frozen titles, search on "Titles" in Help.

Grouping worksheets

To see how commands and actions affect data in grouped worksheets, view them in perspective.

When you group worksheets, 1-2-3 applies the following styles and settings in the current worksheet to all other worksheets in the file: number formats, fonts and text attributes, colors, alignments, row height, column width, protection settings, frozen titles, and page breaks. After grouping worksheets, if you change any of these settings in one worksheet, *all* the worksheets change.

Grouping worksheets is a convenient way to make all the worksheets in a file look the same. For example, suppose you're setting up a multiple-sheet file so that each worksheet contains expense figures for a different month. When creating the file, you can style one worksheet in the file; then, with the cell pointer in that worksheet, group worksheets to apply the same styles to all other worksheets. Before entering data, you can ungroup the worksheets.

Caution   You can lose data if you forget that worksheets are grouped. For example, if you delete a column or row in one worksheet, you delete it in all grouped worksheets. Also, don't group worksheets if you want to keep styles or other settings unique to a particular worksheet. Ungrouping does *not* restore the styles and settings applied to a worksheet before grouping.

To group worksheets

1. Choose Style Worksheet Defaults.

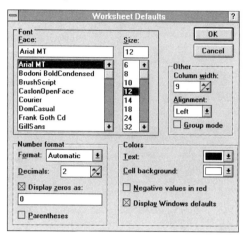

2. Under Other, select the Group mode check box.
3. Choose OK.

The Group indicator appears in the status bar.

To ungroup worksheets

1. Choose Style Worksheet Defaults.
2. Deselect the Group mode check box.
3. Choose OK.

The Group indicator disappears from the status bar.

Saving a file

The data you enter in a worksheet is temporary until you save it. It's a good idea to save a file frequently as you work on it. This way, you have a recent copy on disk and, in case of a power failure or other accident, you won't lose much data.

[?] **Help** You can save files automatically at a time interval you specify using Tools User Setup. For more information, search on "Autosave" in Help.

To save a file

1. Make sure the cell pointer is in the file you want to save.

2. Choose File Save As.

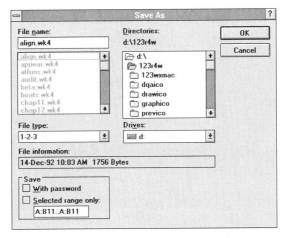

If you previously saved the file, you can choose File Save to save the current file without changing the file name and without using a dialog box.

3. Accept the default file name, or specify a new name in the File name text box.

   A file name can contain up to eight characters. You can use any combination of letters, numbers, _ (underscores), and - (hyphens). Since 1-2-3 isn't case-sensitive for file names, you can use any combination of uppercase and lowercase letters. 1-2-3 accepts spaces in file names, but using spaces isn't recommended.

4. If you want, specify a different drive or directory using the Drives drop-down box and the Directories list box.

   ? **Help**   For more information about naming a file, search on "Naming files" in Help.

5. Choose OK.

   If you specified a file name that already exists, 1-2-3 asks whether you want to cancel saving the current file, replace the data in the existing file with the data in the current file, or create a backup of the existing file before replacing data in it.

   Note   For information about saving a file with a password, see "Preventing others from opening a file" page 147.

   ? **Help**   You can extract data from the current file by saving it as a file on disk. To extract data, select the "Selected range only" check box in the Save As dialog box. For more information about extracting data, search on "Extracting data" in Help.

Closing a file

When you finish working in a file, it's a good idea to close it. Closing files you're not using saves memory and keeps your workspace from getting cluttered.

To close a file

1. Make sure that the cell pointer is in the file you want to close.

2. Choose File Close, or double-click the Control menu box of the Worksheet window.

You can also close a file by pressing **CTRL+F4**.

If you changed the file but didn't save the changes before closing, 1-2-3 indicates that the file has changed and asks whether you want to save the changes before closing.

6

Selecting Worksheet Areas

Selecting an area of the worksheet tells 1-2-3 what part of the worksheet you want your next action to affect. A selection can be as small as a single cell or as large as all the cells in all the worksheets in the file. This chapter describes how to select ranges, collections, columns, rows, and worksheets.

Selecting a single cell

The rectangular highlight in the worksheet is the **cell pointer**. The cell pointer marks the **current cell**. To enter data in a cell or perform a command on a cell, you must make it the current cell. You select a cell by moving the cell pointer there. 1-2-3 depresses the current cell's row number and column letter, and the selection indicator displays the address of the selected cell.

Cell address appears in ——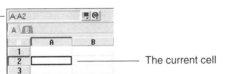
the selection indicator

—— The current cell

A **cell address** consists of a worksheet letter followed by : (colon), a column letter, and a row number. If you're referring to an address in the current worksheet, you can leave out the worksheet letter. For example, you can refer to A:A2 as A2 when worksheet A is the current worksheet.

To select a single cell

If you change to perspective view (described on page 52), you can click a cell in any visible worksheet.

Mouse

1. Click the cell.

    If the cell isn't in view, use the scroll bars to move it into view, and then click it. If the cell is in another worksheet, click the tab of the worksheet, and then click the cell.

Keyboard

1. Press ↑, ↓, →, ←, or other pointer-movement keys to move the cell pointer to the cell. If the cell is in another worksheet, use **CTRL+PG UP** or **CTRL+PG DN** to display the worksheet, and then move the cell pointer to the cell.

Selecting a range

A **range** is a block of cells that can be as small as a single cell or as large as all the worksheets in a file. A **range address** consists of the addresses of the first and last cells in the range, separated by two periods. For example, the address of the range shown below is A:A2..A:C4.

Range address in the —— selection indicator

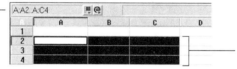

Range A:A2..A:C4

You can select a range contained entirely in a single worksheet or a range that spans two or more adjacent worksheets in a single file, a **3D range**. For example, the 3D range A:A2..C:C4 spans three worksheets.

The easiest way to make a command work on a range is to select the range before choosing a command. Some commands, such as Tools Chart, require you to select the range before choosing the command. You can also select a range from a dialog box. For more information about selecting a range from a dialog box, see "To enter a range in a text box" on page 32.

To select a range

*Another quick way to select a range is to click the first cell and **SHIFT**+click the last cell; or hold down **SHIFT** and press ↑, ↓, →, ← to highlight the range.*

1. Point to a cell in one corner of the range:

    Mouse   Move the mouse pointer to the cell.

    Keyboard   Press ↑, ↓, →, ←, or the other pointer-movement keys to move the cell pointer to the cell.

2. Anchor the cell pointer:

    Mouse   Press and hold the mouse button.

    Keyboard   Press F4.

3. Highlight the range:

    Mouse   While holding down the mouse button, drag across the worksheet. Release the mouse button when the range you want is highlighted.

    Keyboard   Press ↑, ↓, →, ← until you have highlighted the range you want. Press ENTER.

To select a 3D range with the mouse

1. Move the cell pointer to one corner of the range in the first worksheet.

    For example, click cell A:A2.

2. Drag across the worksheet and release the mouse button when you've highlighted the range you want.

    For example, highlight A:A2..A:C4.

3. Extend the selection to the last worksheet in the range by holding down SHIFT and clicking the worksheet tab.

    For example, hold down SHIFT and click the tab for worksheet C, highlighting the 3D range A:A2..C:C4.

To select a 3D range with the keyboard

1. Press ↑, ↓, →, ←, or other pointer-movement keys to move the cell pointer to one corner of the range in the first worksheet.

   For example, move the cell pointer to cell A:A2.

2. Anchor the cell pointer by pressing F4.

To see the file in perspective view, choose View Split, select Perspective, and choose OK.

3. Highlight the range in the first worksheet by pressing ↑, ↓, →, ←.

   For example, highlight A:A2..A:C4.

4. Move to the last worksheet in the range by pressing CTRL+PG UP or CTRL+PG DN. Press ENTER to highlight the entire 3D range.

   For example, after highlighting A:A2..A:C4, press CTRL+PG UP twice to move to worksheet C, and press ENTER to highlight the range A:A2..C:C4, as shown below.

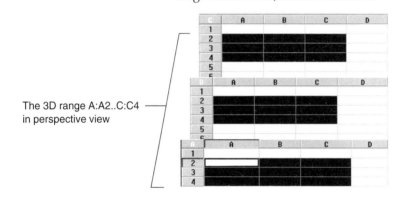

The 3D range A:A2..C:C4 in perspective view

To reshape a selection

Mouse

1. Hold down SHIFT and click any cell, or hold down SHIFT and drag to any cell to extend or shrink the selection to that cell.

Keyboard

1. Press F4 or hold down SHIFT, and press ↑, ↓, →, ← CTRL+PG UP or CTRL+PG DN to extend or shrink the selection.

   Press → and ← to extend the selection one column to the right or left; press ↑ and ↓ to extend the selection one row up or down. Use CTRL+PG UP and CTRL+PG DN to extend the selection one worksheet forward or back.

Selecting a collection

A **collection** contains more than one range on one or more worksheets. The ranges in a collection can touch, not touch, or overlap. You can select a collection containing ranges in a single worksheet and ranges that span worksheets. Most of the Edit commands and Style commands can act on collections.

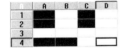

A collection's address consists of the addresses of all the ranges in the collection separated by , (commas) or ; (semi-colons). For example, the address of the collection at left is A1..A2,A4..B4,C1..C2,D4..D4. The address of the 3D collection in the illustration below is A:A2..A:B3, A:C4..A:C5, B:A2..B:B3, B:C3..B:C5.

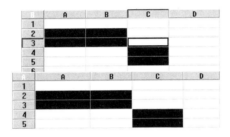

To select a collection

1. Select the first range in the collection.

2. If necessary, display another worksheet by holding down CTRL and clicking the worksheet tab.

3. Hold down CTRL and click a cell or drag across the range you want to add to the collection.

   To remove a range from a collection, hold down CTRL and click the range you want to remove.

4. Repeat step 3 until you've selected the entire collection.

   Note   Using the mouse is the only way to select a collection.

Selecting columns and rows

A **column** is a series of cells extending from the top to the bottom of the worksheet. A **row** is a series of cells extending from the left edge to the right edge of the worksheet. You can select a single column or row, a range of columns or rows, or a collection of columns or rows.

Some commands work specifically on columns or rows. For example, you can move or delete entire columns and rows. Select a column or row and press the right mouse button to see a menu of the most common commands that work on columns and rows.

Note   Using the mouse is the only way to select entire columns and rows.

To select a single column or row

1. Click the column letter or row number.

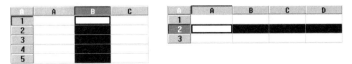

To select a range of columns or rows

1. Do one of the following:

    • Point to the letter or number of the first column or row in the range; drag across the worksheet to the last column letter or row number; release the mouse button.

    • Click the letter or number of the first column or row in the range; if necessary, scroll to the last column or row in the range; SHIFT+click the last column letter or row number.

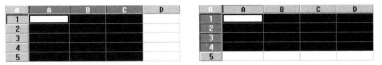

**To select a
collection of
columns or rows**

1. Select the first column or row, or range of columns or rows in the collection.
2. If necessary, scroll to the next column or row you want to select.
3. Hold down CTRL and click the letter or number of the next column or row; or drag across column letters or row numbers to select the next range of columns or rows.
4. Repeat steps 2 and 3 until you've selected the entire collection of columns or rows.

**Selecting
worksheets**

Selecting a worksheet selects all the cells in the worksheet. The cell pointer moves to the first cell in a selected worksheet.

Note   Using the mouse is the only way to select entire worksheets.

**To select a single
worksheet**

1. Click the worksheet letter.

Click here to select
the entire worksheet

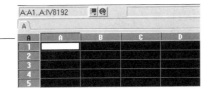

**To select a range of
worksheets**

1. Click the letter of the first worksheet in the range.
2. Hold down SHIFT and click the tab of the last worksheet in the range.

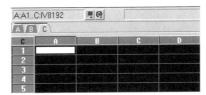

To select a collection of worksheets

1. Click the letter of the first worksheet in the collection.
2. Move to the next worksheet in the collection by holding down CTRL and clicking the worksheet tab.
3. CTRL+click the worksheet letter.
4. Repeat steps 2 and 3 until you've selected the entire collection of worksheets.

Summary of selection techniques

The table below summarizes the techniques for selecting various areas in a file.

To select	Do this
Cell	Click the cell; or use ↑, ↓, →, ← to move the cell pointer to the cell.
Range	Drag across the range; or press **F4**, use ↑, ↓, →, ← to highlight the range, and press **ENTER**.
3D range	Select the range in the first worksheet, then **SHIFT**+click the tab of the last worksheet in the range.
Collection	Select the first range, then hold down **CTRL** and select the other ranges.
Column or row	Click the column letter or row number.
Worksheet	Click the worksheet letter in the worksheet frame.

7

Entering and Editing Data

You build a spreadsheet by entering data, such as numbers, text, dates, and times. You can edit data, copy it, and move it. You can also enter and edit data by inserting and deleting columns, rows, and ranges. After entering data, you can find and replace text, and check spelling. This chapter describes techniques for entering, editing, and checking data.

Entering data

You can enter numbers, text, dates, times, formulas, and @functions. As you enter data, it appears in both the contents box and the current cell. Click in the contents box to enter data there, or select a cell to enter data directly in the cell. The insertion point, a | (vertical bar), appears where you're entering the data.

Entry appears in the contents box ...

... and in the cell

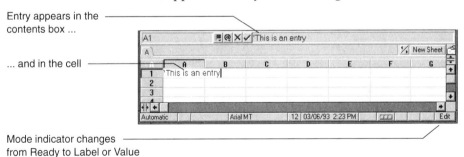

Mode indicator changes from Ready to Label or Value

When you enter data in the contents box, the box expands to the right until it reaches the edge of the window. Then it expands downward to display more characters up to a limit of 512. When you enter and edit data directly in a cell, the cell expands to the right until it reaches the edge of the window and then begins to scroll.

Cancel   Confirm

While you're entering data, 1-2-3 displays the Cancel and Confirm buttons in the edit line. You can click these buttons to cancel or confirm an entry. You can also confirm an entry by clicking another cell, or by pressing ENTER, or ↑, ↓, →, ← or the other pointer-movement keys.

When you click the Confirm button or press ENTER in a single-cell range, the cell pointer stays in the cell where you entered the data. When you press ↑, ↓, →, or ←, the cell pointer moves one cell in the direction of the arrow. When you enter data in a multiple-cell range or in a collection, pressing ENTER moves the cell pointer to the next cell in the current range.

If your entry is valid, 1-2-3 enters it in the cell, and the mode indicator changes to Ready. If your entry isn't valid, 1-2-3 beeps and places the insertion point where you made an error. The cell contents remain in the contents box or the cell until you correct or cancel the entry. To cancel an entry, click the Cancel button or press ESC.

Entering numbers

Numeric entries are called **values**. Values can be numbers, formulas, or @functions. You can enter and calculate with numbers from 10^{-4931} to 10^{4932}, but 1-2-3 can only display numbers from 10^{-99} to $9.99*10^{99}$. If 1-2-3 can't display a number, it displays *** (asterisks) instead. **Formulas** calculate or combine numbers and text. **@Functions** are built-in formulas that calculate with numbers and text. See Chapters 9 and 10 for information about entering formulas and @functions.

To add a note to a value entry, type ; (semicolon) immediately after the entry and then type your note. The note appears in the contents box but not in the cell.

When you enter numbers, 1-2-3 formats them automatically as Comma, Currency, Percent, or Scientific, depending on the symbols you use. For example, if you enter $37.00, 1-2-3 can tell from the $ (dollar sign) that you want this number to appear in Currency format. If you enter 37%, 1-2-3 can tell from the % (percent symbol) that you want this number to appear in Percent format. If you enter a plain number or a decimal, such as 7.875, 1-2-3 enters the number without thousands separators, percentage, or currency symbols.

If you don't want 1-2-3 to format your entries automatically, choose Tools User Setup and deselect the "Use Automatic format" check box.

To enter numbers

1. Select the cell where you want to enter the number:

    Mouse   Click the cell.

    Keyboard   Use ↑, ↓, →, ←, or the other pointer-movement keys to move the cell pointer to the cell.

*If you make a mistake as you type, press **BACKSPACE**. You can also press **ESC** to delete the entire entry.*

2. Enter the number.

    Begin with a number from 0 to 9 or a decimal point. Start a negative number with – (minus sign).

3. Confirm the entry:

    Mouse   Click the Confirm button or click another cell.

    Keyboard   Press **ENTER** or ↑, ↓, →, ←.

If you enter a number with more than 15 decimals, 1-2-3 rounds it to 15 decimals. If a number appears in the form *n*E+*n*, or a number with decimal places appears rounded, or if you see *** (asterisks) in the cell, it means the entry is too long to fit in the column. 1-2-3 stores the entire entry in the cell but can't display it.

If the number is within the limits that 1-2-3 can display, you can see the number by widening the column. Double-click the column border to the right of the column letter. For more information on widening columns, see "Changing column width" on page 125. Also, you can change the appearance of the number by using Style Number Format. For more information, see "To change the number format of a range or collection" on page 116.

Entering text

Text entries are called **labels**. In addition to letters, labels can contain numbers, or a combination of numbers and letters. For example, you can enter Victor Shing, or 201 Newbury Street, or $19,803 as labels.

By default, labels are left-aligned and values are right-aligned. You can use Style Alignment to change the alignment of labels and values.

If the first character you enter is a letter, 1-2-3 automatically precedes the entry with a **label-prefix character** to signal that the entry is a label. If you want to enter numbers as a label, you must start your entry with a label-prefix character.

For example, to enter 20,000 as a label, you must type a label-prefix character before typing 20,000. Each of the label-prefix characters has a different effect, as shown in the following table.

Label-prefix character	How the text aligns	Effect
'	Kathy	Left alignment
"	Kathy	Right alignment
^	Kathy	Center alignment
\	KathyKathyKathy	Label repeats

To enter text

1. Select the cell where you want to enter the text:

   Mouse   Click the cell.

   Keyboard   Use ↑, ↓, →, ←, or the other pointer-movement keys to move the cell pointer to the cell.

If you make a mistake as you type, press **BACKSPACE.** *You can also press* **ESC** *to delete the entire entry.*

2. Enter the text.

   If your entry doesn't start with a letter, be sure to begin the entry with a label-prefix character. You can use any of the label-prefix characters shown in the table above. You can enter up to 512 characters.

3. Confirm the entry:

    Mouse   Click the Confirm button or click another cell.

   Keyboard   Press ENTER or ↑, ↓, →, ←.

If the cells to the right of the label are blank, 1-2-3 displays the part of the label that overlaps those cells. If the label is too long to fit in the cell and the cell to the right contains data, 1-2-3 displays as much of the label as possible. To see the entire label, widen the column by double-clicking the column border to the right of the column letter. For more information on widening columns, see "Changing column width" on page 125.

Entering dates and times

You can enter a date or time, for example April 9, 1948 or 11:10 PM, as either a label or a value. When you enter dates or times as labels, remember to enter a label-prefix character first, if the date or time begins with a number.

When you enter a date or time as a value, you can use it in calculations and change its appearance by changing its number format. For example, you can calculate the number of days between two dates, or quickly change the appearance of a date from 4/9/48 to April 9, 1948. You can also use @functions, such as @DATE and @TIME, to enter dates and times and calculate with them.

1-2-3 automatically formats dates entered as 09-Apr-93, 09-Apr, or 04/09/93. 1-2-3 also automatically formats times entered in any of the standard time formats except hh.mm (hour.minutes).

If 1-2-3 doesn't automatically format a date or time when you enter it, a date or time number, such as 34068, appears in the cell. A **date number** is an integer that represents a date between January 1, 1900 and December 31, 2099. **Time numbers** are decimal numbers ranging from .0 (12:00:00 AM) to .9999884 (11:59:59 PM).

To enter a date or time

1. Select the cell where you want to enter the date or time:

   Mouse   Click the cell.

   Keyboard   Use ↑, ↓, →, ←, or the other pointer-movement keys to move the cell pointer to the cell.

2. Enter the date or time.

   For example, you can enter @DATE(93,2,14), 14-Feb-93, @TIME(14,33,0), 14:33, or 2:33 PM.

3. Confirm the entry:

    Mouse   Click the Confirm button or click another cell.

   Keyboard   Press ENTER or ↑, ↓, →, ←.

   If a date or time number appears in the cell, you can change the appearance of the number by using Style Number Format. For more information, see "To change the number format of a range or collection" on page 116.

    Shortcut   Select the cell and click the icon shown at left to enter the current date in MM/DD/YY format.

Entering data automatically

You can automatically fill a range with a sequence of data based on what's already in the range. For example, if you select a range whose top left cell contains the label January, 1-2-3 automatically fills the rest of the range with February, March, April, and so on. The illustration below shows the effects of filling ranges by example.

Before

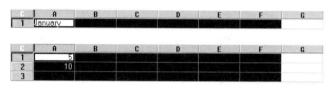

After

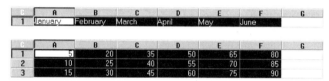

? Help   You can also fill a range automatically by using Range Fill to enter a sequence of numbers, dates, times, or percentages. For more information, search on "Filling ranges with values" in Help.

To fill a range by example

1. Select a range that includes the data you want to use as an example and the cells you want to fill.

    *   To create a sequence that increments each entry by 1 (for example, January, February, March), make sure the first cell in the range contains the data you want 1-2-3 to use to calculate the sequence.

    *   To create a sequence that increments each entry by a value other than 1 (for example, 5, 10, 15), make sure the first two cells in the range contain the data you want 1-2-3 to use to calculate the sequence.

        If 1-2-3 can't recognize the relationship between the data in the first two cells in the range (for example, Monday, February), it uses only the data in the first cell to calculate the sequence.

    Caution   1-2-3 writes over existing data in the fill range.

2. Choose Range Fill by Example.

1-2-3 fills the cells in the range from top to bottom in a column and from left to right in a row. If you specify a 3D fill range, 1-2-3 fills the range in the first worksheet, continues the sequence in the second worksheet, and so on until reaching the end of the range.

? Help   You can also create custom fill sequences. For more information, search on "Custom fill sequences" in Help.

Editing data

To change data or correct mistakes, you can replace an entry entirely or edit it. To replace an entry, select the cell, type the new entry, and press ENTER. You can edit data directly in the cell, or in the contents box, or you can switch between them by clicking in either area. You can also delete data, find and replace text, and check your spelling.

To edit in a cell

1. Double-click the cell you want to edit, or select the cell and press F2 (EDIT).

The insertion point appears in the cell. The cell contents also appear in the contents box.

You can also select characters by dragging across them; then press **BACKSPACE** *or* **DEL** *to delete the selected characters, or enter new text to replace them.*

2. Edit the entry.

Press BACKSPACE to delete characters to the left of the insertion point, or press DEL to delete characters to the right. Then enter replacement characters. If necessary, you can use → and ← to scroll through the cell's contents.

3. Click the Confirm button or press ENTER.

To edit in the contents box

Editing in the contents box is convenient when the entry is wider than the window and would require a great deal of scrolling.

1. Select the cell you want to edit.

The cell contents appear in the contents box.

To highlight a word, double-click it.

2. Click the contents box at the point where you want to begin editing, or press F2 (EDIT).

The insertion point appears where you clicked in the contents box.

3. Edit the entry.

Press BACKSPACE to delete characters to the left of the insertion point, or press DEL to delete characters to the right. Then enter replacement characters. If necessary, you can use → and ← to scroll through the entry in the contents box.

 4. Click the Confirm button or press ENTER.

To delete data

1. Select the range or collection.

2. Choose Edit Clear.

3. Select an option.

- "Cell contents only" deletes only cell contents, leaving all styles intact.

- Styles leaves the cell contacts intact and deletes number formats, text attributes, line styles and colors, alignment, background colors and patterns, and protection settings.

- Both deletes both cell contents and styles.

4. Choose OK.

If you delete a value that a formula refers to, the formula results in ERR. Any other formulas that depend on this invalid formula also result in ERR. For more information, see "Moving formulas" on page 105.

  Shortcut   Click the trash can icon shown at left or press DEL to delete cell contents without displaying the dialog box. Click the eraser icon to delete styles without displaying the dialog box.

To find and replace text

You can search through the cells in your worksheet to find and replace characters.

 1. Choose Edit Find & Replace.

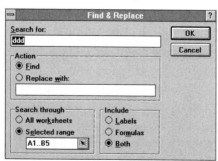

2. In the "Search for" text box, enter the characters you want to find.

   You can enter up to 512 characters.

3. Under Action, select the action you want 1-2-3 to perform.
   - Find highlights occurrences of the characters in the search area.
   - "Replace with" replaces occurrences of the characters with the characters you enter in the "Replace with" text box. Enter the replacement characters in the "Replace with" text box.

4. Under Include, select the kinds of entries you want to search.
   - Labels searches only in cells containing labels.
   - Formulas searches only in cells containing formulas.
   - Both searches labels and formulas.

5. Under Search through, select All worksheets or Selected range.

   If you select Selected range, specify the range.

6. Choose OK.

   1-2-3 highlights the first occurrence of the search characters and displays the Find dialog box if you selected Find in step 3, or the Replace dialog box if you selected "Replace with."

7. In the Find dialog box, choose Find Next to highlight the next occurrence of the search characters, or Close to stop the search and return to Ready mode.

8. In the Replace dialog box, choose one of the following:
   - Replace replaces the highlighted characters with the replacement characters and highlights the next occurrence of the search characters.
   - Replace All replaces all remaining occurrences of the search characters with the replacement characters, without highlighting any more occurrences of the search characters.
   - Find Next moves to the next occurrence of the search characters and doesn't replace the highlighted occurrence.
   - Close stops the search and returns to Ready mode.

1-2-3 displays a message when it can't find another occurrence of the search characters.

To check spelling
You can correct misspelled words and check for duplicate words, such as "the the" in worksheet entries, charts, text blocks, and query tables.

1. To limit the area where 1-2-3 checks, select a range.

2. Choose Tools Spell Check.

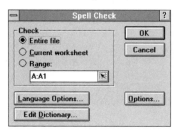

3. Under Check, select an option.
   - Entire file checks all cells, charts, and text blocks in the current file. Select this option to check spelling in charts.
   - Current worksheet checks all cells and text blocks in the current worksheet.
   - Range checks cells, query tables, and text blocks within the selected range.

4. Choose OK.

   1-2-3 begins checking the worksheet for spelling errors and duplicate words. If it finds a word that's not in the language dictionary or a duplicate word, 1-2-3 highlights the word in the worksheet and displays the following dialog box:

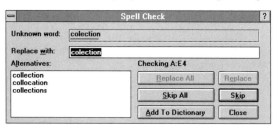

5. Do one of the following:

- To change the word, select an alternative word from the Alternatives list box, or enter an alternative in the "Replace with" text box. Then choose Replace to replace only this occurrence of the unrecognized word or Replace All to replace all occurrences of the unrecognized word.
- To keep a word unchanged, choose Skip or Skip All.
- To add the word to the user dictionary, choose Add To Dictionary.
- To delete a repeated word, press DEL and then choose Replace.
- To stop checking spelling and save any corrections you've made up to that point, choose Close.

When 1-2-3 finishes checking spelling, it displays a message.

? **Help**   You can add words to the user dictionary, use a different default language dictionary, and select various spell check options. For more information, search on "Spelling" in Help.

Copying data

After you've entered data once, you can copy it to other places in the worksheet. Copying data saves time and prevents typing errors. Copying always leaves what you copied unchanged. You can copy ranges, columns, rows, and drawn objects such as charts. For information about copying drawn objects, see page 183. Also, when you copy data, it can affect your formulas. For more information, see "Copying and moving formulas" on page 101.

You can copy data by dragging a copy to another location, by using the Clipboard, or by filling adjacent cells. Dragging is a quick and easy way to copy data to a single location in the current worksheet.

The **Clipboard** is a temporary storage area for data that you remove or copy using Edit Cut or Edit Copy. You can use Edit Paste to copy data from the Clipboard to as many locations as you want, including worksheets in other active files. The copied or cut data remains on the Clipboard until you replace it by using Edit Cut or Edit Copy again.

? **Help**   For information about copying data from the current file and extracting it to a file on disk, search on "Extracting data" in Help.

To copy data by dragging

1. Select the range.
2. Move the mouse pointer to the edge of the selected range so that the pointer changes to a hand, as shown below.

You can cancel dragging by pressing ESC before you release the mouse button.

3. Hold down CTRL, press the mouse button, and drag a copy of the selected range.

   While you drag, the mouse pointer changes to a fist with a + (plus sign), and the range appears as an outline.

4. Release the mouse button when the outline of the range is where you want to put the copy.

   Caution   1-2-3 writes over any existing data in the destination range.

To copy data using the Clipboard

1. Select the range.
2. Choose Edit Copy or press CTRL+C.

   1-2-3 places a copy of the data on the Clipboard.

3. Select the destination for the copied data.

   You need to select only the top left cell of the destination range. The destination range can be in the same file, in another file, or in another active Windows application.

   Caution   1-2-3 writes over any existing data in the destination range.

4. Choose Edit Paste or press CTRL+V.

The contents of the Clipboard appear in the destination range. To paste the data into other ranges, repeat steps 3 and 4.

If the destination range has room for more than one copy of the source range, 1-2-3 repeats the copied data until the destination range is full. For example, if you copy the quarterly headings to a range containing three rows, they appear three times, as shown below.

To copy data to adjacent cells

You can copy the contents of the top row or leftmost column of the range to the remaining cells in the range. This is especially useful for copying formulas and @functions.

1. Select a range.

   Include the cells you want to copy and the adjacent area down or to the right that you want to fill with the copied data. For example, you can select the range A6..D6 to copy the formula in cell A6 to cells B6, C6, and D6.

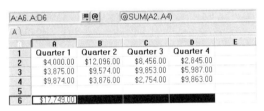

2. Do one of the following:

   - To copy the leftmost column of the selection into the selected adjacent columns to the right, choose Edit Copy Right.
   - To copy the top row of the selection into the selected adjacent rows below, choose Edit Copy Down.

   For example, to copy the formula in cell A6 to cells B6, C6, and D6, choose Edit Copy Right.

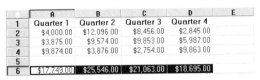

? **Help**   You can also copy data to adjacent cells up or to the left, or to adjacent worksheets. For more information, search on "Copying data" in Help.

Moving data

You can rearrange your worksheet data by moving it. When you move data, 1-2-3 leaves the source range blank and enters the data, including styles, in the destination. You can move data either by dragging it or by cutting and pasting it using the Clipboard. For information about the Clipboard, see page 77.

Because you make only one selection and don't use the Clipboard, dragging is the quickest way to move data in the current worksheet. You can drag ranges, columns, rows, charts, drawn objects, and query tables. You can also drag chart elements including titles, footnotes, legends, and pie slices. For more information about moving drawn objects, see page 183.

When you drag a range of data, it writes over any data in the destination range. When you drag entire columns or rows, 1-2-3 inserts them instead of writing over data in the destination range. When you move data, it can affect your formulas. For more information, see "Copying and moving formulas" on page 101.

When you use the Clipboard, you can paste data to as many locations as you want. The cut data remains on the Clipboard until you replace it by using Edit Copy or Edit Cut again.

To move data by dragging

1. Select the range.

2. Move the mouse pointer to the edge of the selected range so that the pointer changes to a hand, as shown below.

3. Hold down the mouse button and drag the selected range.

   While you drag, the mouse pointer changes to a fist and the range appears as an outline.

You can cancel dragging by pressing ESC before you release the mouse button.

4. Release the mouse button when the outline of the range is where you want to move the data.

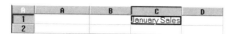

Caution   1-2-3 writes over any existing data in the destination range.

To move data using the Clipboard

1. Select the range.

2. Choose Edit Cut or press CTRL+X.

   1-2-3 places the data on the Clipboard and removes it from the worksheet.

3. Select the destination range.

   You need to select only the top left cell of the destination range.

   Caution   1-2-3 writes over existing data in the destination range.

4. Choose Edit Paste or press CTRL+V.

   The contents of the Clipboard appear in the destination range. To paste the data into other ranges, repeat steps 3 and 4.

Inserting and deleting columns, rows, and ranges

You can insert and delete entire columns and rows. You can also insert or delete a selected range in a worksheet. When you insert a selected range, an adjacent range of the same proportions shifts to the right or down to make room for the inserted range. When you delete a selected range, an adjacent range of the same proportions shifts left or upwards to take the place of the deleted range.

Caution   If Group mode is on, adding or deleting columns or rows affects the same range in all worksheets in the file. For more information about Group mode, see "Grouping worksheets" on page 55.

You can also insert and delete entire worksheets. For more information, see page 45.

To insert columns or rows

1. Select as many entire columns or rows as you want to insert.

	A	B	C	D
1		January	February	March
2	Boston	943	782	490
3	Chicago	570	874	567
4	New York	350	654	932

2. Choose Edit Insert or press CTRL+GRAY PLUS on the numeric keypad.

1-2-3 inserts the number of columns or rows you selected, placing new columns to the left of the columns you selected or new rows above the rows you selected.

To delete columns or rows

1. Select the columns or rows you want to delete.

2. Choose Edit Delete or press CTRL+GRAY MINUS on the numeric keypad.

   1-2-3 deletes the selected columns or rows, along with any data they contain. The columns to the right or the rows below take the place of what you deleted.

To insert a range

1. Select a range where you want to insert a range of the same proportions.

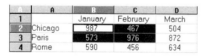

2. Choose Edit Insert or press CTRL+GRAY PLUS.

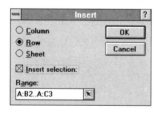

3. Select the Insert selection check box.

4. Do one of the following:
   - To shift the selected range to the right, select Column.

A	B	C	D	E	F
1		January	February	March		
2 Chicago				987	467	504
3 Paris				573	976	872
4 Rome		590	456	634		

   - To shift the selected range down, select Row.

A	B	C	D
1		January	February	March
2 Chicago				504
3 Paris				872
4 Rome				634
5		987	467	
6		573	976	
		590	456	

5. Choose OK.

To delete a range

1. Select the range you want to delete.
2. Choose Edit Delete or press CTRL+GRAY MINUS.
3. Select the Delete selection check box.
4. Do one of the following:
   - If you want the range to the right of the deleted range to shift left, select Column.
   - If you want the range below the deleted range to shift upwards, select Row.
5. Choose OK.

How inserting and deleting affects formulas

Inserting or deleting columns, rows, and worksheets may move formulas or the values they refer to. 1-2-3 adjusts each formula so that it continues to refer to the same values as before. When you insert rows, columns, or worksheets in the middle of a range that a formula refers to, 1-2-3 adjusts the formula to include the new cells in the range.

If you insert rows or columns just *under* or *next to* a range a formula refers to, *you* must adjust the formula if you want it to include the inserted cells.

If you delete a column, row, or worksheet containing a range that a formula refers to, the formula results in ERR. Any other formulas that depend on this invalid formula also result in ERR. For more information, see "Moving formulas" on page 105.

?	**Related Help topics**

You can rearrange data by **transposing** it, which means converting rows into columns and columns into rows. For more information, search on "Transposing data" in Help.

You can use Edit Paste Special to paste the styles and contents of a range separately. For more information, search on "Pasting data" in Help.

Also, Tutorial lessons 1 and 2 include exercises for entering and editing data. Choose Help Tutorial to start the Tutorial.

8

Working with Range Names

You can name a range and then use the name in place of the address. Range names are easy to remember and enter, and they're convenient for building formulas, going to and selecting data, and printing specific areas of a file. You also name ranges to use with Version Manager. This chapter describes how to name a range, go to and select a named range, enter a range name in a dialog box, and delete range names.

What is a range name?

A **range name** is a word you substitute for an address. You can use range names instead of addresses in formulas, @functions, macros, and dialog boxes. In the illustration below, the name of range B2..B5 is Hats, and the range name appears in an @function.

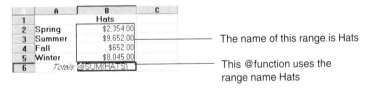

The name of this range is Hats

This @function uses the range name Hats

Naming ranges

You can name a range by typing the name. You can also name several single-cell ranges at once, using labels in adjacent cells. After you name a range, 1-2-3 substitutes the name for the address in any existing formulas containing the address.

For example, if you name B2..B5 HATS, 1-2-3 changes the formula @SUM(B2..B5) to @SUM(HATS). For more information about using range names in formulas and @functions, see page 98.

The number of range names you can create in a file is limited only by the amount of available memory. You can have different names for the same range, but you can't use the same name for more than one range in the same file. If you give a range another name, it doesn't replace the old name in formulas. You can also delete existing names.

When you insert or delete columns or rows within a named range, 1-2-3 changes the range associated with the name. For example, if the name of A6..C6 is Terms, and you insert a column between columns B and C, Terms becomes A6..D6.

If you move data into the first or last cell of a named range, the range name is no longer associated with that range. Also, if you delete a column, row, or worksheet that contains the first or last cell of a range, the range name is no longer associated with that range. Formulas that contain range names not associated with a range result in ERR.

? **Help**   For more information about ERR, search on "ERR" in Help.

Range name guidelines

Use the following guidelines when naming ranges:

- Range names can be up to 15 characters long.

- You can enter names in uppercase characters, lowercase characters, or a combination. When you enter the name, 1-2-3 changes it to uppercase.

- You can use letters, numbers, and _ (underscores) in range names, but don't start a range name with a number.

- Don't start a range name with ! (exclamation point) and don't include , (comma), ; (semicolon), . (period), or the characters +, −, *, /, &, >, <, @, #, or { in a range name.

- Don't use spaces in range names. Use underscores instead.

- If you're not using the range name in formulas or macros, you can use − (hyphen) in the name, but don't begin a name with a hyphen.

- Don't use @function names, macro command keywords such as BEEP, or the names of keys, such as HOME.

- Don't create names that look like cell addresses, such as Q2 for Quarter 2, or FY93 for Fiscal Year 1993.

To name a range by typing

1. Select the range.
2. Choose Range Name.

3. Type the name in the Name text box.
4. Choose Add.

    1-2-3 adds the name to the list of existing named ranges.

5. Choose OK.

To name a range using adjacent labels

You can name single-cell ranges using labels you've entered in adjacent cells. This method is convenient for naming more than one single-cell range at a time. The labels can be to the right, to the left, above, or below the cells you want to name. In the illustration below, the labels name the cells to the right.

Use the labels in A1, A2, and A3...      ...to name the adjacent cells to the right: B1, B2, and B3

1. Select the range containing the labels.
2. Choose Range Name.
3. In the For cells drop-down box, select a direction: To the right, To the left, Above, or Below.
4. Choose Use Labels.
5. Choose OK.

Each label in the range becomes the name of the adjacent cell in the specified direction.

Using range names

This section describes how to go to and select a named range, enter a range name in a dialog box, and delete range names.

To go to and select a named range

1. Do one of the following:

    *   To go to and select a named range in the current file, click the navigator and select a name from the list.

    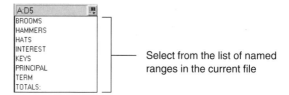

    Select from the list of named ranges in the current file

    *   To go to and select a named range in the current file or in another active file, choose Edit Go To or press F5 (GOTO); select a range name; and choose OK.

    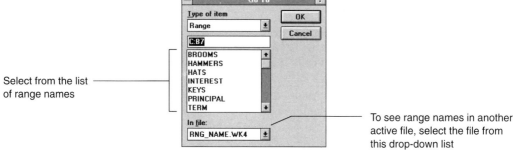

    Select from the list of range names

    To see range names in another active file, select the file from this drop-down list

    1-2-3 moves the cell pointer to the first cell of the range and selects the entire range. If the range is outside the visible area of the worksheet, 1-2-3 scrolls the worksheet so the top left cell of the range appears in the top left corner of the active window.

To enter a range name in a dialog box

After choosing a command, you can enter a range name instead of a range address in the dialog box. You can type the name, use the navigator, or press F3 (NAME).

1. In the dialog box, select the range text box where you want to enter the range name.

2. Do one of the following:

    - Type the range name.

      If the range is in another active file, include the file name enclosed in << >> (angle brackets); for example, <<DBTABLE.WK4>>SALES.

    - Click the navigator and select the name of a range in the current file.

    - Press **F3 (NAME)**, select a range name; and choose OK.

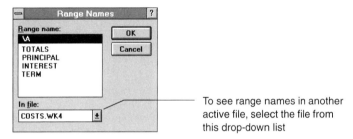

To see range names in another active file, select the file from this drop-down list

To delete range names

You can delete range names in the current file one at a time or all at once.

1. Choose Range Name.

2. Do one of the following:

    - To delete a range name in the current file, select the name from the Existing named ranges list box and choose Delete.

    - To delete all the range names in the current file, choose Delete All.

3. Choose OK.

When you delete a range name, the data in the range doesn't change. If you delete a range name used in a formula, 1-2-3 replaces the range name with its associated address. For example, if SALES is the name of B14..H14, and you delete the name SALES, 1-2-3 changes @SUM(SALES) to @SUM(B14..H14).

Note   A named range can also have one or more versions for creating scenarios. If you delete a named range, 1-2-3 deletes all versions of the range. For more information about versions and scenarios, see Chapter 22.

9 Calculating with Formulas

Formulas are the basis of all calculations in 1-2-3. When you calculate with a formula, your data is dynamic. If you change a value a formula refers to, 1-2-3 automatically recalculates the formula. This chapter describes the types of formulas you can use, the rules for entering formulas, and how to enter, copy, and move formulas.

What is a formula?

A **formula** is a worksheet entry that calculates data. The result of a formula is a number or text. A formula can contain numbers, text, operators, cell addresses, range names, @functions, and other formulas.

The formula calculation can be a simple mathematical calculation, such as subtracting one number from another, or a more complicated calculation, such as determining the net present value of a series of future cash flows.

Types of formulas

You can enter three types of formulas in 1-2-3: numeric, text, and logical.

Numeric formulas perform calculations with values. Most of the formulas in a typical worksheet are numeric formulas. Numeric formulas use +, −, *, /, and ^ for addition, subtraction, multiplication, division, and exponentiation. The illustration below shows some examples of simple numeric formulas.

B4 ⊞ @ X ✓ 25+5	Result is 30
B4 ⊞ @ X ✓ 15+A1	Result is 10 if A1 contains 5
B4 ⊞ @ X ✓ 22*A1/A2	Result is 11 if A1 contains 5 and A2 contains 10

1-2-3 can calculate any numeric formula whose value is from 9.99E–4931 (9.99*10^{-4931}) through 1.19E+4932 (1.19*10^{4932}). However, the value of the formula must be from 1E–99 (1*10^{-99}) through 9.99E+99 (9.99*10^{99}) for 1-2-3 to display it; otherwise, 1-2-3 displays *** (asterisks) in the cell containing the formula.

The number of decimal places 1-2-3 displays for a calculated value depends on the number format of the cell. 1-2-3 calculates the value to a precision of between 18 and 19 total digits regardless of how many it displays. You can use an @function, such as @ROUND, to specify a different precision.

You use **text formulas** to manipulate text. In a text formula, you must enclose text in " " (quotation marks). Text formulas use & (ampersand) to combine strings of text. You can use text formulas to combine in one cell the text from several cells, to change the case of text characters, or to find occurrences of certain text characters in cells. The illustration below shows two examples of text formulas.

A:B4	🔲@✕✔ +"New "&D6	Result is New Balance if D6 contains the text Balance

A:B4	🔲@✕✔ +"New "&"Balance"	Result is New Balance

Logical formulas are statements that evaluate a condition. They result in 1 if true and 0 if false. You can use them to test whether a value meets a condition before using it in other formulas. Logical formulas use =, <, >, <=, >=, and <>, as well as #AND#, #OR#, and #NOT# to evaluate various conditions. The figure below shows some examples of logical formulas.

B4	🔲@✕✔ 5>4	Result is 1 (true)

B4	🔲@✕✔ 5>A1	Result is 1 when the value in A1 is less than 5

B4	🔲@✕✔ +A1=1#AND#A2=2	Result is 1 if A1 contains 1 and A2 contains 2, but result is 0 if either cell contains a different value

B4	🔲@✕✔ +A1=1#OR#A2=2	Result is 1 if A1 contains 1 or if A2 contains 2

B4	🔲@✕✔ #NOT#A1=0	Result is 1 if A1 is any value but zero

Building a formula

Operands

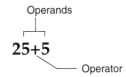

25+5

Operator

Nested parentheses

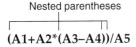

(A1+A2*(A3−A4))/A5

To build a formula, you use the following three basic elements:

- **Operands** are values or text that the formula operates upon. Although you can enter values or text directly into a formula, you can often make a formula more useful by entering instead the addresses or names of cells that contain the values or text. For information, see "Referring to cells and ranges in formulas" on page 97.

- **Operators** are mathematical symbols, text characters, or logical statements that tell 1-2-3 what to do with the operands in a formula. The **arithmetic operators** are +, −, *, /, ^ for addition, subtraction, multiplication, division, and exponentiation. The **text operator** for combining text is & (ampersand). The **logical operators** are =, <, >, <>, >=, <=, #NOT#, #AND#, and #OR#.

- **Separators** are for combining various operations and multiple formulas in one formula. You can use separators such as parentheses in complex formulas to tell 1-2-3 the order in which you want the formulas calculated.

In the example at left, the inside formula is set off from the outside formula with parentheses. In a formula, one or more pairs of parentheses enclosed in another pair of parentheses are called **nested parentheses**.

Entering a formula

This section describes the guidelines and procedure for entering a formula, and some common errors.

Guidelines for entering formulas

Use the following guidelines when entering a formula:

- A formula can begin with a number or one of the characters +, −, =, (, @, ., $, #. @ (at sign) indicates an @function; . (period) indicates a decimal; $ (dollar sign) indicates an absolute reference; # (number sign) indicates the beginning of a logical formula.

- When the first element of a formula is a cell address or range name, you must begin the formula with +, −, =, (, or $. For example, +B7/B8, -B7*B8, (JAN-20), and $JAN/B8 are all valid formulas.

- When the first character in a text formula is a " (quotation mark), you must begin the formula with (or +. For example, ("Ms. "&LAST), and +"Ms. "&LAST are both valid formulas.

- When a formula looks like a date in month/day/year, day/month/year, or year-month-day format, begin the formula with +; otherwise, 1-2-3 enters a date or date number instead of the formula. For example, +9/25/90 is a valid formula.

- A formula can't contain spaces except within text enclosed in " " (quotation marks) in text formulas and text @functions.

- To enter an @function in a formula, you can select it from the @function selector in the edit line; or you can type @, press F3 (NAME), and then select the @function. See Chapter 10 for information about @functions.

- 1-2-3 assigns the value 0 to blank cells whose addresses are used in formulas and @functions, except statistical and text @functions. Most statistical @functions ignore blank cells, and text @functions evaluate to ERR.

To enter a formula

You enter a formula in a cell much as you enter any data in a worksheet. Once you've entered a formula in a cell, 1-2-3 displays the formula in the contents box and the formula's result in the cell. Unless you format the cell as text or edit in the cell, the formula itself appears only in the contents box.

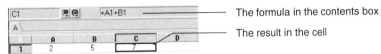

The formula in the contents box

The result in the cell

1. Select the cell where you want to enter the formula.

2. Enter + to begin the formula.

Beginning a formula with = is the same as beginning it with +.

You can also begin the formula with a number or the characters –, =, @, ., (, #, $. The mode indicator changes to Value.

3. Enter the first operand (cell A1 in the example).

4. Enter the first operator (+ in the example).

To add a note to the formula, type ; (semicolon) immediately after the formula and then type the note. The note appears in the contents box only, unless you format the cell as text.

5. Enter the next operand (cell B1 in the example).

6. Repeat steps 4 and 5 until the formula is complete.

The example uses only two operands and one operator, but a formula can contain several operands, operators, and parentheses as needed, using up to 512 characters. Enter spaces only within text enclosed in quotation marks.

 7. When the formula is complete, click the Confirm button or press ENTER.

If the result of the formula is too long to fit in the cell, 1-2-3 displays *** (asterisks). To display the formula result, widen the column by double-clicking the column border to the right of the column letter. For more information, see "Changing column width" on page 125.

Caution Because you can select ranges for a formula with the mouse or by using ↑, ↓, →, ←, confirming a formula entry by clicking another cell or by using ↑, ↓, →, ← may not produce the results you intend. For more information about selecting ranges for a formula, see "Referring to cells and ranges in formulas" on page 97.

Some common errors in formulas

When you try to enter a formula containing an error, 1-2-3 beeps and doesn't accept the formula, or the formula results in ERR. If 1-2-3 beeps, the insertion point remains in the formula so you can examine the formula for errors such as extra spaces, missing operators, or missing parentheses. You can edit a formula as you edit any data.

The table below suggests solutions for common errors that can occur when you enter a formula.

What you did	*Try this*
Why does this formula result in ERR?	
You used zero as a denominator.	Don't divide by zero.
You used an undefined range name or text that you haven't yet defined as a range name.	Link the name with an address. For information, see "Naming ranges" on page 85.
In a text formula, you referred to a cell that contains a value.	Correct the formula to refer to a cell that contains text, or correct the cell so it contains text.
You referred to a file that doesn't exist.	Create the file or refer to an existing file using a file reference. For more information on file references, see "Referring to other files in formulas" on page 98.
You deleted a range name referred to in the formula, or moved data into its first or last cell.	Correct the address to refer to the data in its new location.
Other Problems	
Your numeric formula looks like a date to 1-2-3, for example 11/30, or 30–Aug (if Aug is a range name).	Enclose the formula in parentheses or start with + or =, for example +30–Aug or (11/30).
You entered a formula that begins with a range name, and it didn't evaluate.	Enclose the formula in parentheses or start it with +, –, or =.
You entered an address one way, for example with a worksheet letter in the address, but 1-2-3 changed the way the address looks, or changed the address to a range name.	Don't worry. 1-2-3 sometimes adjusts references you enter to show what's relevant. For example, if you have only one worksheet, 1-2-3 doesn't show worksheet letters in the formula. This doesn't affect your formulas.

Referring to cells and ranges in formulas

You don't have to enter the values and text that a formula calculates directly into the formula. Instead, you can use addresses or names of single cells that contain the data you want to use in your calculations. With @functions, you can use multiple-cell as well as single-cell addresses.

A cell address in a formula is called a **reference** because the formula refers to data in this cell. Every time you change the data in a cell referred to by a formula, the result of the formula changes, as shown below.

The formula in B3 subtracts the contents of B2 from B1

When the value in B1 changes, the result of the formula in B3 also changes

To enter an address in a formula

You can enter a cell or range address in a formula by typing it, or you can select the range with the mouse or keyboard so that 1-2-3 enters the address for you. Selecting helps you avoid typing errors.

1. Select a cell and begin entering the formula by typing an operator.

2. Select the cell or range you want to refer to:

    Mouse   Click the cell or drag to select a range.

    Keyboard   Use ↑, ↓, →, ← to move the cell pointer to the cell. For a range, move to a cell at the corner of the range, press . (period), and use ↑, ↓, →, ← to highlight the other cells. You can also type the address into the formula.

3. You can enter other operators and addresses, and separators as needed, up to 512 characters.

 4. Click the Confirm button, or press ENTER.

1-2-3 enters the result of the formula in the cell.

To enter a range name in a formula

To locate and change occurrences of a range name in formulas, use Edit Find & Replace.

You can enter a range name in a formula in place of an address. Suppose you have two ranges named PRICE and COST in a worksheet. The formula below uses range names to subtract the average of the COST range from the average of the PRICE range. You can enter the range names in the formula by selecting them from the navigator.

Select from the navigator to enter a range name in a formula

Price ——————— Cost

If you plan to use a range name in a formula, you can use it as a placeholder in the formula before you define the range name. The formula results in ERR until you define the range name.

1. Begin entering a formula.

   Enter the formula up to the operator or ((open parenthesis) that precedes the range name you want to enter.

2. Do one of the following:

   • Click the navigator and select the range name from the list.

   • Press F3 (NAME) and select the range name from the list.

   • Type the range name.

3. Complete the formula.

Referring to other files in formulas

Sharing data in formulas is easier and faster within the same file. If you don't need to keep linked data in separate files, put it all in a multiple-sheet file.

Formulas can refer to ranges in other 1-2-3 files as well as ranges in the current file. This is called a **file reference**. A formula in one file that refers to a range in another file **links** the two files. A formula can refer to an active file or to a file on disk.

For example, if you're doing a complex set of tax calculations depending on rates that might change with new tax legislation, you can create a separate file containing a list of the various tax rates. Then you can create links to these rates in files that do the tax calculations. When you change the tax rates, 1-2-3 automatically updates all the formulas that refer to these rates.

To refer to another file in a formula

1. Enter the formula up to the operator or ((open parenthesis) that precedes the file reference.

2. Do one of the following:

    -   If the other file is visible, use the mouse to select the range.
    -   Press **CTRL+PG UP** or **CTRL+PG DN** to go to the other file and use the keyboard to select the range.
    -   Type the file reference using the following format:

        +<<*filename*.WK?>>*range*

        where *filename*.WK? is the name and extension of the file and *range* is the address or range name of the data you want to reference; for example, <<SALES.WK4>>A:E2 in the illustration below.

    Note   You can specify the *filename* with or without a path and you can link to .WK4, .WK3, or .WK1 files.

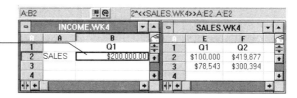

Formula in B2 of INCOME refers to data in cell E2 of SALES

 3. Click the Confirm button or press **ENTER**.

Any changes you make to data in the SALES file are automatically reflected in the formula in B2 of the INCOME file. For example, if the value in A:E2 in the SALES file changes, then the value of the formula in A:B2 in the INCOME file changes as shown in the illustration below.

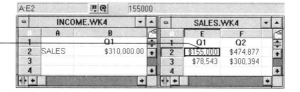

Changing the value in E2 of SALES changes the value of the formula in B2 of INCOME

To update file links

If Tools User Setup Recalculation is set to Automatic, when you open a file that refers to other active files, 1-2-3 automatically updates all the file links. If you open a file that has links to a file on disk, you need to update the links manually so the file uses current data from the linked files. When you update file links, 1-2-3 updates all the links in the file; you can't update links individually. For more information about recalculating formulas, see page 105.

1. Choose Edit Links.
2. Select File links from the Link type drop-down box.
3. Choose Update All.
4. Choose Close.

How 1-2-3 calculates a formula

Precedence numbers represent the order in which 1-2-3 performs operations in a formula. The lower the precedence number, the earlier 1-2-3 performs the operation. 1-2-3 performs operations with the same precedence number sequentially from left to right. The following table shows the order of precedence for all operators you can use in formulas.

Precedence number	Operation	Operator
1	Exponentiation	^
2	Identification of value as negative or positive	− +
3	Multiplication and division	* /
4	Addition and subtraction	+ −
5	Equal-to and not-equal-to tests	= <>
5	Less-than and greater-than tests	< >
5	Less-than-or-equal-to test	<=
5	Greater-than-or-equal-to test	>=
6	Logical-NOT test	#NOT#
7	Logical-AND and logical-OR tests	#AND# #OR#
7	Text concatenation	&

Overriding order of precedence

You can override precedence order in a formula by enclosing operations in parentheses. 1-2-3 performs operations enclosed in parentheses first. Within each set of parentheses, the precedence numbers listed in the table on the previous page apply.

The illustration below shows the order in which 1-2-3 performs the operations in a formula containing nested parentheses and operators with different precedence numbers.

4th   1st   2nd   3rd   5th

$$A1+((A2+A3)*A4)/A5-A6$$

Copying and moving formulas

You can copy a formula and use it in other cells, or move it to a new location in the worksheet. You can copy or move formulas to different cells of the same worksheet, to different worksheets, or to different files. You copy a formula the same way you copy other data. For information, see "Copying data" on page 77. This section describes how copying and moving formulas affects cell references.

When you copy a formula containing addresses, the addresses automatically adjust to their new location(s) in the worksheet. Addresses that adjust when you copy them to new locations are called **relative references**.

Sometimes you want to copy formulas to other locations but want to make sure they always refer to the same worksheets, rows, and columns. Addresses that always refer to the same worksheets, rows, and columns no matter where you put them are called **absolute references**.

Absolute symbol

$A:$B$25

You can make relative references absolute by adding a $ (dollar sign) to the worksheet letter or name, to the column letter, and to the row number, as shown in the figure to the left. You can create a **mixed reference** by making part of an address absolute and leaving other parts relative, for example $A:B$25.

Copying formulas with relative references

An ordinary cell address, for example, A:B25, is all relative. When you copy a formula containing relative references and paste it in a new location, 1-2-3 automatically adjusts the cell and range addresses in the formula to refer to cells relative to the formula's new location, as shown in the next illustration.

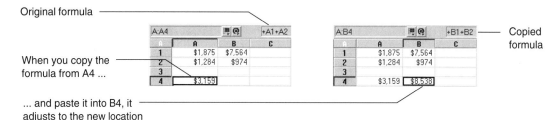

Original formula

When you copy the formula from A4 ...

... and paste it into B4, it adjusts to the new location

Copied formula

If you want to use the same formula in many cells, you can copy the original formula and paste it into several cells at once. For example, you can copy a formula in column A and then paste it into columns B through D. 1-2-3 adjusts the addresses for each new location.

Copying formulas with absolute references

Sometimes you want a formula always to refer to the same cells, no matter where and how many times you copy and paste it. To ensure that a formula refers to the same cells even if you copy it, you can change the references to absolute references.

To make references absolute, add a $ (dollar sign) before each element in the reference, or select the reference and press **F4 (ABS)**. File names are always absolute references.

Suppose you're calculating the interest on a series of principal values, and you want to use the same interest rate each time. The illustration below shows how you can make an absolute reference to the cell containing the interest rate. The formula in B4 contains an absolute reference to the interest rate in A2. When you copy this formula and paste it into cells in column B, the copied formulas also refer to A2.

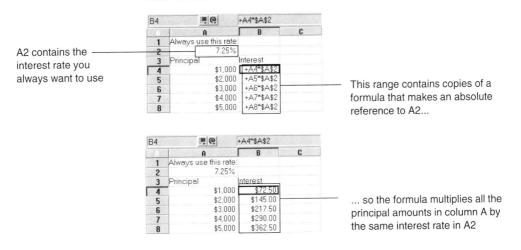

A2 contains the interest rate you always want to use

This range contains copies of a formula that makes an absolute reference to A2...

... so the formula multiplies all the principal amounts in column A by the same interest rate in A2

Copying formulas with mixed references

When you copy or move a formula that refers to a range, you may want part of the address to stay the same in the new formula and part of the address to change. For example, you may want the column letter to stay the same but the row number to change. You do this by using a mixed reference.

A mixed reference contains some absolute and some relative elements, for example an absolute column letter and a relative row number. To make parts of a reference absolute, add a $ (dollar sign) before the part you want to be absolute, or press F4 (ABS) repeatedly until it's correct.

Suppose you want to calculate interest, as in the previous example, but using three different interest rates. You can use the same formula to do all the calculations, as long as it contains mixed references.

The formula in the illustration below, +$A4*B$1, mixes absolute and relative references. It makes a relative reference to the column and an absolute reference to the row containing the interest rates. So 1-2-3 moves across a column each time, but looks in the same row. It also makes a relative reference to the row and an absolute reference to the column containing the various principal values. So 1-2-3 moves down a row each time but looks in the same column.

The formula refers to the interest rate by relative column, absolute row

B4		🔲 @	+$A4*B$1			
	A		B	C	D	E
1	Try these interest rates:		7.50%	8.00%	8.50%	
2						
3	Principal					
4	$1,000		$75	$80	$85	
5	$2,000		$150	$160	$170	
6	$3,000		$225	$240	$255	
7	$4,000		$300	$320	$340	
8	$5,000		$375	$400	$425	

The formula refers to the principals by absolute column, relative row

To copy and paste the results of a formula

Occasionally you want to copy a formula and paste the results of the formula, not the formula itself, into another cell. This is useful when you need only the results for further calculations.

1. Select the cell or range that contains the formula or formulas whose results you want to copy.

2. Choose Edit Copy.

3. Select the cell or range where you want to paste the results of the formula or formulas.

To convert a formula to its value, double-click the cell containing the formula and press **F9 (CALC)**.

4. Choose Edit Paste Special.

5. Under Paste, select Formulas as values.

6. Choose OK.

Shortcut   Do the first 3 steps of the procedure above, and then click the icon at left to paste formulas as values.

Moving formulas

Moving data affects formulas in different ways depending on whether you move the formulas, the cells they refer to, or both. You move formulas and data for formulas the same way you move other data. For information about moving data, see page 80.

Keep in mind the following when moving formulas and data for formulas:

- If you move a formula, but not the data it refers to, the references in the formula don't change. For example, if you move the formula +A1+B3 from cell C10 to cell D10, the formula remains +A1+B3.
- If you move the data that a formula refers to, 1-2-3 adjusts the formula. For example, if cell C10 contains +A1+B3 and you move the contents of cell A1 to cell Q25, the formula in cell C10 changes to +Q25+B3.
- If you move a formula and the data it refers to, 1-2-3 adjusts all references, including absolute references. For example, if cell A3 contains the formula +$A$1+A2 and you move the range A1..A3 to B1..B3, the formula in cell B3 is +$B$1+B2.

Recalculating formulas

The Tools User Setup Recalculation setting determines how 1-2-3 recalculates your formulas when you change data they refer to.

- When Tools User Setup Recalculation is set to Automatic (the default), 1-2-3 immediately recalculates formulas whenever you change data they refer to. Automatic recalculation occurs in the background, so you can continue your work while it's happening.

  The Calc button appears in the status bar whenever 1-2-3 is performing an automatic recalculation.

- When Tools User Setup Recalculation is set to Manual, 1-2-3 recalculates formulas only when you press F9 (CALC), or click the Calc button in the status bar, or click the icon at left. Manual recalculation occurs in the foreground, so you must wait for 1-2-3 to complete it before continuing your work.

  With manual recalculation, the Calc button appears in the status bar whenever you change worksheet data. This reminds you that some of your formulas may now need updating.

Note   These recalculation methods apply only to formulas that refer to data in active files. See "To update file links" on page 100 for information about how 1-2-3 recalculates formulas linked to files on disk.

Whenever 1-2-3 performs a recalculation pass, it recalculates only those formulas affected by the changes in data; it skips over any formulas not affected by those changes. This technique, called **optimal recalculation**, can minimize recalculation time considerably, especially in large worksheets that contain many unrelated formulas.

? **Related Help topics**

You can also change the order in which 1-2-3 recalculates the worksheet, setting it to recalculate by column, by row, or natural. For more information on recalculation methods, search on "Recalculation order" in Help.

Also, Lesson 1 in the Tutorial includes an exercise for building formulas. Choose Help Tutorial to start the Tutorial.

10 Calculating with @Functions

1-2-3 provides a set of more than 200 built-in formulas called @functions. The @function selector in the edit line provides an easy, reliable way to enter @functions. This chapter describes the format for @functions, how to enter an @function, how to customize the @Function menu, and how to use Help to find detailed information about each @function.

> ? **Help**   To browse through @functions by category in Help, search on "@Functions" and select the topic "@Function Categories."

What is an @function?

An **@function** is a built-in formula in 1-2-3 that performs a specialized calculation. @Functions are a quick, easy way to build powerful worksheets. You can use an @function by itself, combine it with other @functions and formulas, or use it in a macro.

Some @functions are simple; for example, @SUM(D2..D7) adds the values in the range D2..D7 which is easier than writing out the formula +D2+D3+D4+D5+D6+D7. Other @functions calculate complex formulas. For example, @NPV calculates the net present value of a series of future cash-flow values.

@Function format

The format for most @functions has the following three parts:

- The @ (at sign), which you must enter as the first character
- The name of the @function
- One or more arguments enclosed in ( ) (parentheses)

Some @functions, such as @NOW, @RAND, and @TRUE, don't have arguments.

Parts of an @function

The examples below show the different parts of an @function.

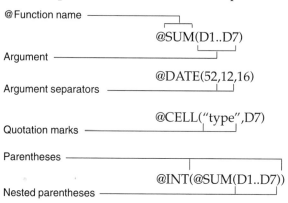

An **argument** is data you provide for 1-2-3 to use when it calculates the @function. Depending on the particular @function, an argument can be a single value, a range of cells, text, or another @function. The arguments in an @function can be any length as long as the total number of characters in the cell containing the @function doesn't exceed 512.

When an @function has arguments, they can be required or optional. You must enter required arguments when you use the @function. You can omit optional arguments. In the documentation, optional arguments are enclosed in [ ] (brackets).

If an @function contains more than one optional argument, you must use the arguments sequentially. You can't use an optional argument without using the optional arguments that precede it. You can, however, use an optional argument without using subsequent optional arguments. For example, the syntax of @VDB is

@VDB(*cost,salvage,life,start,end,*[*rate*],[*switch*])

The *rate* and *switch* arguments are optional. You can't use the *switch* argument without using the preceding *rate* argument. You can, however, use *rate* without using *switch*.

Argument separators separate two or more arguments. You can use three types of argument separators: , (comma), ; (semicolon), and . (period). A semicolon is always a valid argument separator. In addition, you can set either a period or comma as the argument separator.

The argument separator can't be the same as the decimal separator. Some countries use a comma as the decimal separator, while others use a period. So, if you use files with varying international settings for the decimal separator, it's best to use a semicolon as the argument separator.

[?] **Help**   For information about changing the argument separator, search on "Argument separators" in Help.

Quotation marks enclose the text for text arguments. For example, in the text @function @LOWER("Sales Forecast"), you enclose the text argument Sales Forecast in " " (quotation marks). 1-2-3 assumes that text not enclosed in quotation marks is a range name.

Parentheses enclose @function arguments. **Nested parentheses** enclose an @function that you use as an argument for another @function. For example, you use nested parentheses when you make @SUM and its argument the argument for @INT as follows: @INT(@SUM(D1..D7)).

Argument types

1-2-3 @functions accept the following four types of arguments:

- A **condition** is an expression that uses a logical operator (=, <, >, <>, >=, <=, #NOT#, #AND#, and #OR#), or the address or name of a cell containing such an expression. You can also use a formula, @function, number, range name, cell address, or text as a condition argument. The @function evaluates the condition argument and proceeds according to whether it is true or false.

- A **location** is the address or name of a range, or a formula or @function that produces the address or name of a range. A location argument can refer to a single-cell or a multiple-cell range in one or more worksheets in a single file.

- **Text** is any sequence of letters, numbers, and symbols enclosed in quotation marks, the address or name of a cell that contains a label, or a formula or @function that produces a label. Text @functions use text arguments.

- A **value** is a number, the address or name of a cell that contains a number, or a formula or @function that produces a number.

Entering an @function

You can enter an @function by typing it into a cell or by using the @function selector. Using the @function selector is the easiest, most reliable method because 1-2-3 automatically enters the @function in the correct format with the @function name, parentheses, argument placeholders, and argument separators.

To enter an @function

1. Select the cell where you want to enter the @function.
2. Click the @function selector.

You can also type @ in an empty cell, and then press **F3 (NAME)** *to open the @Function List dialog box.*

3. If the @function you want appears on the @Function menu, choose it and skip to step 7. Otherwise, select List All.

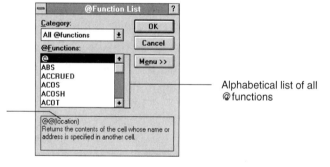

Syntax and description of the selected @function

Alphabetical list of all @functions

4. If you know the category of the @function you want, select the category from the Category drop-down box.

   The @Functions list box displays @functions in the category that you picked.

5. Select the @function from the @Functions list box.

6. Choose OK.

1-2-3 enters the @function name, placeholders for required and optional arguments, and argument separators. 1-2-3 highlights the first argument placeholder so it's ready for you to specify your actual argument.

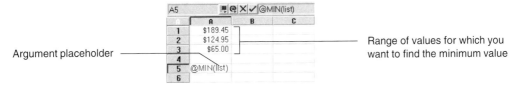

Argument placeholder

Range of values for which you want to find the minimum value

7. Replace the placeholders for required and optional arguments with your actual argument.

You can type a range address or name, choose a name from the navigator, or select a range in the worksheet. In the illustration above, *list* is the placeholder for a required argument. The actual argument is the range for which you want to find the minimum value with @MIN, A1..A3.

 8. Click the Confirm button, or press **ENTER**.

The result, not the @function, appears in the cell. If the result of the @function is too long to fit in the cell, 1-2-3 displays *** (asterisks). To display the result, widen the column by double-clicking the column border to the right of the column letter. For more information, see "Changing column width" on page 125.

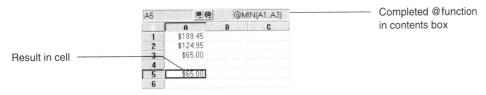

Result in cell

Completed @function in contents box

Customizing the @Function menu

You can customize the @Function menu by adding and removing @functions at the top level of the menu. You can also add and remove separator lines between @functions in the menu. Adding frequently used @functions to the menu saves time because you can choose them without having to display a dialog box.

To add an @function to the menu

1. Click the @function selector.

2. Choose List All.

3. If you know the category of the @function you want to add, select the category from the Category drop-down box.

4. Choose Menu >>.

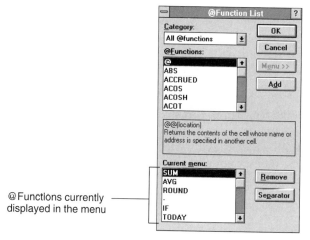

@Functions currently displayed in the menu

5. Select the @function from the @Functions list box.

6. Choose Add.

   1-2-3 appends the @function to the Current menu list.

7. To add a separator line below an @function on the menu, select the @function in the Current menu list, and choose Separator.

8. Choose OK.

The @functions and separators you added now appear in the menu when you click the @function selector.

To remove an @function from the menu

1. Click the @function selector.

2. Choose List All.

3. Choose Menu >>.

4. Select the @function from the Current menu list box.

5. Choose Remove.

6. To remove a separator, select it in the Current menu list, and choose Remove.

7. Choose OK.

The @functions and separators you removed no longer appear in the menu when you click the @function selector.

Learning about each @function

Help provides detailed information about each of the more than 200 @functions. The *User's Guide* doesn't list individual @functions.

To find information about an @function

1. In an empty cell, type @

2. Press F3 (NAME).

    The @Function List dialog box appears, containing an alphabetical list of all @functions.

3. Select the @function you want in the @Functions list box.

4. Press F1 (HELP).

1-2-3 displays a Help topic with detailed information about the @function including syntax, arguments, notes, and examples. To print the Help topic, choose File Print Topic in the Help window.

For a list of the formulas that 1-2-3 uses to calculate some statistical and financial @functions, see Appendix C.

11

Changing the Worksheet's Appearance

You can enhance the appearance of your worksheets on screen and in print and make your presentations more effective. For example, you can change fonts, add colors and patterns, and put borders around ranges. This chapter describes how to style the worksheet, change column width and row height, and hide parts of the worksheet.

Note If Group mode is on, changes to a range's number format, fonts and attributes, colors and patterns, borders, alignment, row height, column width, protection setting, and hidden status affect the same range in all worksheets in the file.

Changing the appearance of numbers

You can change the appearance of numbers, dates, and times by changing number formats. **Number formats** differentiate one kind of numeric data from another; for example, currency from percentages.

You can change the default number format for an entire file, or for the current worksheet. You can also change the number format for a selected range or collection, and parts of a query table or chart.

The initial default number format is Automatic. 1-2-3 automatically formats data as Comma, Currency, Percent, or Scientific, depending on the symbol you use when you enter the data. For example, if you enter a number followed by a % (percent symbol), 1-2-3 automatically formats the number as Percent.

1-2-3 automatically formats dates entered as 09-Apr-93, 09-Apr, or 04/09/93, and times entered in any of the standard time formats except hh.mm (hour.minutes).

? **Help** The sample box in the Number Format dialog box shows how each format changes the appearance of a number. For a detailed description of each number format, search on "Number formats" in Help.

Note Formats affect only the onscreen and printed appearance of numbers, dates, and times; they don't affect the way 1-2-3 stores these values or uses them in calculations.

To change the default number format

You can change the default number format; for example, from Automatic to General. General format displays negative numbers with a – (minus sign), no thousands separators, and no trailing zeros to the right of the decimal point.

1. Choose Tools User Setup.

2. Deselect the Use Automatic format check box.

3. Choose OK.

1-2-3 uses the specified number format as the default until you change it.

To change a worksheet's default number format

You can change the default number format for the current worksheet.

1. Choose Style Worksheet Defaults.

2. Under Number Format, choose a format from the Format drop-down box.

3. Choose OK.

To change the number format of a range or collection

1. Select the range or collection.

2. Choose Style Number Format.

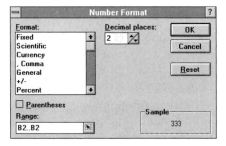

You can also click the format and decimal selectors on the status bar.

3. Select a format from the Format list box.

    The dialog box displays a sample of the format.

4. If you select Fixed, Scientific, Currency, Comma, or Percent, the Decimal places text box appears. Click the arrows or enter the number of decimal places (0 through 15) you want 1-2-3 to display.

5. To display values enclosed in parentheses, select the Parentheses check box.

6. To reset a range's format to the current default format for the worksheet, choose Reset.

7. Choose OK.

Shortcut   Select the range or collection and click one of the SmartIcons shown at left to apply Currency, Percentage, or Comma format with two decimal places.

> **Note**   If you select a format that adds characters such as $ (dollar sign) or , (comma), the width of the cell may not be large enough to display the number and the extra characters. In this case, 1-2-3 replaces the number with *** (asterisks). To display the number, widen the column by double-clicking the column border to the right of the column letter. For more information, see "Changing column width" on page 125.

Changing font and attributes

Fonts and attributes determine how characters look on the screen and in print. A **font** is a typeface of a particular size, such as Times, 12 point or Helvetica, 10 point. **Attributes** are style characteristics such as boldface, underlining, italics, and color. You can change the font and attributes for a selected range or collection, as shown below.

	A	B	C	D	E	F
1						
2			Howard's Fine Hats			
3						
4		Berets	Boaters	Borsalinos	Bowlers	
5	April	$235	$320	$78	$585	
6	May	$421	$465	$109	$2,100	
7	June	$237	$677	$230	$7,000	
8						
9	Totals:	$893	$1,462	$417	$9,685	

To change font and attributes

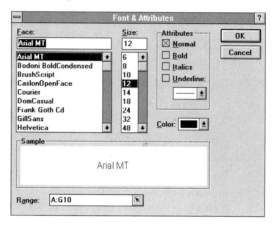

1. Select the range or collection.
2. Choose Style Font & Attributes.

You can also use the typeface and point-size selectors on the status bar.

3. Select a typeface from the Face list box.
4. Select a point size from the Size list box.
5. To add bold, italics, or underlining, select the Bold, Italics, or Underline check box.
6. If you selected Underline, select a line style from the Underline drop-down box.
7. To remove bold, italics, or underline, select Normal.
8. Select a color from the Color drop-down box.
9. Choose OK.

Shortcut   To apply text attributes, select the range or collection and click the SmartIcons shown below.

| Bold | Italics | Single underline | Double underline | Remove bold, italics, and underline |

Changing colors and patterns

Applying a color to a range accentuates the range on screen and draws attention to the data. For example, you can emphasize a range by changing its background color and pattern. It's also an effective way to group similar data visually. For example, you can set headings in one color and numbers in another.

? **Help**   You can also change the color 1-2-3 uses to display grid lines. For more information, search on "Grid lines" in Help.

To change colors and patterns

1. Select the range or collection.
2. Choose Style Lines & Color.

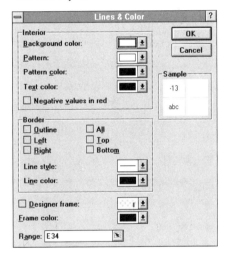

3. To change the background color, select a color from the Background color drop-down box.
4. To change the background pattern, select a pattern from the Pattern drop-down box.
5. To change the color of the background pattern, select a color from the Pattern color drop-down box.
6. To change the color of data in the range, select a color from the Text color drop-down box.
7. To display negative values in red, select the Negative values in red check box.
8. Choose OK.

Adding borders and frames

To emphasize a range and the data in it, you can add borders and designer frames. As shown below, you can choose from a variety of frames and border styles, and you can add borders to different edges of a range.

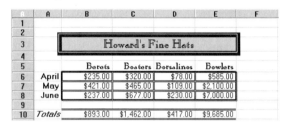

To add borders and frames

1. Select the range or collection.
2. Choose Style Lines & Color.
3. Under Border, select one or more options.
   - Outline draws a line around the outside edge of the range.
   - Left, Right, Top, and Bottom draw a line along the specified edge of each cell in the range.
   - All draws a line around all edges of each cell in the range.

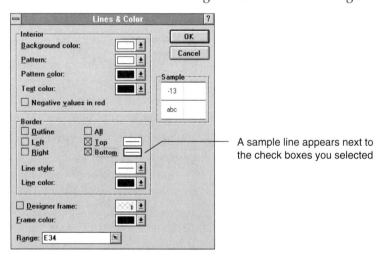

A sample line appears next to the check boxes you selected

4. To apply a style and color to a border line, click the sample line next to the check box; then select a style from the Line style drop-down box and a color from the Line color drop-down box.

5. To add a designer frame to the range or collection, select a frame from the Designer frame drop-down box.

6. To apply a color to the designer frame, select a color from the Frame color drop-down box.

7. Choose OK.

To remove borders and frames, select the range or collection; choose Style Lines & Color; deselect the borders and frame options; choose OK.

> **Note**   If you put a border around a 3D range, 1-2-3 treats the selection as a group of two-dimensional ranges, putting borders in each worksheet separately.

  Shortcut   Select a range and click the SmartIcons at left to add an outline or a drop shadow to the range.

Changing alignment

You can change the alignment for both values and labels in a range. By default, 1-2-3 aligns values horizontally to the right and labels horizontally to the left; and aligns both values and labels vertically to the bottom. The illustration below shows examples of different alignments.

Horizontally left-aligned   —— Quarter 1

Horizontally centered   ——   Quarter 2

Horizontally right-aligned   —— Quarter 3

Evenly spaced   ——   Quarter   4

Quarter 1 ——————   Vertically top-aligned

Quarter 2 ——————   Vertically centered

Quarter 3 ——————   Vertically bottom-aligned

To change alignment

1. Select the range or collection.

2. Choose Style Alignment.

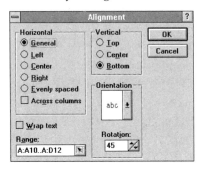

You can also use label-prefix characters to align text horizontally. For more information, see "Entering text" on page 69.

3. Under Horizontal, select an option.

   • General aligns labels to the left and values to the right.

   • Left

   • Center

   • Right

   • Evenly spaced stretches data evenly across the cell. It has no effect on data that ends with a . (period), ! (exclamation point), ? (question mark), or : (colon).

4. Select the Across columns check box to align the data in the leftmost cell across the columns in the range, according to the horizontal alignment.

   For example, when the horizontal alignment is Center, Across columns centers the data in the leftmost cell across the entire range, as shown below.

Before

	A	B	C	D	E	F
1	Yearly Totals					
2		1990	1991	1992	1993	
3	Dublin	$578,395	$674,873	$589,654	$764,321	
4	London	$476,456	$325,687	$567,234	$764,321	

After

	A	B	C	D	E	F
1			Yearly Totals			
2		1990	1991	1992	1993	
3	Dublin	$578,395	$674,873	$589,654	$764,321	
4	London	$476,456	$325,687	$567,234	$764,321	

Note   When you select Across columns, make sure the cells to the right of the label you want to align are blank. If these cells contain data, 1-2-3 displays the label as left-aligned.

Before

This text needs to be wrapped

After

This text needs to
be wrapped

5. To wrap text within a cell, select the Wrap text check box. 1-2-3 adjusts row height to fit the wrapped text.

6. Under Vertical, select Top, Center, or Bottom to align data vertically in a cell.

   Note   Data appears vertically aligned in a cell only when the height of the row containing the cell is larger than the largest font in the row.

7. To rotate the text in a cell, select an orientation from the Orientation drop-down box. If you want, specify a rotation angle from 0 to 90 in the Rotation text box.

8. Choose OK.

Shortcut   To align data, select the range or collection and click one of the SmartIcons below.

Left   Center   Right   Evenly   Rotate
                                             spaced

Using named styles

You can name the styles of a selected cell and then apply this named style to a selected range or collection. A named style can include the number format, font and attributes, colors, patterns, borders, frames, and alignment of the selected cell. You can define 16 named styles.

? **Help**   You can also style a range with one of the built-in templates in the style gallery. For more information, search on "Templates" in Help.

To define or delete named styles

1. Select a cell whose style you want to define as a named style.

2. Choose Style Named Style.

3. Enter a name of up to 35 characters in the Style name text box.

4. Choose Define.

   You can use the range selector to select another cell whose style you want to define as a named style; then repeat steps 3 and 4.

5. To delete a named style, select it from the Existing styles list box and choose Clear.

   Deleting a named style doesn't affect any of the ranges where you previously applied this style.

6. Choose Close.

To apply a named style

1. Select the range where you want to apply a named style.

2. Choose Style Named Style.

3. Select a named style from the Existing styles list box.

4. Choose OK.

You can also use the style selector on the status bar to apply a named style to a selected range or collection.

Copying and deleting styles

You can copy a range and paste the styles from that range into another range without pasting the data. This is a quick way to duplicate the styles of one range in another range. The styles you can paste this way are number format, font and attributes, colors, patterns, borders, alignment, named style, and protection setting.

When you paste styles into a range, any data in the range changes to conform to the pasted styles. Any new data you enter in the range appears according to the pasted styles.

You can also delete styles from a range without deleting the data in the range. When you delete styles in a range, 1-2-3 resets the range to the default styles.

To copy styles

1. Select the range whose styles you want to copy.
2. Choose Edit Copy.
3. Select the range or collection you want to paste the styles into.
4. Choose Edit Paste Special.
5. Under Paste, select Styles only.
6. Choose OK.

Shortcut   Select the range whose styles you want to copy, click the icon at left, and select the range you want to paste the styles into.

To delete styles

1. Select the range or collection whose styles you want to delete.
2. Choose Edit Clear.
3. Select Styles.
4. Choose OK.

Shortcut   Select the range and click the icon at left to delete the styles.

Changing column width

When a value is too wide to fit in a cell, it appears in scientific notation or as a line of **** (asterisks). To display the value, you must widen the column.

You can change the width of columns by dragging, or by using Style Column Width. Use Style Column Width to change the column to a specific width, reset to the default width, or set the width to fit the largest entry in the column.

To change a column by dragging

To change the column width to fit the largest entry in the column, double-click the border to the right of the column letter.

1. Move the mouse pointer to the letter of the column.
2. Point at the right column border.

    The mouse pointer changes to a black two-headed horizontal arrow.
3. Drag left to narrow the column or right to widen it.
4. Release the mouse button when the column is the width you want.

To change more than one column by dragging

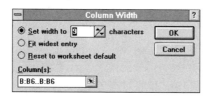

1. Select the columns.
2. Point to a border between any of the column letters in the selected columns.

   The mouse pointer changes to a black two-headed horizontal arrow.

3. Drag left to narrow the column or right to widen it.
4. Release the mouse button when the column is the width you want.

1-2-3 changes the width of all the selected columns to match the one you dragged.

To change columns to a specified width

1. Select a range that includes cells in the columns you want to change.
2. Choose Style Column Width.

   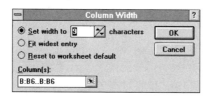

3. Select an option.
   - "Set width to" adjusts the column to the width you specify. Click the arrows or enter a number from 1 to 240 in the characters text box.
   - "Fit widest entry" adjusts each column to the width of the widest entry in that column.
   - "Reset to worksheet default" adjusts the columns to the default width defined with Style Worksheet Defaults.

4. Choose OK.

   ? Help   For more information about how fonts, values, and labels can affect column width, search on "Width" in Help.

Changing row height

1-2-3 automatically adjusts row height to match the height of the data you put in the row. You can also change row height manually by dragging a row border or by using Style Row Height.

To change a row by dragging

To reset the row height to fit the largest font in the row, double-click the border below the row number.

1. Move the mouse pointer to the number of the row.
2. Point to the lower border of the row.

   The mouse pointer changes to a black two-headed vertical arrow.
3. Drag up to narrow the row or down to widen it.
4. Release the mouse button when the row is the height you want.

To change more than one row by dragging

1. Select the rows.
2. Point to a border between any of the row numbers in the selected rows.

   The mouse pointer changes to a black two-headed vertical arrow.
3. Drag up to narrow the row or down to widen it.
4. Release the mouse button when the row is the height you want.

1-2-3 changes the height of all the selected rows to match the one you dragged.

To change rows to a specified height

1. Select a range that includes cells in the rows you want to change.
2. Choose Style Row Height.

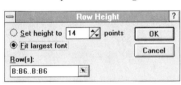

3. Select an option.

- "Set height to" changes row height to the height you specify. Click the arrows or enter a height from 1 through 255 in the points text box.

  When you set the row height to a specific number of points, it no longer automatically adjusts to fit the largest font in the row.

- "Fit largest font" resets the height of each selected row to the height of the largest font in the row.

4. Choose OK.

Hiding data

You can hide data in a range so that the range appears blank. You can also hide a column or a worksheet so that the entire column or worksheet disappears from the worksheet display. You can't hide a row.

Hiding data is a good way to keep other users of your file focused on what you want them to see rather than on confidential or distracting data. For example, suppose you have a file with two worksheets in it. The first worksheet contains data and a chart. The second contains macros and calculations. To help other users focus on the chart and data that you want them to see, hide the worksheet containing the macros and calculations.

You can perform 1-2-3 operations on ranges in hidden columns or worksheets by typing the address or range name in a dialog box or by selecting the surrounding columns or worksheets. Formulas that refer to data in hidden columns or worksheets continue to work correctly. To make formulas refer to ranges in hidden columns or worksheets, type the address in the formula instead of selecting the range.

You can prevent changes to hidden data by protecting it and sealing the file. For more information about sealing a file, see page 145.

Caution   If hidden data isn't protected and sealed, you can accidentally change it. For example, you can accidentally delete text, or change settings such as font and color. If you enter new data in a hidden cell, the new entry replaces the old one but is still hidden. When you redisplay the hidden cell, it will show the changed data or settings.

To hide data in a range

1. Select the range or collection.

2. Choose Style Number Format.

3. Select Hidden from the Format list box.

4. Choose OK.

The contents of the range are no longer visible. If you select a cell in this hidden range, however, the contents of the cell appear in the contents box, unless the file is sealed.

The selected range is hidden —

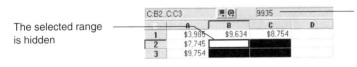

The contents of the current cell appear in the contents box

Note   If you print a range that contains hidden cells, the contents of the hidden cells don't print.

To hide columns or worksheets

When you hide a worksheet, 1-2-3 hides the tab for that worksheet. When you hide a column, 1-2-3 hides the letter for that column, as shown below. You can't move the cell pointer to hidden columns or worksheets unless you redisplay them.

Column D is hidden —

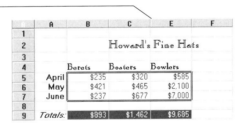

1. Select a range.

The range needs to include only one cell in each of the columns or worksheets you want to hide.

2. Choose Style Hide.

You can also hide columns by dragging one column border to the left until it overlaps the columns you want to hide.

3. Select Column or Sheet.

4. Choose OK.

    Note   If you print a range that contains hidden columns or worksheets, the hidden columns or worksheets don't print.

To display hidden columns or worksheets

1. Select columns or worksheets surrounding the columns or worksheets you want to display.

    For example, to display hidden column D, select at least one cell in columns C and E. To display worksheets B and C, select worksheets A and D.

2. Choose Style Hide.

3. Select Column or Sheet.

4. Choose Show.

[?] Related Help topics

There are many default settings that can affect the appearance of data and the worksheet. For information about setting defaults, search on "Default settings" in Help.

For a tutorial lesson about ways to enhance a worksheet's appearance, choose Help Tutorial and select Lesson 3.

12

Printing Data

You can print ranges, charts, drawn objects, and query tables. To enhance your printed pages, you can add headers, footers, print titles and page breaks; shrink and enlarge printed data; change the page orientation; and save named page settings for printing. You can also preview printing and print directly from the Print Preview window. This chapter describes how to print data, preview printing, and enhance your printed pages.

Quick printing

The quickest way to print is to use the default settings. Generally, printing requires only the default printer and default page settings. You can customize the page settings as described later in this chapter. However, you can also print right away without changing any defaults.

You can print the current worksheet, the entire file, a range, or a collection. By default, 1-2-3 prints any charts, drawn objects, and query tables within your print ranges. For information about changing this default, see "To hide or show worksheet elements in print" on page 142. You can also print a chart, drawn object, or query table by itself without any worksheet data.

Note Before you print, make sure a printer was installed during the Windows installation procedure. To see if a printer is installed on your system, choose File Printer Setup. 1-2-3 displays the names of all installed printers in the Printers list box. If the list box doesn't display any printer names, see your Windows documentation for information about using the Windows Control Panel to install a printer.

To print the current worksheet or file

1. Move the cell pointer to the worksheet or file.

2. Choose File Print or press CTRL+P.

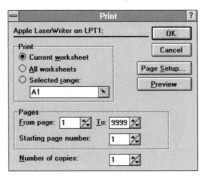

3. Under Print, select an option.

   - Current worksheet prints the active area of the current worksheet.

   - All worksheets prints the entire file.

4. Choose OK.

1-2-3 prints the current worksheet or the entire file, including all cell contents, charts, drawn objects, and query tables.

To print a selected range or collection

1. Select the range or collection.

   If you want to print a long label, make sure you select the cells the label overlaps, as well as the cell containing the label. For example, to print a long label entered in A2 that overlaps B2 and C2, be sure to include cells A2, B2, and C2 in the range.

   If you want to print a chart, drawn object, or query table make sure that it's *completely* within the range or collection.

2. Choose File Print or press CTRL+P.

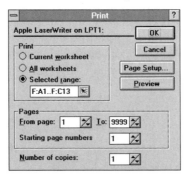

3. Choose OK.

1-2-3 prints the range or collection, including all cell contents, charts, drawn objects, and query tables.

To print charts or query tables only

You can select charts and query tables to print without printing data in cells. As well as charts, the drawn objects you can print are lines, arrows, shapes, text blocks, pictures, and embedded objects. Printing charts, drawn objects, and query tables without other data is useful when you want to make overhead transparencies or prints for a presentation.

1. Select one or more charts, drawn objects, or query tables.

 2. Choose File Print or press **CTRL+P**.

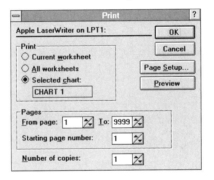

3. Choose OK.

1-2-3 prints the chart, drawn object, or query table starting at the top left corner of the page.

Print previewing

Before printing, you can preview how your pages will look when printed. Previewing is useful for checking that page breaks occur where you want them. It's also useful for checking that headers, footers, and the layout of printed pages is what you want.

When 1-2-3 displays a preview of the printed page, if the setup isn't what you want, you can use an icon to display the Page Setup dialog box. You can also use icons in the Print Preview window to display the next page or previous page, to zoom in and zoom out, and to print.

To preview pages

1. Select what you want to preview.

   Move the cell pointer to the worksheet or file you want to preview; or select a range, collection, chart, drawn object, or query table.

2. Choose File Print Preview.

   Depending on what you selected to preview, 1-2-3 displays a dialog box like the one shown below.

A range was selected for previewing ————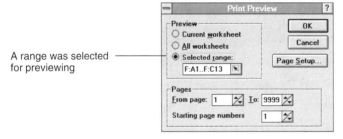

3. Under Preview, select Current worksheet, All worksheets, or Selected range, chart, drawn object, or query table.

4. To change the default pages to preview, specify them under Pages.

5. Choose OK.

1-2-3 displays the Print Preview window.

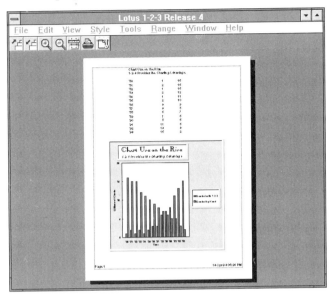

6. Use the icons, as described below:

Click	Or press	To
	ENTER or **PG DN**	Display the next page
	PG UP	Display the previous page
	GRAY MINUS	Zoom out
	GRAY PLUS	Zoom in
		Change the page setup
		Print
	ESC	Close the Print Preview window

After zooming a page, you can use $\uparrow$, $\downarrow$, $\rightarrow$, $\leftarrow$ to move around the page. To return to the original unzoomed state, press * (asterisk).

Adding headers and footers

A **header** is text printed below the top margin of each page, and a **footer** is text printed above the bottom margin. You can enter up to 512 characters of text in a header or footer; however, 1-2-3 doesn't print any text that extends beyond the right margin of the printed page.

As well as entering text in the headers and footers, you can use the buttons in the Page Setup dialog box to enter the date or time of printing, the page number, the file name, or data from a cell in the worksheet.

If you type @ (at sign) or + (plus sign) to enter the date or time or use a button in the Page Setup dialog box, 1-2-3 updates the date and time each time you print. If you don't want the date and time to update each time you print, you can type them in.

Also, you can combine the date, time, page number, and file name with other header and footer text that you type. For example, you can type Page and then enter # (number sign) or click the page number button. You can't combine the contents of a cell with other text you type.

To add headers and footers

1.   Choose File Page Setup.

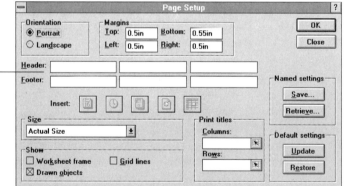

Enter headers and footers in these boxes to align text to the left, center, and right

2.   Next to Header or Footer, enter text in one or more of the text boxes.

You can also do any of the following:

To enter	Click	Or type
The date of printing		@ (at sign)
The time of printing		+ (plus sign)
The page number		# (pound sign)
The file name		^ (caret)
The contents of a cell	...then type the address or name of a cell	\ (backslash) ...then type the address or name of a cell

3. Choose OK.

Note You can't use a | (vertical bar) character in a header or footer. Also, to display @ (at sign), + (plus sign), # (pound sign), ^ (caret), or \ (backslash) in a header or footer, enter an ' (apostrophe) immediately before the character. For example, enter '# to display #.

Adding and removing page breaks

1-2-3 automatically paginates what you're printing based on how many complete columns and rows can fit on the current page. Page breaks never occur partway through columns or rows.

After you preview or print a worksheet, the automatic page breaks appear as dashed lines in the worksheet. If the pages don't automatically break where you want, you can add page breaks to keep related data together or to print certain data on separate pages.

Note You can also change the way pages break by setting different print margins (see page 141), shrinking or enlarging printed data (see page 141), and by changing the page orientation (see page 142).

To add a page break

1. Select a cell below the row or to the right of the column where you want the page to break.

2. Choose Style Page Break.

3. Do one or both of the following:

   • To add a page break above the row containing the selected cell, select the Row check box.

   • To add a page break to the left of the column containing the selected cell, select the Column check box.

4. Choose OK.

  Shortcut   The SmartIcons at left insert page breaks above or to the left of the current cell.

When you print the data, 1-2-3 starts a new page at the location you specified. For example, the following illustration shows a dashed line indicating a page break along the row above and the column to the left of the selected cell.

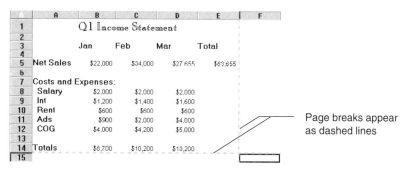

Page breaks appear as dashed lines

Note   1-2-3 doesn't automatically break pages between worksheets in a multiple-sheet file. To start each worksheet on a new page, insert a page break at the top of each worksheet after worksheet A.

To remove a page break

1. Select a cell below the row and to the right of the column where the page breaks.

2. Choose Style Page Break.

3. Deselect the Row check box, the Column check box, or both check boxes.

4. Choose OK.

Adding print titles

Adding print titles to printed pages is like freezing titles in your onscreen worksheet. Print titles help you keep track of the categories of data in your printed worksheet. You can specify columns as vertical print titles, rows as horizontal print titles, or both. Columns print along the left edge, and rows along the top edge of each page.

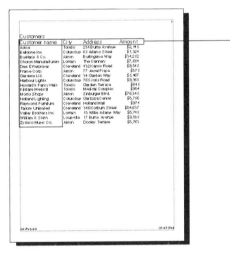

Ranges in the left column and top row are set as print titles and appear on every printed page

You can select as many contiguous columns and rows as you like and add them as print titles. It's practical to set only a few columns and rows as titles, however, so you can still fit all the data you want to print.

1-2-3 uses as print titles only the rows and columns that correspond to your print range. For example, if you specify D3..D15 as a print range and column A as a print title, 1-2-3 prints the contents of A3..A15 as the print title.

To add print titles

Don't include the print titles in your print range, or 1-2-3 will print them twice.

1. Choose File Page Setup.

2. Under Print titles, specify a range for vertical titles in the Columns text box and a range for horizontal titles in the Rows text box.

    The range you specify needs to include only one cell from each column or row.

3. Choose OK.

Shortcut   Select a range and click one of the SmartIcons at left to set the selected column or row as a vertical or horizontal print title.

Enhancing your printed pages

You can enhance the appearance of your printed pages by customizing the page settings. You can change print margins; shrink or enlarge printed data; hide or show the worksheet frame, grid lines, and drawn objects; and change the page orientation.

You change page settings by choosing File Page Setup. You can also go to Page Setup from the Print dialog box and the Print Preview window. In all cases, the following dialog box appears:

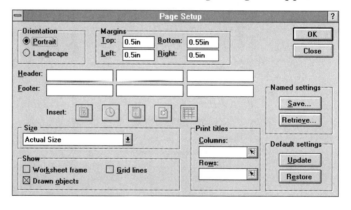

To change print margins

You can change the top, bottom, left, and right print margins. Most printers require about half an inch on all sides. If the printer you're using has minimum margins larger than what you enter, edges of your printed pages may be cut off. If this happens, enter larger margins.

1. Choose File Page Setup.

2. Under Margins, click the arrows or enter a measurement for each print margin in the Top, Bottom, Left, or Right text boxes.

    To specify a margin in millimeters or centimeters, type mm or cm after the measurement number.

3. Choose OK.

To shrink or enlarge printed data

You can reduce the size of printed worksheet data to fit all columns on a single page, all rows on a single page, or everything on a single page. You can also shrink or enlarge printed data by a percentage. When you shrink data to fit on a single page, keep in mind that the more data you try to fit, the smaller and more difficult it becomes to read. You can also shrink or enlarge a printed chart, or drawn object.

To shrink or enlarge a range, collection, or worksheet

1. Choose File Page Setup.

2. Under Size, select an option.

    You can also try changing the page orientation to landscape to fit a large number of columns on the page. See page 142 for information.

    - Actual size prints the selection in the size it appeared on screen, starting at the top left corner of the page.
    - Fit all to page fits all the data on a single printed page.
    - Fit columns to page shrinks all the columns of data to fit on a single printed page. The printed output is more than a single page if the number of rows exceeds what can fit on one page.
    - Fit rows to page shrinks all the rows of data to fit on a single printed page. The printed output is more than a single page if the number of columns exceeds what can fit on one page.
    - Manually scale shrinks or enlarges the printed data by a percentage, from 15 to 1000, you enter in the text box. For example, enter 75 to shrink the selection to 75% of its original size.

3. Choose OK.

Shortcut   The SmartIcons at left change the page setting to fit all columns, all rows, or all data on a single page.

To shrink or enlarge a chart or drawn object

1. Choose File Page Setup.

2. Under Size, select an option.

   • Actual size prints the object in the size it appeared on screen, starting at the top left corner of the page. A large chart or other drawn object may require more than a single printed page.

   • Fill page shrinks or expands the object, changing its proportions, to fit on one page.

   • Fill page but keep proportions shrinks or enlarges the selected object, but maintains its proportions.

To hide or show worksheet elements in print

You can print a worksheet showing the worksheet frame, grid lines, charts and other drawn objects; or you can hide these elements for printing. For example, for your own reference, one printed version of a worksheet could show grid lines and the worksheet frame and hide drawn objects. Another version, for presentation, could hide the frame and grid lines, but show all the charts and other drawn objects.

1. Choose File Page Setup.

2. Under Show, select or deselect one or more options: Worksheet frame, Grid lines, Drawn objects.

3. Choose OK.

To change page orientation

You can change the orientation of printed pages from **portrait** (upright) to **landscape** (sideways). If you have many columns of data, landscape printing may help you fit all the columns on a single page. You can also try reducing data to fit it on a single page. For information about reducing the size of printed data, see page 141.

1. Choose File Page Setup.

2. Under Orientation, select an option.

   • Landscape prints sideways.

   • Portrait prints upright.

3. Choose OK.

Shortcut   The SmartIcons at left change the page orientation to landscape or portrait.

Using named page settings

After you've used the page setup options to create page settings, you can name the page settings and save them to use any time you print. This way you can easily apply a complex combination of page settings to different data. You can also use named page settings to print the same data in different ways; for example, with grid lines and without. Named page settings include the print range and all the options you can set in the Page Setup dialog box.

To name and save page settings

1. Choose File Page Setup.
2. Under Named settings, choose Save.

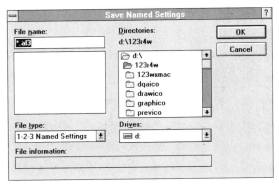

3. Enter a name of up to 15 characters in the File name text box.
4. Choose OK.

   You return to the Page Setup dialog box.

5. Choose OK.

1-2-3 saves the named page settings in a file with the extension .AL3.

To use named page settings

1. Choose File Page Setup.
2. Under Named settings, choose Retrieve.

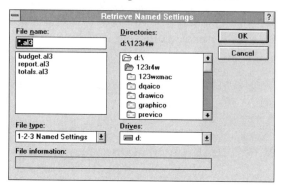

3. Select a named setting from the File name list box.
4. Choose OK.

   You return to the Page Setup dialog box.
5. Choose OK.

The settings you retrieved are now the current page settings; 1-2-3 will print according to these settings until you change them.

? Related Help topics

You can use File Printer Setup to change the default printer. For more information search on "Printers" in Help and select the "File Printer Setup" topic.

You can also change or restore the default page settings. For information, search on "Default page settings" in Help.

13

Protecting Data

Sometimes your files contain data you don't want others to change or see. For example, you want to prevent others from changing a set of formulas, or you want to limit who can open a file containing confidential financial data. This chapter describes how to protect data by sealing a file or by preventing others from opening a file.

Sealing a file

Sealing a file prevents changes to cell contents, styles, and settings. When you seal a file, others can open the file. However, unless they know the password, they can't change data in the file except in ranges you specifically unprotected before you sealed the file.

When a file is sealed, you can't show hidden worksheets and columns, or insert and delete rows, columns, or worksheets. You also can't change protection settings, file reservation status, range names, style settings, formats, alignments, column width, row height, page breaks, frozen titles, drawn objects, or query tables.

Caution   Remember your password for sealing a file. When you seal a file with a password, you can unseal it again *only* if you enter the exact password.

To seal a file

1.   Choose File Protect.

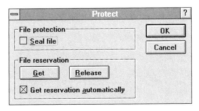

2.   Under File protection, select the Seal file check box.

3. Choose OK.

1-2-3 prompts you to enter a password to seal the file.

4. Enter a password in the Password text box.

A password can include 15 characters or less. 1-2-3 displays an * (asterisk) for each character as you enter the password. 1-2-3 is case-sensitive for passwords, so you must remember the exact combination of uppercase or lowercase letters you use when you create the password.

5. Enter the same password in the Verify text box.

6. Choose OK.

1-2-3 dims the menu commands for any actions that you can't perform when a file is sealed.

Note   Sealing a file with a password is different from saving a file with a password. For information about saving a file with a password, see page 147.

To seal a file and leave specifled ranges unprotected

When you seal a file, you can leave specified ranges unprotected so others can enter data in these ranges. Others can change the contents of the specified ranges, but not the styles.

1. Select the range or collection where you want to allow changes.

2. Choose Style Protection.

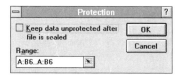

3. Select the "Keep data unprotected after file is sealed" check box.

4. Choose OK.

5. Use File Protect to seal the file as described on page 145.

After you seal the file, the status bar displays Pr when the cell pointer is on a protected cell, and U when the cell pointer is on an unprotected cell.

To reprotect ranges

1. Unseal the file by choosing File Protect, deselecting the Seal file check box, and choosing OK.

   1-2-3 prompts you to enter a password to unseal the file.

2. Enter the password and choose OK.

3. Select the unprotected range or collection you want to reprotect.

4. Choose Style Protection.

5. Deselect the "Keep data unprotected after file is sealed" check box.

6. Choose OK.

7. Use File Protect to seal the file again, as described on page 145.

Preventing others from opening a file

You can limit who can open a file by saving it with a **password**. Only users who know the password can open, copy, or print the file. You can attach a password to a file when you save it with File Save As.

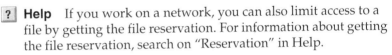 **Help**   If you work on a network, you can also limit access to a file by getting the file reservation. For information about getting the file reservation, search on "Reservation" in Help.

To limit access to a file

1. Make sure the cell pointer is in the file you want to save.

2. Choose File Save As.

3. Under Save, select the "With password" check box.

4. Choose OK.

   1-2-3 displays the Password dialog box.

5. Enter a password in the Password text box.

   A password can include 15 characters or less. 1-2-3 displays an * (asterisk) for each character as you enter the password. 1-2-3 is case-sensitive for passwords, so you must remember the exact combination of uppercase or lowercase letters you use when you create the password.

6. Enter the same password in the Verify text box.

7. Choose OK.

Caution Remember your password. When you save a file with a password, you can open it again *only* if you enter the exact password. Any user who knows the password can change or remove it. If you try unsuccessfully to open a password-protected file, check to see if another user who knew the original password changed it.

To delete a password

1. Make sure the cell pointer is in the file whose password you want to delete.

2. Choose File Save As.

3. Under Save, deselect the "With password" check box.

4. Choose OK.

Note Only users who know the password can open the file and delete the password.

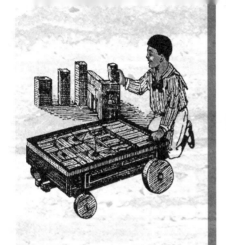

Part III
Using Charts

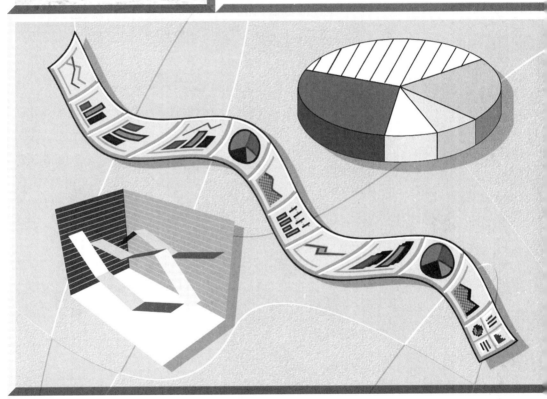

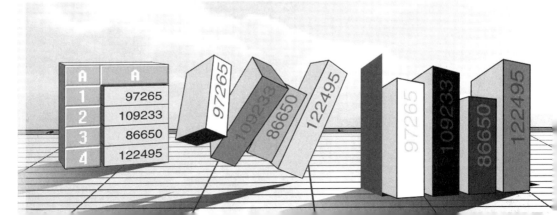

14

Creating Charts

1-2-3 produces presentation-quality charts right on the worksheet. You can create many different chart types in 2D and 3D, and you can change easily from one type to another. This chapter describes how to create 1-2-3 charts, change chart types, and use chart names.

> **Note** You work with charts as with other drawn objects. For information about selecting, sizing, moving, copying, deleting, and styling drawn objects, see Chapters 16 and 17. For information about printing charts, see "Quick printing" on page 131. To save a chart, save the file containing the chart.

What is a chart?

A **chart** is a visual representation of worksheet data. Charts reveal the significance of data and make it easier to identify trends and relationships. They're also dynamic; when you change the data a chart is based on, 1-2-3 updates the chart.

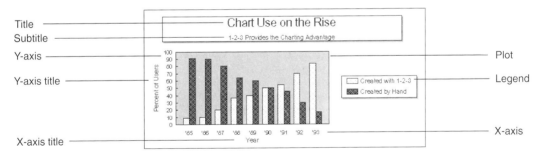

Most charts plot data against a horizontal x-axis and a vertical y-axis. The **x-axis** can include a scale or categories such as years, geographic areas, or age ranges. The **y-axis** can define the scale of values plotted in the chart. You can show units of measure, such as years or kilos, and title each axis to describe the categories or units plotted against it. You can also include labels for the chart title, subtitle, legend, and footnote.

Creating a chart

You can quickly create a chart from a selected range of data. When you create a chart, 1-2-3 plots each row or column of data in the selected range as a **data series**, a group of bars, lines, areas, or pie slices. A chart can contain up to 23 data series. 1-2-3 plots data series according to the following rules:

- If the selected range contains more rows of data than columns of data, 1-2-3 plots the data series by columns.

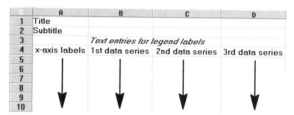

- If the selected range contains more columns of data than rows of data, or the same number of columns and rows of data, 1-2-3 plots the data series by rows.

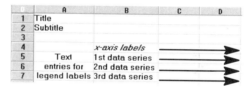

- 1-2-3 doesn't count blank columns or rows in the selected range. For example, 1-2-3 plots the data series shown below by columns. There are an equal number of rows and columns in the selected range, but two of the columns are blank.

? **Help**   You can use Chart Ranges to define data series that don't follow these rules. For information about how to define, delete, and change data series, search on "Data ranges" in Help.

If you select only numeric data and create a chart, 1-2-3 creates a default title, axis labels, and legend, as shown below.

This range ...

... produces this chart

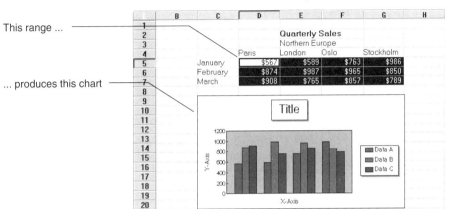

If your selected range includes column and row headings, and text above or to the left of the numeric data, 1-2-3 uses the text to create the axis labels, title, subtitle, and legend, as shown below.

This range ...

... produces this chart

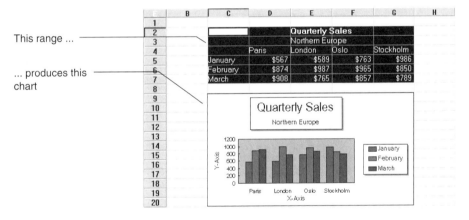

To create a chart

When you create a chart, 1-2-3 uses the initial default chart type, a bar chart. You can change the default, as described on page 155.

1. Select the range or collection of data you want to chart.

    If you want, include text for the axis labels, title, subtitle, and legend.

2. Choose Tools Chart.

In the worksheet, the mouse pointer changes to the one shown below.

To cancel a chart while creating it, press **ESC**.

3. Do one of the following:

- To create the chart in the default size, click the worksheet where you want the top left corner of the chart to appear.
- To size the chart yourself, drag across the worksheet and release the mouse button when the chart is the size you want.

If the chart covers data, you can drag or size the chart when you want to see the data. To delete a chart, select it and choose Edit Cut or press **DEL**.

Changing the chart type

1-2-3 provides many different types of charts, including 3D bar, line, area, and pie charts. After creating a chart, you can change it to the type you want. The type you choose depends on how you want to present your data. This section describes how to change from one type of chart to another and how to change the default chart type.

To change chart type

1. Click the chart to select it.

2. Choose Chart Type.

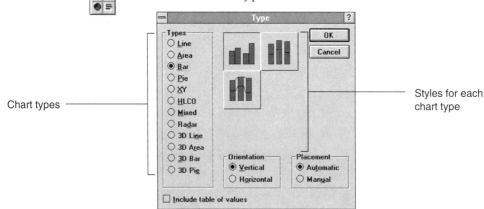

Chart types

Styles for each chart type

3. Under Types, select a chart type.

4. Select one of the style buttons for the chart type.

5. Under Orientation, select an option.

    • Vertical displays the x-axis across the bottom of the chart.

    • Horizontal displays the x-axis along the left side of the chart.

    Note   Orientation has no effect on pie charts or radar charts.

6. If you previously moved the plot and want to return it to the default position, select Automatic under Placement.

7. To display data values under the chart, select the "Include table of values" check box.

8. Choose OK.

1-2-3 displays the chart as the new chart type.

Shortcut   Select the chart and click one of the SmartIcons shown below to change the chart type. If the icon doesn't appear in your set of SmartIcons, you can use Tools SmartIcons to add it.

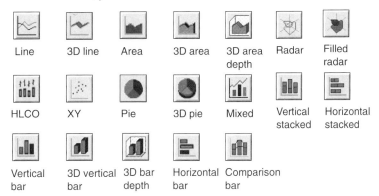

| Line | 3D line | Area | 3D area | 3D area depth | Radar | Filled radar |

| HLCO | XY | Pie | 3D pie | Mixed | Vertical stacked | Horizontal stacked |

| Vertical bar | 3D vertical bar | 3D bar depth | Horizontal bar | Comparison bar |

To change the default chart type

1. Create a chart using Tools Chart.

2. Change the chart to the type you want as the default.

3. Choose Chart Set Preferred.

1-2-3 uses the chart type you selected as the default for new charts. To change an existing chart to the default type, select it and choose Chart Set Preferred.

Types of charts

This section describes and illustrates all the different chart types. It also includes a table to help you choose the chart type that best presents your data.

Bar charts

Bar charts are the most common type of business chart. Each type of bar chart illustrates a specific relationship among the data in your worksheet.

Standard bar charts emphasize individual values. The x-axis can show time progressing from left to right. The chart on the left below shows a set of sales data plotted for each year between 1989 and 1993. If you have more than one data range, 1-2-3 creates a clustered bar chart and displays each data range in a different pattern or color, as shown below on the right. Using clustered bars lets you compare several points in time.

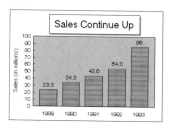
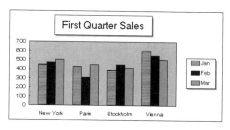

Use a **stacked bar chart** when you want to compare totals in addition to individual values for each period. The bars in a stacked bar chart represent totals, and the segments in each bar represent the parts that comprise the total. For example, the charts below use the same data to show the total sales for each quarter, as well as the sales figures for each hair care product. The chart on the right shows the relative contributions of each product as a percent of sales.

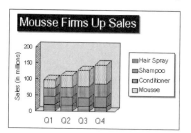
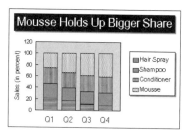

Use a **comparison bar chart** when you want a stacked bar chart that emphasizes the differences between corresponding segments in each bar.

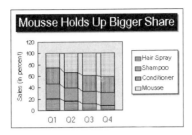

Line and area charts

Line and area charts show the changes in a set of data over time. Like bar charts, line and area charts often show time progressing from left to right on the x-axis. These charts work especially well when you have many data elements.

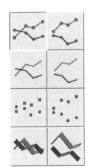 When you draw a **line chart**, 1-2-3 plots each element in a data series as a **data point** and connects the data points with a line. 1-2-3 can represent each data point with a symbol, such as a square or a triangle. You can change these symbols by selecting the line and choosing Style Lines & Color.

Using line charts, you can analyze actual values as well as compare the slope of lines to measure the rate of change. You can add visual interest to simple line charts by making them 3D.

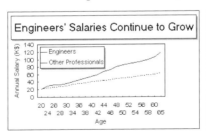

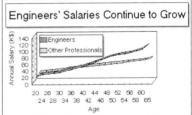

Area charts show trends in data over time by emphasizing the area under the curve created by each data series. Like line charts, area charts downplay individual values. The first area chart below reveals that training costs, although less than salary costs, are increasing faster than salaries. The second chart shows that total sales are improving, despite changes in individual sales offices.

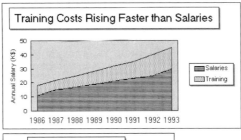

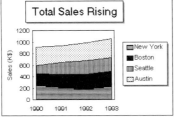

Mixed charts

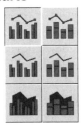

A **mixed chart** can combine parts from a line chart, a bar chart, or an area chart. This lets you plot data in two forms on the same chart. In the example below, the bars show that the company has moved from a loss to profitability over five years, the line shows the trend for expenses, and the area shows the total revenues. You can also create bar/area, and bar/line combinations.

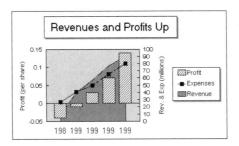

? Help   You can create your own mixed charts by using Chart Ranges to change the type of individual data ranges to line, area, or bar. For more information, search on "Data ranges" in Help.

XY charts

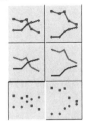

XY charts are similar to line charts, except that the data points are plotted against a numeric x-axis. An XY chart whose points are plotted without a connecting line is called a **scatter chart**.

You use an XY chart to see if there is a correlation between large sets of data. If the data points cluster around an imaginary line, then a correlation exists. The more points approach the "line," the stronger the correlation. The chart on the left below shows a correlation; the chart on the right shows no clear correlation.

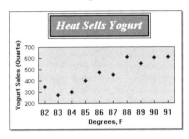
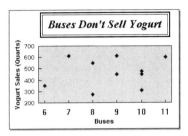

Pie charts

Pie charts compare parts to the whole. 1-2-3 charts each data point or element as a slice in the pie. The size of a slice corresponds to the percentage of the data range it represents. You can include a legend that identifies each slice, or you can include labels that show the actual percentages or values that each slice represents.

You can also explode slices to set them apart from the rest of the pie. The data series can proceed in clockwise or counter-clockwise order. The charts below show the increasing popularity of video rentals, as compared to other kinds of entertainment.

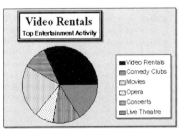
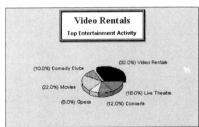

HLCO charts

High-Low-Close-Open (HLCO) charts are also called stock market charts. Use HLCO charts to track data that fluctuates over time, such as stocks, commodities, air temperature, and currency rates. HLCO charts show both ranges and data points.

A **whisker HLCO chart** consists of a set of vertical bars, with two markers on each bar. Each vertical bar shows the range of values between the first and second data series (the high and low values). The left marker shows the third data series (the ending or closing value) and the right marker shows the fourth data series (the starting or opening value).

The fifth data series is plotted as a bar chart below the HLCO chart, and represents trading volume in stock market charts. Any additional data series are plotted as line graphs in the HLCO portion of the chart.

The marker on the left
shows the opening value

The top of each bar
shows the high value

The bottom of each bar
shows the low value

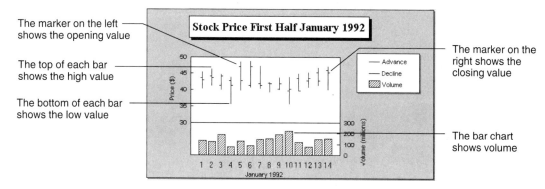

The marker on the
right shows the
closing value

The bar chart
shows volume

A **candlestick HLCO chart** provides the same information but shows the third and fourth data series (close and open) as a widened vertical bar spanning the range between close and open. The vertical bar is white if Close is higher than Open ("Advance"), and solid blue if Closed is lower than Open ("Decline"). The rest of the chart format is the same as the whisker HLCO.

The widened vertical bar shows the range between open and close

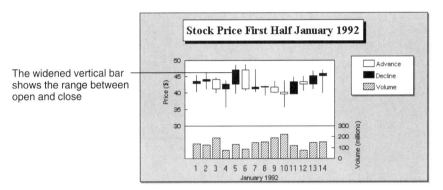

Radar charts

A **radar chart** is a line or area chart wrapped around a central point. Each axis represents a set of data points. Because they plot data as a function of distance from a central point, radar charts are useful for showing the symmetry or uniformity of data. For example, the line radar chart below shows the actual yield of Florida oranges over a 6-month period plotted against projected yields for these periods.

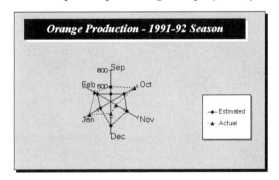

The area radar chart below shows sales results for each of three offices, along with the total sales for all three offices, over a five-month period.

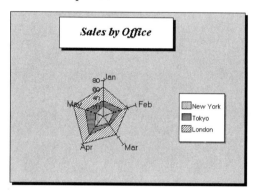

Choosing the best type of chart

When charting data, think about which chart type most clearly represents the data. The table below describes when it's best to use a particular chart type.

To show	Use this chart type	For example
Items that change over time	Line, bar, mixed bar/line, stacked bar, area, HLCO	Annual sales from 1988–1993; 30-day stock trend
Items at a specific point in time	Horizontal bar, horizontal stacked bar	1993 sales for 5 products; 1993 costs by month
Parts of the whole	Pie, 100% horizontal stacked bar, 100% area	Market share by company; percent of office space used in New York by industry
Frequency distributions	Bar	Number of homes in various price ranges; number of employees in various age ranges
Relationships between variables	Bar, scatter (XY)	Level of education compared to hours spent watching TV; average drop in asking price for home versus length of time on market
Ranges of data	Bar, HLCO	Daily temperature ranges in February for Juneau, Alaska
Symmetry or uniformity of data	Radar	Individual performance versus group performance

Naming and finding charts

1-2-3 automatically assigns default names to all charts, starting with Chart 1. You can change the default name to a more descriptive one. This section describes how to rename a chart and how to find a chart by using the name. Going to a chart by name is particularly useful for finding charts in large files.

To rename a chart

1. Select the chart.
2. Choose Chart Name.
3. Enter a name in the Chart name text box.

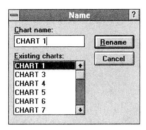

   You can't use the same name for more than one chart in the current file.
4. Choose Rename.

To find a chart

1. Choose Edit Go To.
2. From the Type of item drop-down box, select Chart.

3. If the chart is in another active file, select the file name from the In file drop-down box.
4. Select the name of the chart.

1-2-3 displays and selects the chart.

[?] Related Help topics

Tutorial lesson 4 gives you hands-on practice in creating and working with charts. To start the Tutorial, choose Help Tutorial.

15 Enhancing Charts

You can customize a chart by working directly with its elements. For example, you can style, size, and move the title, footnotes and legend. You can also change the axis scale and tick marks. This chapter describes how to enhance your charts to present your data in the clearest, most attractive way.

Styling chart elements

The illustration below shows the elements of a chart that you can work with and enhance.

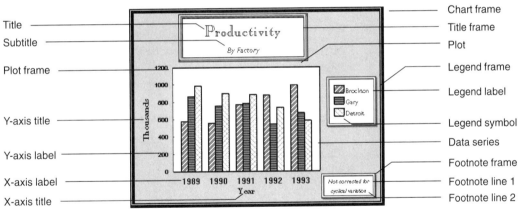

To see the styling options available for a particular chart element, select it and press the right mouse button.

You can style chart elements the same way you style other drawn objects. For example, you can use Style Lines & Color to add designer frames and interior colors and patterns to any framed chart element. For more information about working with drawn objects, see Chapters 16 and 17. You can also style text in a chart. For example, you can select the chart title and use Style Font & Attributes to change the font.

Working with titles, footnotes, and legends

As described on page 153, you can create a chart with a default title and legend labels, or you can include text for these elements and a subtitle in the range that you select to chart. This section describes how to add footnotes to a chart and how to change titles, footnotes, and legend labels.

To add or change titles and footnotes

1. Select the chart.

2. Choose Chart Headings.

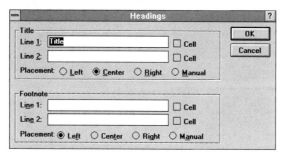

3. To add or change the title and subtitle, do one of the following:

    • Under Title, enter the chart title in the Line 1 text box and the subtitle in the Line 2 text box.

    • Under Title, select the Cell check boxes next to Line 1 and Line 2; then specify the name or address of a cell containing text for the title in the Line 1 text box, and text for the subtitle in the Line 2 text box.

    Titles and footnotes can contain any numbers, letters, and special characters.

4. To add or change a footnote, repeat step 3 using the Line 1 and Line 2 text boxes under Footnote.

5. Choose OK.

To move titles and footnotes

The quickest, easiest way to move a chart title or footnote is to drag it. You can also use the Headings dialog box as described below.

1. Double-click the title or footnote; or select the chart and choose Chart Headings.

2. Under Title or Footnote, select a placement option: Left, Center, or Right.

   Manual indicates that you previously dragged the title or footnote.

3. Choose OK.

To change individual legend labels

1. Double-click the legend; or select the chart and choose Chart Legend.

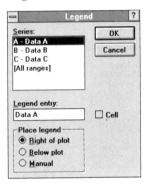

2. In the Series list box, select a data series.

3. In the Legend entry text box, do one of the following:
   - Enter the label.
   - Select the Cell check box; then specify the name or address of a cell containing text for the legend entry.

4. To change the location of the legend, select an option under Place legend: Right of plot or Below plot.

   Manual indicates that you previously dragged the title or footnote.

5. Choose OK.

   Note For information about changing legend labels for a pie chart, see page 173.

**To change all
legend labels**

1. Double-click the legend; or select the chart and choose Chart Legend.

2. In the Series list box, select All ranges.

3. In the Legend entry text box, specify the range containing the labels.

4. To change the location of the legend, select an option under Place legend: Right of plot or Below plot.

   Manual indicates that you previously dragged the title or footnote.

5. Choose OK.

**Changing axis
titles**

When you create any chart except a pie or radar chart, 1-2-3 supplies the default axis titles, "X-Axis" and "Y-Axis." You can change the axis titles to describe the data plotted against each axis.

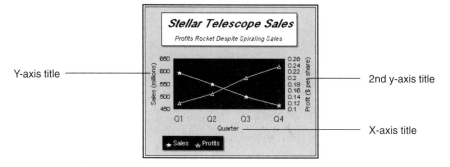

Y-axis title

2nd y-axis title

X-axis title

To change an axis title

1. Double-click the axis title; or select the chart and choose Chart Axis X-Axis, Y-Axis, or 2nd Y-Axis.

   Depending on the axis you selected or the command you chose, 1-2-3 displays a dialog box like the following one:

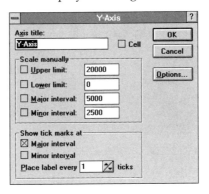

2. Do one of the following:

   • Enter a new title in the Axis title text box.

   • Select the Cell check box; then in the Axis title text box, specify the name or address of a cell containing text for the axis title.

3. Choose OK.

Adding and changing units titles

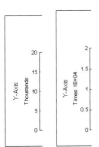

Automatic   Manual

Units titles define the scale for each axis; for example, "in thousands," "millionths," "years," and "miles per hour." You can use text or an exponent as a units title.

1-2-3 displays the units title in standard units. For example, using an exponent of 3 displays a units title of Thousands (10^3). An exponent of –6 displays a units title of Millionths (10^{-6}). When an exponent isn't a multiple of 3, it doesn't correspond neatly to these units titles. In this case, 1-2-3 can automatically adjust the exponent up or down and change the axis labels accordingly.

For example, if you enter axis labels ranging from 10,000 to 90,000 with an exponent of 4, and select Automatic, 1-2-3 automatically changes the exponent to 3, multiplies the axis labels by 10, and changes the units title to Thousands. If you specify an exponent over 15, 1-2-3 uses scientific notation. For example, 1-2-3 shortens an exponent of 23, or 1×10^{23}, to 1E+23.

To add or change a units title

1. Double-click the axis where you want to add a units title; or select the chart and choose Chart Axis X-Axis, Y-Axis, or 2nd Y-Axis.

2. Choose Options.

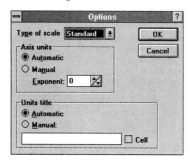

If the chart already has a units title, double-click it to display the Options dialog box.

3. Under Axis units, select an option.

   • Automatic

   • Manual lets you set the exponent. Click the arrows or enter a number in the Exponent text box.

4. Under Units title, select an option.

   • Automatic

   • Manual lets you specify a title. In the text box, enter text for the title; or select the Cell check box, and specify the name or address of a cell containing the text.

5. Choose OK.

Changing the axis scale

When you create a chart, 1-2-3 sets the scale of the axes. You can change the type of scale for a numerical axis to any of the following:

• A **linear** or **standard** scale, in which the numbers increase or decrease by a fixed number of units.

• A **log** scale, in which the numbers increase or decrease logarithmically.

• A **100%** scale, in which the values range from 0 through 100% and represent percentages instead of absolute values. You can use 100% scales for area, line, radar, mixed, and stacked and unstacked bar charts.

You can also change the upper and lower value limits of the scale and the intervals between the major and minor tick marks. The illustration below shows a chart using a standard scale with settings for upper and lower limits and intervals between major and minor tick marks.

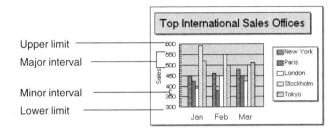

To set the axis scale manually

1. Double-click the axis; or select the chart and choose Chart Axis X-Axis, Y-Axis, or 2nd Y-Axis.

2. To change the type of scale, choose Options and select an option from the Type of scale drop-down box. Then choose OK.

3. To create a scale displaying only data that falls within specified upper and lower limits, specify a number in the Upper limit and Lower limit text boxes under Scale manually.

4. To change intervals between tick marks, enter the interval in the Major interval and Minor interval text boxes under Scale manually.

5. Choose OK.

   Note   If the upper limit is lower than the lower limit, 1-2-3 displays a blank rectangle in place of the chart.

Positioning tick marks and labels

Tick marks show a chart's scale. You can show major and minor tick marks, such as years and months, for each axis.

Major tick marks

Minor tick marks

Axis labels

0   150   300   450

To position the tick marks, 1-2-3 calculates the major and minor interval automatically for each axis, unless you change the intervals manually as described above. **Axis labels** identify the major tick marks on an axis. You can label every major tick mark, every other one, every third one, and so on.

To set tick marks and axis labels

If your axis labels are values, use Style Number Format to change their format without changing the format of the data in the worksheet.

1. Select the chart and choose Chart Axis X-Axis, Y-Axis, or 2nd Y-Axis.

2. Under "Show tick marks at," select one or both options:
   - Major interval
   - Minor interval

3. Next to "Place label every," click the arrows or enter a number in the text box.

4. Choose OK.

Enhancing pie charts

By default, 1-2-3 displays a legend and percentages in a pie chart. If you include x-axis labels in the selected range, 1-2-3 uses the text for the legend labels, as shown below.

This range ...

... produces this chart

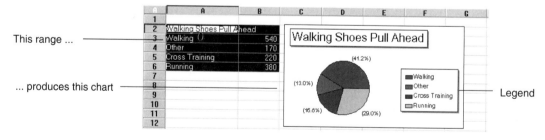

Legend

You can enhance pie charts by displaying labels and values for each pie slice and by exploding individual slices. Labeling each pie slice takes the place of the legend. **Exploding** a pie slice emphasizes it by pulling it out of the pie. You can explode a slice manually by dragging it, or you can explode all pie slices by a percentage you specify.

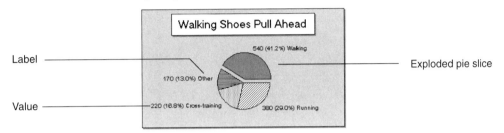

Label

Value

Exploded pie slice

To label each pie slice

Instead of including a legend in a pie chart, you can label each pie slice.

1. Select the chart.

2. Choose Chart Data Labels.

To change the color of a pie slice, select it and use Style Lines & Color.

3. Under Show, select Contents of X data range.

4. To include values, select Values under Show.

5. Choose OK.

[?] **Help**   You can also show percentages for individual slices using a range, called a C range, that you set up in the worksheet. For information about setting up a C range, search on "C range" in Help.

To explode all pie slices

The quickest, easiest way to explode a single pie slice is to drag it. When you want to explode all pie slices by a specific percentage, you can use Chart Data Labels as described below.

1. Select the chart.

2. Choose Chart Data Labels.

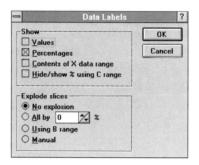

3. Under Explode slices, select "All by," and click the arrows or enter a percentage in the text box.

4. Choose OK.

To reset exploded pie slices, choose Chart Data Labels, select No explosion, and choose OK.

? **Help** You can also use a range of values in the worksheet to explode pie slices. For information, search on "Exploding pie slices" in Help.

? ## Related Help topics

You can add grid lines to a chart at major and minor intervals. For information, search on "Chart grid lines" in Help.

You can add labels for each data point in a data series. For more information, search on "Data labels" in Help.

You can specify a color and pattern for each point in a data series by using Chart Numeric Color and specifying a range. For example, you can highlight a specific bar in a bar chart by making it a different color from all the rest; or you can make the color of a particular bar dependent upon a variable, so the bar changes color when the variable exceeds a specified limit. For more information, search on "Colors" in Help and select the topic "Setting up a Colors Range."

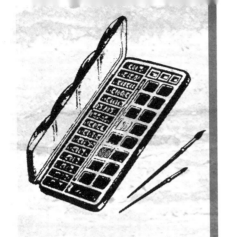

Part IV
Using Graphics

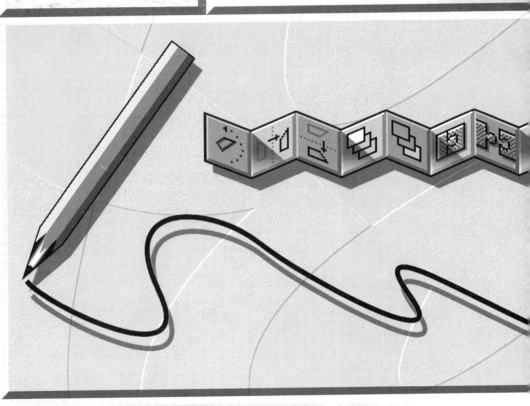

16 Creating Graphics

You can use graphics to enhance your presentation of data in 1-2-3. This chapter gives you basic information about how to create and work with drawn objects, such as lines, arrows, shapes, and text blocks. Chapter 17 gives you more advanced information about styling and manipulating drawn objects.

What are drawn objects?

Drawn objects are graphic elements you can use to enhance your worksheet data, as shown in the illustration below.

When you create and arrange drawn objects on a worksheet, they appear and print as part of the worksheet. In a multiple-sheet file, you can have different drawn objects on every worksheet.

You can create lines, arrows, shapes, and text blocks. The types of lines you can draw are plain lines, polylines, arcs, and freehand drawings. The shapes you can draw are rectangles, rounded rectangles, squares, polygons, ellipses, and circles. You can also copy a picture from another program to the Clipboard and paste it into a 1-2-3 worksheet.

Charts, chart elements, macro buttons, and embedded objects are also types of drawn objects. For information about creating and using charts, see Chapters 14 and 15. For information about creating and using macro buttons, see Chapter 26. For information about creating embedded objects, see Chapter 27.

Creating lines, arcs, and arrows

You can use arrows to point out important data in your worksheet. You can use lines to create shapes such as triangles. As you draw a line, arc, or arrow you can drag it to any size or angle. When drawing an arc, drag in the direction you want the arc to curve. When you draw an arrow, the arrow head appears at the end where you stop dragging.

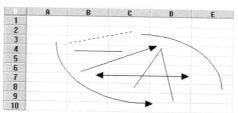

To create a line, arc, or arrow

*For horizontal, vertical, or 45-degree lines or arrows, hold down **SHIFT** as you drag.*

1. Choose Tools Draw Line, Tools Draw Arc, or Tools Draw Arrow.

2. Move the mouse pointer where you want to begin drawing the line, arc, or arrow.

3. Drag across the worksheet to where you want to end the line, arc, or arrow.

4. Release the mouse button.

Shortcut   You can use the SmartIcons shown at left in place of step 1 to create lines, arcs, and arrows.

Creating rectangles and ellipses

You can use rectangles, rounded rectangles, and ellipses to surround areas of your worksheet, or to create designs such as logos.

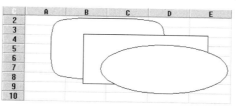

To create a rectangle or ellipse

To draw a square instead of a rectangle or a circle instead of an ellipse, hold down **SHIFT** *as you drag.*

1. Choose Tools Draw Rectangle, Tools Draw Rounded Rectangle, or Tools Draw Ellipse.

2. Move the mouse pointer where you want to begin drawing the shape.

3. Drag across the worksheet where you want the shape to appear.

4. Release the mouse button.

Shortcut   You can use the SmartIcons shown at left to create a rectangle, rounded rectangle, or an ellipse.

Creating polylines and polygons

A **polyline** is an open shape consisting of straight or freehand line segments. A **polygon** is a closed shape with any number of straight or freehand line segments as sides. A polyline or polygon can be a combination of straight and freehand line segments.

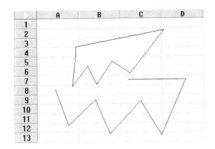

To create a polyline or polygon

For horizontal, vertical, or 45-degree lines, hold down **SHIFT** *as you drag.*

1. Choose Tools Draw Polyline or Tools Draw Polygon.

2. Move the mouse pointer where you want to begin drawing the first line segment.

3. To draw a straight line segment, drag across the worksheet to where you want to end the line. To draw a freehand line segment, hold down **CTRL** while dragging.

4. Release the mouse button.

5. Drag or **CTRL**+drag to draw each line segment.

6. Double-click to complete the polyline or polygon.

You don't have to draw the last line segment in a polygon; 1-2-3 automatically connects the last line segment you drew to the first.

Shortcut   You can use the SmartIcons at left in place of step 1 to create a polygon or polyline.

Drawing freehand

You can draw freehand on the worksheet to create any shapes you want.

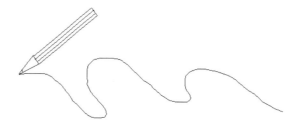

To draw freehand

1. Choose Tools Draw Freehand.
2. Move the mouse pointer where you want to begin the freehand drawing.
3. Drag across the worksheet.
4. Release the mouse button where you want the drawing to end.

Using text blocks

Text blocks are like notes you stick on a page to add comments or emphasize important information. You can size the text block and place it anywhere on the worksheet. You can edit text in a text block and style it.

To create a text block

1. Choose Tools Draw Text.
2. Move the mouse pointer where you want to begin the text block.
3. Do one of the following:
    *   Click to create the text block in the default size.
    *   Drag across the worksheet and release the mouse button when the text block is the size you want.

    1-2-3 displays the text block with the insertion point, a blinking vertical bar, in the top left corner.
4. Enter text by typing or by pasting it in.

    For example, you can copy text from a cell and paste it into the text block.
5. When you finish entering text, click the worksheet.

To edit text in a text block

1. Select the text block.
2. Double-click the text block to start editing.
3. Edit the text.
4. When you finish editing, click the worksheet.

To change the appearance of a text block

1. Select the text block.
2. Do one of the following:
   - To change the type face, size, color, or attributes of the text in the text block, choose Style Font & Attributes.
   - To change the alignment, choose Style Alignment.
   - To apply edge styles, colors, and designer frames to the text block, choose Style Lines & Color.

   Note You can't apply different fonts, attributes, and colors to different parts of the text in a text block. You can apply only one font, attribute, and color to all the text. For more information about applying styles, see Chapter 11.

Bringing Pictures into 1-2-3

You can bring a picture from another program into 1-2-3. For example, you can create or edit a picture in Windows Paintbrush, copy it to the Clipboard, and paste it into your 1-2-3 worksheet or on a drawn object or chart.

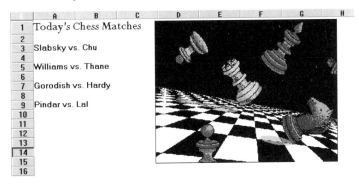

To bring a picture into 1-2-3

1. Make sure the Clipboard contains a copy of the picture.
2. Click the worksheet where you want to place the top left corner of the picture.
3. Choose Edit Paste.

The picture appears on the worksheet. You can select, size, move, and delete it like any other drawn object.

Working with drawn objects

This section describes basic tasks you perform when working with drawn objects, such as selecting, copying, moving, sizing, and deleting them. The more advanced tasks, such as styling, grouping, rotating, and flipping drawn objects are described in the next chapter.

Working with a drawn object doesn't affect the worksheet area behind the object. For example, if you move or size an object, it doesn't move or size the worksheet cells behind the object. Moving or sizing the cells behind a drawn object can affect the object, depending on how the object is fastened to the cells. For more information about fastening drawn objects to cells, see page 191.

To select drawn objects

*To select more than one drawn object, click the first one and hold down **SHIFT** or **CTRL** while clicking the others; or lasso the objects.*

1. Move the mouse pointer over the drawn object you want to select.
2. Click the object.

Small squares called **handles** appear at the corners, mid-points, and ends of the object. You can use these handles to size the object.

Handles appear around a drawn object

 Note You can't select a macro button by clicking it. You can use the lasso icon shown at left to select a macro button or any other drawn objects. You can also select a macro button by SHIFT+clicking it or CTRL+clicking it.

To copy drawn objects

To copy a selected drawn object in the current worksheet, press **INS**.

You can copy drawn objects and paste them into the current worksheet or into another worksheet or active file.

1. Select one or more drawn objects.
2. Choose Edit Copy.
3. Select a cell where you want to paste the object.
4. Choose Edit Paste.

To move drawn objects in the current worksheet

To cancel the move, press **ESC** *before you release the mouse button.*

1. Select one or more drawn objects.

    To move more than one drawn object, position the mouse pointer over any one of the selected objects.

2. Drag the object by any part except the handles.
3. Release the mouse button when the object is where you want it.

As you drag a drawn object, an outline of the object appears, and the mouse pointer changes as shown below.

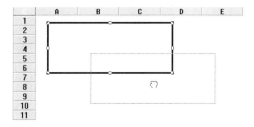

To move drawn objects to another worksheet or file

1. Select one or more drawn objects.
2. Choose Edit Cut.
3. Select a cell in the worksheet where you want to paste the object.
4. Choose Edit Paste.

To size drawn objects

You can change the size of any drawn object. You can change width, height, or both for all objects other than lines or arrows.

1. Select one or more drawn objects.

To cancel sizing, press ESC *before you release the mouse button. If you don't like the results after sizing, press* CTRL+Z *to restore the object to its original size.*

2. Drag a handle in the direction you want to size the object.

   When you select multiple drawn objects, you can size them all by dragging a handle of one object.

   To maintain the proportions of a drawn object, hold down SHIFT and drag a corner handle in the direction you want to size the object.

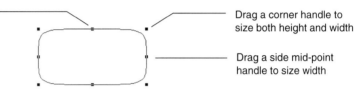

Drag a top or bottom mid-point handle to size height

Drag a corner handle to size both height and width

Drag a side mid-point handle to size width

3. Release the mouse button when the object is the size you want.

To delete drawn objects

1. Select one or more drawn objects.

2. Choose Edit Clear or press DEL.

   Note   When you delete a drawn object with Edit Clear or DEL, 1-2-3 doesn't put the object on the Clipboard. Choose Edit Cut when you want to delete a drawn object and put it on the Clipboard.

17   Enhancing Graphics

You can enhance drawn objects with a variety of visual effects. This chapter describes how to change lines and edges, add designer frames, and change patterns and colors. It also describes how to shuffle drawn objects, flip them, rotate them, group them, lock them, and fasten them to underlying cells. For basic information about how to create and work with drawn objects, see Chapter 16.

Changing lines or edges

You can change the style and width of lines, arrows, polylines, arcs, and freehand drawings. You can also change the style and width of the edge of shapes, charts, pictures, embedded objects, or text blocks. The thicker the line or edge, the more prominent the object appears.

To change lines or edges

Double-click a drawn object to display the Lines & Color dialog box for styling the object.

1. Select one or more drawn objects.

2. Choose Style Lines & Color.

3. Select a style from the Line style drop-down box under Edge or Line.

4. Select a width from the Line width drop-down box under Edge or Line.

5. If you selected an arrow or line, select an arrowhead style from the Arrowheads drop-down box under Edge or Line.

6. Choose OK.

To add a designer frame

A **designer frame** is a graphic enhancement that appears like a frame around the edges of a square, rectangle, picture, text block, embedded object, chart, and chart title, footnote, and legend.

1. Select one or more drawn objects.
2. Choose Style Lines & Color.
3. Select a frame from the Designer frame drop-down box.
4. Choose OK.

Changing fill patterns

A fill pattern can add interest to a drawn object. You can choose from 64 different patterns for the interior of solid and closed drawn objects, such as shapes, text blocks, pictures, and a series of bars in a bar chart. You can also fill an arc, polyline, or freehand drawing with a pattern.

The transparent fill pattern, shown at left, is the default fill for the interior of shapes. When the fill is transparent, other drawn objects or worksheet data can show through the object. For example, you can emphasize data in a cell by putting a circle around the cell.

You can use the four patterns shown at left to create a gradient fill pattern. A gradient pattern changes gradually from the background color to the pattern color, starting from right to left, left to right, bottom to top, or top to bottom.

> **Note**   When you change the fill pattern of a chart or text block, remember to choose a pattern that doesn't obscure the information inside.

To change fill patterns

1. Select one or more drawn objects.
2. Choose Style Lines & Color.
3. Under Interior, select a pattern from the Pattern drop-down box.
4. Choose OK.

Changing colors

You can change the color of lines, arrows, arcs, or freehand drawings. You can change the color of the edges of closed shapes, charts, pictures, or text blocks.

Closed drawn objects and arcs, polylines, and freehand drawings can also have a background color and a pattern color. The **background color** is the color inside the object behind any pattern in the object. The **pattern color** is the color of the pattern in the object. Also, if you added a designer frame to an object, you can change the color of the frame.

If you apply colors to your worksheet, you can print the results on a color printer, or create color slides or overheads. Even if you don't plan to print a worksheet in color, you can use color to enhance the online appearance of your worksheets, particularly if you plan to have other people use your worksheets on a color monitor.

> **Note**   Depending on your monitor, all colors can appear as shades of gray.

To change line and edge color

1. Select one or more drawn objects.
2. Choose Style Lines & Color.
3. Under Edge or Line, select a color from the Line color drop-down box.
4. If the object has a designer frame, select a color from the Frame color drop-down box.
5. Choose OK.

To change background and pattern color

1. Select one or more drawn objects.
2. Choose Style Lines & Color.
3. Under Interior, do one or both of the following:
   - Select a color for the background from the Background color drop-down box.
   - Select a color for the pattern from the Pattern color drop-down box.
4. Choose OK.

Arranging drawn objects

You can use the Edit Arrange commands to shuffle overlapping drawn objects, flip or rotate objects, group objects so you can work with them as a unit, and lock objects to prevent accidental change. You can also fasten and unfasten objects to the worksheet cells behind them so you can move or resize cells and objects together.

To shuffle drawn objects

You can rearrange overlapping objects by sending the object in front to the back and vice versa. For example, if you create a rounded rectangle that covers an ellipse, you can shuffle the ellipse to the front of the rectangle, as shown below.

Before Shuffling   **After Shuffling**

To bring a drawn object in front of other objects

1.   Select one or more drawn objects.

 2.   Choose Edit Arrange Bring to Front.

To send a drawn object in back of other objects

1.   Select one or more drawn objects.

2.   Choose Edit Arrange Send to Back.

To flip drawn objects

You can flip drawn objects horizontally or vertically. Flipping an object horizontally turns the object backward. Flipping an object vertically turns the object upside down.

1. Select one or more drawn objects.

2. Do either of the following:

- To flip drawn objects horizontally, choose Edit Arrange Flip Left-Right.

- To flip drawn objects vertically, choose Edit Arrange Flip Top-Bottom.

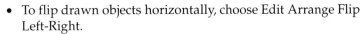

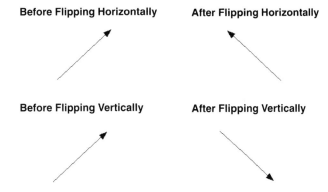

Note   You can't flip charts, embedded objects, macro buttons, query tables, pictures, or text blocks.

To rotate drawn objects

You can rotate a drawn object on its axis.

1. Select one or more drawn objects.

2. Choose Edit Arrange Rotate.

3. Move the mouse pointer in the direction you want to rotate the object.

    To rotate the object in 45-degree increments, hold down SHIFT as you move the mouse pointer.

4. Release the mouse button when the object is in the position you want.

Shortcut   Select the drawn object and click the icon shown at left to rotate the object.

Before Rotating   **After Rotating**

Note   You can't rotate embedded objects, macro buttons, pictures, or query tables.

To group or ungroup drawn objects

You can group objects so you can move, size, and style them together as a group instead of one by one. You can select several objects to move or style them all at once; however, this isn't the same as grouping them.

Grouped objects stay together until you ungroup them, even when you deselect them or save and close the file. When you reopen the file, you can still select the objects as a group.

To group drawn objects

1. Select the objects you want to group.

2. Choose Edit Arrange Group.

Before Grouping   **After Grouping**

Each object has its own set of handles

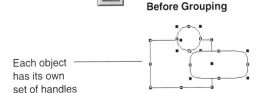
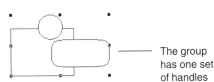

The group has one set of handles

To ungroup drawn objects

1. Select one or more groups.

2. Choose Edit Arrange Ungroup.

Each object appears with its own set of handles.

To lock or unlock drawn objects

Locking a drawn object prevents you or another user from accidentally moving, sizing, or deleting the object. When an object is locked, you can't change any of its styles with the Style Lines & Color command and you can't change its arrangement with any of the Edit Arrange commands.

To lock drawn objects

1. Select one or more drawn objects.

2. Choose Edit Arrange Lock.

When you select a locked drawn object, its handles are shaped liked diamonds rather than squares, as shown below.

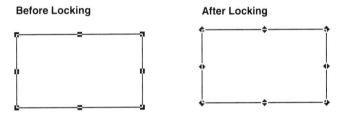

To unlock drawn objects

1. Select one or more drawn objects.

2. Choose Edit Arrange Unlock.

To fasten drawn objects

When you create a drawn object, 1-2-3 fastens it by default to the cells behind its top left and bottom right corners. The corner of a drawn object is the corner formed by its handles. A drawn object fastened in this way always moves and sizes with the cells behind it.

A fastened object can move and change size when you insert or delete cells, columns, and rows, or when you change column widths and row heights, as shown below.

This rectangle is fastened to the top left and bottom right cells

The rectangle resizes when you widen column A

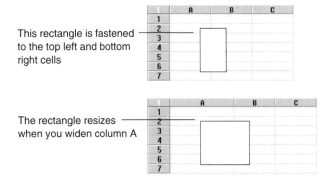

When you size or move a fastened object, 1-2-3 fastens it to the cells behind its new top left and bottom right corners. When you paste a picture into 1-2-3, by default it is fastened to the top left cell only. This means that it moves but doesn't size with the cells.

To change how a drawn object is fastened to the cells behind it

1. Select one or more drawn objects.

2. Choose Edit Arrange Fasten to Cells.

3. Under "Attach object to," select an option.

- Top left and bottom right cells lets you move and size the drawn object when you move, size, or hide the cells behind it.

- Top left cell only lets you move but not size the drawn object when you move, size, or hide the cells behind it.

4. Choose OK.

Shortcut   Select the drawn object and click the icons at left to fasten the object to the top left and bottom right cells, or to the top left cell only.

Part V
Analyzing Data

18

Analyzing Formulas

With the 1-2-3 audit feature, you can analyze the overall logic of a worksheet. Auditing is especially useful when you want to examine someone else's worksheet to identify the formulas and other data that the worksheet is based on. It's also helpful for reviewing your own worksheets when they start to get large and complex. This chapter describes how to use Tools Audit to find and analyze formulas, circular references, and DDE links.

Why audit your worksheets?

With Tools Audit, you can quickly discover the source of errors or inconsistencies, and you can check if any ranges you want to delete are referred to by formulas. It's also useful when you want to modify formulas or their precedent and dependent data.

Using Tools Audit to identify dependent cells can also make what-if analysis easier. When you want to see the effects of changing a value, knowing the dependent cells affected by the change helps you make a speedy check of the results.

Using Tools Audit

To audit your worksheets, you choose Tools Audit and specify the following information in the Audit dialog box:

- What you want to find

  You can find all formulas in your worksheets, formula precedents and dependents, circular references, file links, and DDE links.

- How you want to see the results

  Tools Audit reports the results of an audit either by selecting all cells of the specified type or by displaying a list of these cells.

- Where you want to audit

  You can limit your audit to the current file, or you can audit formulas in all active files.

Select what you want to find

Select how you want to see the results

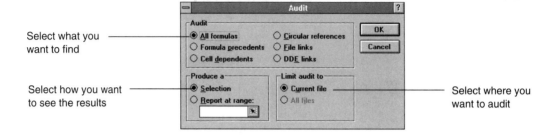

Select where you want to audit

To find all formulas

Finding formulas is useful when you want to identify the formulas and other data a worksheet is based on. It's especially effective when you're examining someone else's worksheet or reviewing your own long after creating it.

1. Choose Tools Audit.

2. Under Audit, select All formulas.

3. Under Produce a, select an option.
   - Selection selects a collection of all cells containing formulas.
   - Report at range displays a list of all cells containing formulas. In the text box, specify a blank range.

     If you specify a single-cell range, 1-2-3 displays the list, one item per cell down the column, starting at the cell you specified. If you specify a multiple-cell range, 1-2-3 displays the list one item per cell, top to bottom and left to right. If there's more data in the list than fits in the range, 1-2-3 truncates the list at the bottom right cell of the range.

4. Under Limit audit to, select an option.
   - Current file searches all worksheets in the current file.
   - All files searches all worksheets in all active files.

     This option is available only if you selected Report at range under "Produce a." 1-2-3 can't produce a selection in more than one file.

5.   Choose OK.

1-2-3 selects or lists all cells containing formulas, or displays a message if it finds no cells containing formulas. To move among selected cells, press **CTRL+ENTER** to go to the next range in the collection and **CTRL+SHIFT+ENTER** to go to the previous range. To deselect the collection, click any cell or press **ESC**.

Shortcut   Click the icon shown at left to select all formulas in the current file.

To find formula precedents

Formula **precedents** are all cells referred to by a formula. For example, suppose cell B5 contains the formula +A3+@SUM(B1..B3). The formula precedents of B5 are A3, B1, B2, and B3 because these cells all contain data referred to by the formula in B5.

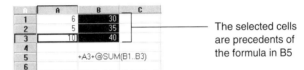

The selected cells are precedents of the formula in B5

1.   Select the range whose formula precedents you want to find.

If you select more than one cell, 1-2-3 finds all precedents of all formulas in the selected range.

2.   Choose Tools Audit.

3.   Under Audit, select Formula precedents.

4.   Under Produce a, select an option.

- Selection selects a collection of all ranges referred to by formulas in the selected range.

- Report at range displays a list of all ranges referred to by formulas in the selected range. In the text box, specify a blank range.

  If you specify a single-cell range, 1-2-3 displays the list, one item per cell down the column, starting at the cell you specified. If you specify a multiple-cell range, 1-2-3 displays the list one item per cell, top to bottom and left to right. If there's more data in the list than fits in the range, 1-2-3 truncates the list at the bottom right cell of the range.

5. Under Limit audit to, select an option.

   • Current file searches all worksheets in the current file.

   • All files searches all worksheets in all active files.

     This option is available only if you selected Report at range under "Produce a." 1-2-3 can't produce a selection in more than one file.

6. Choose OK.

1-2-3 selects or lists all precedents of any formula in the selected range, or displays a message if it finds no cells containing precedents. To move among selected cells, press CTRL+ENTER to go to the next range in the collection and CTRL+SHIFT+ENTER to go to the previous range. To deselect the collection, click any cell or press ESC.

 Shortcut Select a range containing formulas whose precedents you want to find. Click the icon shown at left to select precedents in the current file.

To find cell dependents

Cell **dependents** are cells containing formulas that refer to data in a selected range. For example, suppose C1 contains @SUM(B1..B3), and C2 contains (B1*2)/A1, and C3 contains +B1. The formulas in C1, C2, and C3 all depend on data in B1.

The selected cells are dependents of cell B1

1. Select the range whose dependents you want to find.

   If you select more than one cell, 1-2-3 finds all formulas that depend on any of the data in the selected range.

 2. Choose Tools Audit.

3. Under Audit, select Cell dependents.

4. Under Produce a, select an option.

   • Selection selects a collection of all cells containing formulas that depend on data in the selected range.

- Report at range displays a list of all cells containing formulas that depend on data in the selected range. In the text box, specify a blank range.

  If you specify a single-cell range, 1-2-3 displays the list, one item per cell down the column, starting at the cell you specified. If you specify a multiple-cell range, 1-2-3 displays the list one item per cell, top to bottom and left to right. If there's more data in the list than fits in the range, 1-2-3 truncates the list at the bottom right cell of the range.

5. Under Limit audit to, select an option.

   - Current file searches all worksheets in the current file.
   - All files searches all worksheets in all active files.

     This option is available only if you selected Report at range under "Produce a." 1-2-3 can't produce a selection in more than one file.

6. Choose OK.

1-2-3 selects or lists all cells containing formulas that depend on data in the selected range, or displays a message if it finds no cells containing dependents. To move among selected cells, press **CTRL+ENTER** to go to the next range in the collection and **CTRL+SHIFT+ENTER** to go to the previous range. To deselect the collection, click any cell or press **ESC**.

 Shortcut Select the range whose dependents you want to find. Click the icon shown at left to select all cells in the current file containing formulas that depend on data in the selected range.

To find circular references

A **circular reference** is a formula that refers directly or indirectly to itself. For example, a direct circular reference occurs when you enter the formula +A1+1 in cell A1. An indirect circular reference occurs when the range Net contains the formula +Gross-Bonus, and the range Bonus contains the formula +Net*.1, as shown below.

The selected cells are involved in a circular reference

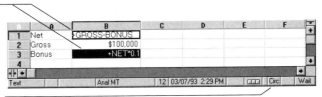

Click the Circ button to go to the first cell of a circular reference

1. Choose Tools Audit.
2. Under Audit, select Circular references.
3. Under Produce a, select an option.
   - Selection selects a collection of all cells containing circular references.
   - Report at range displays a list of all cells containing circular references. In the text box, specify a blank range.

     If you specify a single-cell range, 1-2-3 displays the list, one item per cell down the column, starting at the cell you specified. If you specify a multiple-cell range, 1-2-3 displays the list one item per cell, top to bottom and left to right. If there's more data in the list than fits in the range, 1-2-3 truncates the list at the bottom right cell of the range.
4. Under Limit audit to, select an option.
   - Current file searches all worksheets in the current file.
   - All files searches all worksheets in all active files.

     This option is available only if you selected Report at range under "Produce a." 1-2-3 can't produce a selection in more than one file.
5. Choose OK.

If 1-2-3 finds only one simple circular reference, it selects or lists all cells involved in the circular reference. To move among selected cells, press **CTRL+ENTER** to go to the next range in the collection and **CTRL+SHIFT+ENTER** to go to the previous range. To deselect the collection, click any cell or press **ESC**.

1-2-3 may also find more than one circular reference, or circular references with multiple branches.

If 1-2-3 finds more than one circular reference

The following dialog box appears:

Top left cell of each circular reference ———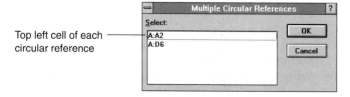

1. In the Select list box, select the address of the circular reference you want to work with.
2. Choose OK.

If the circular reference follows a single path, 1-2-3 selects or lists the cells of the path. If the path has multiple branches, 1-2-3 displays the Multiple Branches dialog box where you can follow a path for further analysis.

> **Note**   To return to the list of circular references, choose Tools Audit again and repeat the audit to generate the Multiple Circular References dialog box.

If 1-2-3 finds multiple branches in a circular reference

The following dialog box appears:

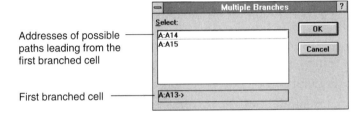

Addresses of possible paths leading from the first branched cell

First branched cell

1.   Select a cell from the list of branches in the Select list box.

2.   Choose OK.

The text box at the bottom of the dialog box displays the address of the cell you selected with an arrow pointing from the address of the first branched cell. The Select list box changes to display the next set of branches.

3.   Repeat steps 1 and 2 until there are no more branches.

The text box at the bottom of the dialog box displays the path of cell addresses you selected in the order you selected them. When there are no more branches, 1-2-3 returns to the worksheet and selects or lists the path of cells you selected.

To find file links

File links are formulas that refer to data in other files. For more information, see "Referring to other files in formulas" on page 98.

1. Choose Tools Audit.
2. Under Audit, select File links.
3. Under Produce a, select an option.
   - Selection selects a collection of all cells containing file links.
   - Report at range displays a list of all cells containing file links. In the text box, specify a blank range.

     If you specify a single-cell range, 1-2-3 displays the list, one item per cell down the column, starting at the cell you specified. If you specify a multiple-cell range, 1-2-3 displays the list one item per cell, top to bottom and left to right. If there's more data in the list than fits in the range, 1-2-3 truncates the list at the bottom right cell of the range.
4. Under Limit audit to, select an option.
   - Current file searches all worksheets in the current file.
   - All files searches all worksheets in all active files.

     This option is available only if you selected Report at range under "Produce a." 1-2-3 can't produce a selection in more than one file.
5. Choose OK.

1-2-3 selects or lists all cells containing formulas that refer to data in other files, or displays a message if it finds no cells containing file links. To move among selected cells, press CTRL+ENTER to go to the next range in the collection and CTRL+SHIFT+ENTER to go to the previous range. To deselect the collection, click any cell or press ESC.

Shortcut   Click the icon shown at left to select all file links in the current file.

To find DDE links

A DDE link is a link between a 1-2-3 file and a file created with another Windows application. For more information, see "Linking 1-2-3 with other applications" on page 329.

1. Choose Tools Audit.

2. Under Audit, select DDE links.

3. Under Produce a, select an option.

   • Selection selects a collection of all cells containing DDE links.

   • Report at range displays a list of all cells containing DDE links. In the text box, specify a blank range.

   If you specify a single-cell range, 1-2-3 displays the list, one item per cell down the column, starting at the cell you specified. If you specify a multiple-cell range, 1-2-3 displays the list one item per cell, top to bottom and left to right. If there's more data in the list than fits in the range, 1-2-3 truncates the list at the bottom right cell of the range.

4. Under Limit audit to, select an option.

   • Current file searches all worksheets in the current file.

   • All files searches all worksheets in all active files.

   This option is available only if you selected Report at range under "Produce a." 1-2-3 can't produce a selection in more than one file.

5. Choose OK.

1-2-3 selects or lists all cells containing DDE links, or displays a message if it finds no cells containing DDE links. To move among selected cells, press CTRL+ENTER to go to the next range in the collection and CTRL+SHIFT+ENTER to go to the previous range. To deselect the collection, click any cell or press ESC.

Shortcut   Click the icon shown at left to select all DDE links in the current file.

19

Performing Statistical Analysis

A 1-2-3 worksheet is useful not only for tracking day-to-day activities, but also for analyzing statistics over time. Statistical analysis involves collecting, organizing, and interpreting numeric data. 1-2-3 has several features that simplify statistical analysis. This chapter describes how to calculate frequency distributions, perform a regression analysis, and invert and multiply data matrixes.

Calculating a frequency distribution

A **frequency distribution** counts how many values in a range fall within certain numeric intervals. The **values range** contains the values to count. The **bin range** contains the numeric intervals within which you want to distribute the values.

For example, suppose you want to count how many of your first quarter monthly sales orders for hats are less than or equal to $3,000, how many are greater than $3,000 and less than or equal to $5,000, and how many are greater than $5,000. The monthly sales orders are the values. The bins, the upper limit of each interval, are 3,000 and 5,000.

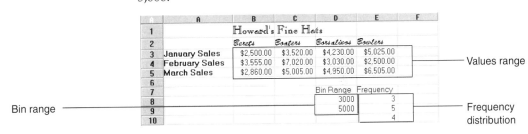

Bin range — Values range / Frequency distribution

The resulting frequency distribution shows how many values are equal to or less than the bin value to the left. 1-2-3 also counts any values that are greater than the largest bin value and displays that number in the cell just below and to the right of the largest bin value.

A frequency distribution always produces one more value than the number of bins. If there are no values for a bin, 1-2-3 enters 0 next to the bin. In the example on the previous page, three orders are less than or equal to $3,000, five are greater than $3,000 and less than or equal to $5,000, and four are greater than $5,000.

To calculate a frequency distribution

Use Range Fill to enter bin values with equal intervals.

1. Enter the values for the bin range in ascending order in a column.

    Put the bin range in a single worksheet. The intervals don't have to be equal. Don't include labels or blank cells in the bin range and leave the column to the right of the bin range blank. When 1-2-3 calculates the frequencies, it enters them in this column and writes over any existing data.

2. Select the range containing the values to analyze.

    The values range can be in one or more worksheets in a file that's active or on disk. 1-2-3 analyzes only the numeric data in the values range and ignores labels and blank cells. The order of the data doesn't matter.

3. Choose Range Analyze Distribution.

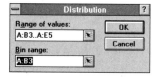

4. Specify the bin range in the Bin range text box.

5. Choose OK.

Performing a regression analysis

A **regression analysis** determines whether one set of data has any relationship, or **correlation**, to another set of data. Once you calculate these relationships, you can make predictions. 1-2-3 performs **multiple linear regression analysis**, which predicts a value for a single dependent variable based on the values of one or more independent variables.

For example, suppose you run an ice cream stand at a tourist location, and you want to predict approximately how many quarts of ice cream you'll sell the next day. You think that your sales depend on three key factors: the number of hours of sunshine, the midday temperature, and the number of buses in a nearby parking lot. These are called **independent variables**. Since you're assuming your sales depend on these values, sales is the **dependent variable**.

You collect data for a six-day period so you can perform a regression analysis. If the correlation between the three factors and sales is strong enough, you can predict future sales based on the values for the independent variables.

To perform a regression analysis, you need to set up three ranges of data: the **y-range** containing the dependent variables, the **x-range** containing the independent variables, and the **output range** where you want 1-2-3 to display the results of the regression analysis. You can enter these ranges in a single worksheet or in different worksheets in the same file.

To set up a regression analysis

1. Enter the values for the dependent variable (y-range) in a single column.

2. Enter the values for the independent variables (x-range).

   You can have from 1 to 75 independent variables. Put the values for each variable in a separate column. Each column must have the same number of rows as the dependent variable, and the columns for the independent variables must all be adjacent.

	A	B	C	D	E	F
1	Day	Ice Cream Sales	Sunshine	Temperature	Buses in Lot	
2	1	250	3	84	10	
3	2	545	5	91	7	
4	3	550	5	89	8	
5	4	450	6	85	10	
6	5	605	6	90	11	
7	6	615	7	88	9	
8						

Y-range contains dependent variables

X-range contains independent variables

3. Decide where you want 1-2-3 to display the results (the output range).

    Make this range nine rows high and four columns wide, with an additional column for each independent variable after the second one.

To find the relationship between variables

1. Choose Range Analyze Regression.

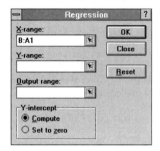

2. In the X-range text box, specify the range containing the independent variables.

3. In the Y-range text box, specify the range containing the values for the dependent variable.

4. In the Output range text box, specify the range where you want 1-2-3 to display the results of the regression analysis.

    Specify an output range nine rows high and four columns wide, with an additional column for each independent variable after the second one. Specify either the entire range or only the first cell.

    Caution 1-2-3 writes over existing data in the output range.

5. To calculate the value of the y-intercept, the point on the y-axis where the predicted regression line crosses, select "Compute" under Y-intercept. To use zero as the value of the dependent variable when the independent variable is zero, select "Set to zero" under Y-intercept.

    Select "Set to zero" only if your dependent variable is zero when all the independent variables are zero.

6. To clear all the settings and enter different ranges, choose Reset.

7. Choose OK.

1-2-3 analyzes the relationship between the dependent variable and the independent variables as shown in the illustration below.

Point where regression line intercepts the y-axis

R² value

Slope for each independent variable

Standard error of each x coefficient

	A	B	C	D	E
1	Day	Ice Cream Sales	Sunshine	Temperature	Buses in Lot
2	1	250	3	84	10
3	2	545	5	91	7
4	3	550	5	89	8
5	4	450	6	85	10
6	5	605	6	90	11
7	6	615	7	88	9
8					
9					
10					
11		Regression Output:			
12	Constant			-2327.9095	
13	Std Err of Y Est			32.6714791	
14	R Squared			0.97722522	
15	No. of Observations			6	
16	Degrees of Freedom			2	
17					
18	X Coefficient(s)	61.17698	28.4478809	0.59564719	
19	Std Err of Coef.	12.18849	6.79391567	11.8965812	

Standard error of estimated y-value

Number of rows of data

Number of observations minus number of independent variables minus 1

The results tell you about the relationships between data. **R Squared** (R^2) tells you how closely the independent and dependent variables are correlated, or how much variation in the dependent variable can be explained by the combination of the independent variables. The value of R^2 is between 0 and 1. The closer the R^2 value is to 1, the more closely the independent variables are related to the dependent variable. Since R^2 is close to 1 in the example above, a strong correlation exists between ice cream sales, the weather, and the number of buses.

Note   If 1-2-3 displays a value less than zero for R^2, you specified a zero intercept when it was not appropriate. Repeat the Range Analyze Regression command, but under Y-intercept, select Compute to have 1-2-3 recalculate the regression and adjust R^2 accordingly.

Once you prove that a relationship exists between the dependent and independent variables, you can use the values for the independent variables to predict values for the dependent variables.

For example, suppose the weather forecast tells you that tomorrow will be cloudy, with only two hours of sunshine and a midday temperature of 84°F. You guess that no more than five buses will visit. You know there's a strong correlation between the weather, the number of buses, and ice cream sales. So, you can use the values for hours of sunshine, the number of buses, and midday temperature to predict tomorrow's sales.

To predict values for dependent variables

1. Enter the predicted value for each independent variable in the cell below the column of existing values. Enter text to identify the forecast, as in B:A8 in the illustration below.

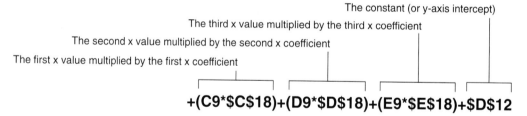

B:B9			(C9*$C$18)+(D9*$D$18)+(E9*$E$18)+$D$12			
	A	**B**	**C**	**D**	**E**	**F**
1	Day	Ice Cream Sales	Sunshine	Temperature	Buses in Lot	
2	1	250	3	84	10	
3	2	545	5	91	7	
4	3	550	5	89	8	
5	4	450	6	85	10	
6	5	605	6	90	11	
7	6	615	7	88	9	
8	Forecast					
9		187.04467354	2	84	5	
10						
11		Regression Output:				
12	Constant			-2327.9095		
13	Std Err of Y Est			32.6714791		
14	R Squared			0.97722522		
15	No. of Observations			6		
16	Degrees of Freedom			2		
17						
18	X Coefficient(s)		61.17698	28.4478809	0.59564719	
19	Std Err of Coef.		12.18849	6.79391567	11.8965812	

Predicted values for independent variables

2. Enter the formula shown below in a blank cell in the dependent variable column. In the figure above, the formula is in cell B:B9.

    The formula refers to the predicted values and the X Coefficients in the output range of the example. The formula may look complicated, but it's really only the sum of the following items:

    The constant (or y-axis intercept)

    The third x value multiplied by the third x coefficient

    The second x value multiplied by the second x coefficient

    The first x value multiplied by the first x coefficient

    +(C9*$C$18)+(D9*$D$18)+(E9*$E$18)+$D$12

    The results of the regression predict that you'll sell approximately 187 quarts of ice cream tomorrow if the weather and number of buses are as forecasted.

    Note   When you use values from the regression output in formulas, select them when building the formula or copy them from the output range. Don't type them over or you may get undesired rounding errors.

Using data matrixes

Finding solutions to problems with many variables requires using data matrixes. A 1-2-3 **matrix** is a multiple-cell range that contains a value in each cell. The range can be in one worksheet or across worksheets (a 3D matrix). Each value represents a constant in a formula or the coefficient for a variable in a formula.

Matrix analysis finds the relationship between two or more sets of variables in one or more formulas. You use the relationships to determine which combination of values will produce the result you want for the formulas.

For example, suppose a bank has three main sources of income: business accounts, house loans, and car loans. The bank also has a venture capital branch that takes money from the bank's total income to provide loans for start-up businesses.

By setting up this problem as a series of simultaneous equations, you can use matrix analysis to determine what percentage each income source contributes to the total venture funds. The following equation represents this relationship:

$x\%*(\text{Business}) + y\%*(\text{House}) + z\%*(\text{Car}) = \text{Total venture funds}$

$x\%$, $y\%$, and $z\%$ are the percentage contributions each of the income sources make to the total venture funds. The x, y, and z percentages are what you want to find.

First, you set up a matrix of values for total income received from each of the three sources, and a corresponding column for the total venture funds received, as shown in the illustration below.

Matrix of income values

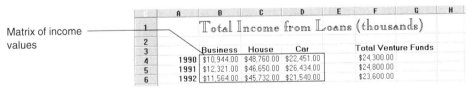

	A	B	C	D	E	F	G	H
1		Total Income from Loans (thousands)						
2								
3		Business	House	Car		Total Venture Funds		
4	1990	$10,944.00	$48,760.00	$22,451.00		$24,300.00		
5	1991	$12,321.00	$46,650.00	$26,434.00		$24,800.00		
6	1992	$11,564.00	$45,732.00	$21,540.00		$23,600.00		

Next, you invert the matrix of income values in range B4..D6. Then you multiply the inverted matrix by the total venture funds to find what percentage each income source contributes to the total venture funds. The following sections describe how to invert and multiply matrixes.

To invert a matrix

1. Select the range containing the matrix you want to invert.

   The matrix must have the same number of columns as rows, and can contain up to 80 columns and 80 rows. The matrix range can be in any file, active or on disk.

2. Choose Range Analyze Invert Matrix.

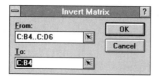

3. Specify the range where you want 1-2-3 to put the inverted matrix in the To text box.

   Specify either the entire range or only the first cell.

   Caution   1-2-3 writes over existing data in the range.

4. Choose OK.

The inverted matrix is the same size as the original matrix, as shown in the illustration below.

Result of inverting the matrix ———

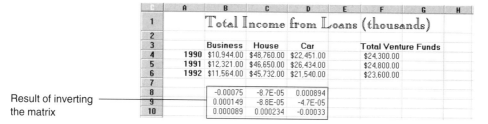

After inverting the matrix, you can solve for the percentage contributions of each income source by multiplying the inverted matrix by the total venture funds received in each of those years.

To multiply matrixes

1. Select the range containing the first matrix you want to multiply.

    The number of columns in this matrix must equal the number of rows in the second matrix. The matrixes can contain up to 80 columns and 80 rows. The range containing this matrix can be in any file, open or on disk.

2. Choose Range Analyze Multiply Matrix.

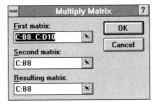

3. Specify the range containing the second matrix you want to multiply in the Second matrix text box.

    The number of rows in this matrix must equal the number of columns in the first matrix. This matrix can be in any file, active or on disk.

4. Specify the range where you want 1-2-3 to put the results in the Resulting matrix text box.

    Specify either the entire range or only the first cell.

    Caution   1-2-3 writes over existing data in the output range.

5. Choose OK.

The result is a matrix with the same number of rows as the first matrix and the same number of columns as the second matrix. The resulting matrix contains the solutions for each variable, as shown in the illustration below.

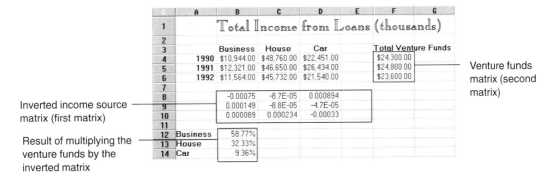

Inverting and multiplying 3D matrixes

When you invert a 3D matrix, the matrix you want to invert and the results range must be square and contain the same number of worksheets. When inverting a 3D matrix, 1-2-3 inverts the matrix in each worksheet of the 3D range and enters the results in each worksheet. The following illustration shows the results of inverting the 3D matrix in B:A1..D:C3.

Original matrix   Inverted matrix

	A	B	C	D	E	F	G	H
1	79	25	90		0.017086	-0.02036	-0.00129	
2	14	15	71	→	-0.00779	-0.00338	0.013248	
3	50	94	71		-0.00172	0.018814	-0.00254	
4								
5								

	A	B	C	D	E	F	G	H
1	15	58	31		-0.0531	0.027425	0.01387805	
2	22	83	14	→	0.00629	0.010253	-0.0037197	
3	86	58	91		0.0462	-0.03245	0.0002443	
4								
5								

	A	B	C	D	E	F	G	H
1	55	80	36		0.026041	-0.04038	0.020019	
2	35	63	49	→	-0.00704	0.013281	-0.01739	
3	49	23	52		-0.02765	0.032173	0.008058	
4								

When you multiply 3D matrixes *both* matrixes must be 3D, and both must contain the same number of worksheets. They must be in the same file but can be in different worksheets. Also, the 3D results matrix must be in the same file as the matrixes you're multiplying but can be in different worksheets.

1-2-3 multiplies the range in the first worksheet of the first matrix by the range in the first worksheet of the second matrix and enters results in the first worksheet; then multiplies the range in the second worksheet of the first matrix by the range in the second worksheet of the second matrix and enters the results in the second worksheet; and so on, as shown in the following illustration.

First matrix   *   Second matrix   =   Results matrix

	A	B	C	D	E	F	G	H	I	J	K
1	22	56	→	80	92	46	→	3216	4320	3084	
2	0	99		26	41	37		2574	4059	3663	
3	23	61						3426	4617	3315	
4	73	15						6230	7331	3913	
5	14	64						2784	3912	3012	

	A	B	C	D	E	F	G	H	I	J	K
1	29	60		94	59	59		8666	3571	4651	
2	79	91	→	99	31	49	→	16435	7482	9120	
3	95	6						9524	5791	5899	
4	3	29						3153	1076	1598	
5	14	6						1910	1012	1120	

	A	B	C	D	E	F	G	H	I	J	K
1	91	71	→	60	58	27	→	11637	7550	3380	
2	22	54		87	32	13		6018	3004	1296	
3	50	47						7089	4404	1961	
4	55	63						8781	5206	2304	
5	41	53						7071	4074	1796	

20

Solving What-If Problems

A what-if problem is based on a question, such as "What if my sales went up 30%? What would happen to my profits?" A what-if problem can require changing one or more values. This chapter describes how to use Backsolver and what-if tables to solve what-if problems. Solver, described in Chapter 21, and Version Manager, described in Chapter 22, are other tools for solving complex what-if problems.

Using Backsolver

Backsolver works backwards from the result of a formula to find the values of one or more variables in the formula. You supply the formula result and specify which variable or variables you want Backsolver to change to arrive at this result. Backsolver then calculates the values of the variable or variables and changes these values in the worksheet.

For example, the worksheet in the illustration below uses @PMT to calculate a monthly loan payment based on a total loan amount of $100,000, an interest rate of 12%, and a term of 30 years. The result of @PMT using these variables is a monthly loan payment of $1,028.61.

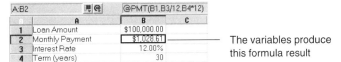

A:B2	🖳 @	@PMT(B1,B3/12,B4*12)	
	A	**B**	**C**
1	Loan Amount	$100,000.00	
2	Monthly Payment	$1,028.61	
3	Interest Rate	12.00%	
4	Term (years)	30	

The variables produce this formula result

What if you can afford a $1,200.00 monthly payment? How does that affect the amount of money you can borrow? The next illustration shows how Backsolver recalculates @PMT to produce a monthly payment of $1,200, and enters the changed loan amount, $116,662, in cell B1.

A:B2	🖳 @	@PMT(B1,B3/12,B4*12)	
	A	**B**	**C**
1	Loan Amount	$116,662.00	
2	Monthly Payment	$1,200.00	
3	Interest Rate	12.00%	
4	Term (years)	30	

Backsolver finds the loan amount that results in a monthly payment of $1,200

As well as using Backsolver to change a single value, you can also change a range of values by the same percentage so a formula results in the value you specify. For example, the worksheet in the illustration below uses @SUM to calculate the total annual expenses of a small company. The result of @SUM using the values in range B3..B9 is $185,949.

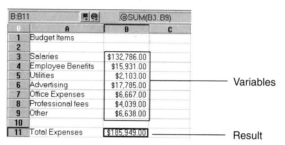

Variables

Result

What if you reduce your total expenses to $179,000? How would that affect the value of each item in your budget? You can use Backsolver to reduce all the values in B3..B9 by the same percentage so that @SUM in B11 results in your specified goal of $179,000. The following illustration shows how Backsolver reduces each value so they add up to $179,000.

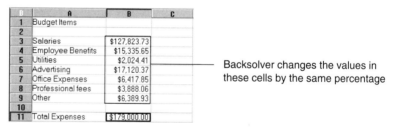

Backsolver changes the values in these cells by the same percentage

To solve a problem with Backsolver, you need to specify the following information:

- The address of the formula you want to solve.

- The result you want for the formula.

- The address of the variable or variables you want Backsolver to change to arrive at your result.

To use Backsolver

1. Choose Range Analyze Backsolver.

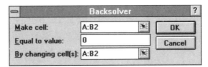

2. In the "Make cell" text box, specify the cell containing the formula you want to backsolve.

3. In the "Equal to value" text box, enter the value you want as the result of the formula.

4. In the "By changing cell(s)" text box, specify the range containing the variables you want to change.

To change the variables back to their original values, press **CTRL+Z** *or choose Edit Undo immediately after using Backsolver.*

5. Choose OK.

Backsolver recalculates the formula to meet the specified result and changes the values of the variables in the worksheet.

> **Note**   If any other formulas depend on the cell(s) that Backsolver changed, 1-2-3 recalculates these formulas.

Using what-if tables

You can set up a **what-if table** to calculate the results of substituting different values in formulas. You can create tables that substitute values for one, two, or three variables in a formula. These are called 1-variable, 2-variable, and 3-variable what-if tables. The tables you create supply 1-2-3 with everything it needs to solve the what-if problem. Then you use Range Analyze What-if to calculate the results.

To create a what-if table, you supply the formulas and the different values for formula variables. Then 1-2-3 calculates the formulas with every combination of values for the variables and enters the results in the worksheet. You can chart the results to find patterns and relationships.

20 Year Mortgage

Loan amount = $80,000
Interest rate = 11%
Monthly
*   payment = $826*

For example, what-if tables come in handy when you're considering mortgage possibilities. Suppose you decide initially not to borrow more than $80,000. Using a formula, you write out calculations showing that if you borrow $80,000 for 20 years at 11% interest, your monthly payments will be $826.

Next you write out the same calculation with a number of different interest rates starting at 9.5% and going up to 11.5% in 0.5% increments. Since lower interest rates mean lower monthly payments, you explore higher mortgage amounts — $90,000 and $100,000. Finally, you repeat all of these calculations varying the term of the loan, using 10, 15, 20, and 30 year terms.

In the illustration below, your calculations show the monthly payment value for every combination of term, interest rate, and loan amount — a total of 72 separate hand-written calculations.

10 Year Mortgage

Loan amount

Interest rate	$80,000	$90,000	$100,000
9.5%	1,035	1,165	1,294
10.0%	1,057	1,189	1,322
10.5%	1,079	1,214	1,349
11.0%	1,102	1,240	1,378
11.5%	1,125	1,265	1,406
12.0%	1,148	1,291	1,435

15 Year Mortgage

Loan amount

Interest rate	$80,000	$90,000	$100,000
9.5%	835	940	1,044
10.0%	860	967	1,075
10.5%	884	995	1,105
11.0%	909	1,023	1,137
11.5%	935	1,051	1,168
12.0%	960	1,080	1,200

20 Year Mortgage

Loan amount

Interest rate	$80,000	$90,000	$100,000
9.5%	746	839	932
10.0%	772	869	965
10.5%	799	899	998
11.0%	826	929	1,032
11.5%	853	960	1,066
12.0%	881	991	1,101

30 Year Mortgage

Loan amount

Interest rate	$80,000	$90,000	$100,000
9.5%	673	757	841
10.0%	702	790	878
10.5%	732	823	915
11.0%	762	857	952
11.5%	792	891	990
12.0%	823	926	1,029

Using a 1-2-3 what-if table gives you the same results in a quicker, more reliable way.

? **Help** For more information about using what-if tables to cross-tabulate information in a 1-2-3 database table, search on "Cross-tabulation" in Help.

Solving a problem by changing one variable

A **1-variable what-if table** displays the result of changing a single variable in one or more formulas. You set up the what-if table by supplying the formulas and the different values you want 1-2-3 to substitute for the variable. You indicate an input cell for 1-2-3 to use during the value substitutions, and then you use Range Analyze What-if to calculate the results.

For example, you can create a 1-variable table that shows the monthly payments for a 30-year mortgage of $80,000 at different interest rates. The variable in this what-if problem is the interest rate. You supply the different values for this variable when you set up the what-if table. The illustration below shows how to set up a 1-variable problem with a table range and an input cell outside the table range.

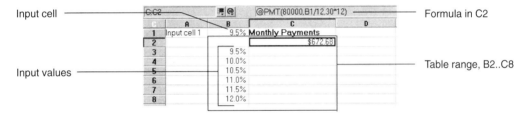

In the example, B1 is the **input cell** where 1-2-3 temporarily stores the different values for the variable while calculating the formula. It's a good idea to label the input cell and enter a sample value to verify that the formula is correct. This also helps you remember where the input cell is and what kind of data it contains. 1-2-3 ignores the sample value when calculating the results.

The table range, B2..C8, includes the input values, the formula, and the cells below the formula where 1-2-3 displays the results. The **input values**, B3..B8, are the various interest rates you want 1-2-3 to substitute in the formula. The formula in C2 uses @PMT.

The formula calculates the payment for a 30-year mortgage of $80,000 at the interest rate in B1. The formula must refer to the input cell, B1. When you use Range Analyze What-if, 1-2-3 substitutes in B1 all the input values you specified, calculates the formula with all these input values, and displays the results in the cells below the formula.

You can also set up a 1-variable table that uses the same input values with more than one formula. The 1-variable table below is the same as the previous one, except it contains an additional formula for calculating monthly interest. You can extend the table range by adding adjacent columns to the right for as many formulas as you want.

Additional formula in D2

Input values

Table range, B2..D8

	A	B	C	D	E
1	Input cell 1	9.5%	Monthly Payments	Monthly Rate	
2			$672.68	0.7917%	
3		9.5%			
4		10.0%			
5		10.5%			
6		11.0%			
7		11.5%			
8		12.0%			

C:D2   +B1/12

To set up a 1-variable what-if table

1. Decide where you want the table range. Make sure you leave enough room for the input values, the formula, and the results.

   Caution   1-2-3 writes over existing data in the results area.

2. Place the input cell outside of the table range. To make the input cell easy to locate, label it by putting text such as "Input cell 1" in the adjacent cell to the left. If you want, enter a sample variable in the input cell to verify that the formula is correct.

When setting up a what-if table, format the cells in the results area as you want the results to appear. For example, format the cells you want to appear as currency and the cells you want to appear as percentages.

3. Enter the formula in the second column of the first row of the table range. If you want to use more than one formula, place each additional formula in an adjacent column to the right, all in the same row.

   Make sure each formula refers to the input cell. For example, if the input cell is B1, the formula must refer to B1.

4. In the first column of the table range, starting in the second row, enter the input values you want 1-2-3 to use in the formula(s).

   Leave the top left cell in the table range blank.

**To calculate a
1-variable table**

1. Select the table range.

   Include only the formulas, input values, and the cells below the formulas. Don't include the input cell.

2. Choose Range Analyze What-if Table.

3. Select 1 from the Number of variables drop-down box.

*You can change the input
values and then press
F8 (TABLE) to recalculate
the same what-if table.*

4. Specify the input cell in the Input cell 1 text box.

5. Choose OK.

1-2-3 substitutes values for the variable in one or more formulas and puts the results in the table. The illustration below shows how the table looks when you're using one formula.

	A	B	C	D
	C:C2		@PMT(80000,B1/12,30*12)	
1	Input cell 1	9.5%	Monthly Payments	
2			$672.68	
3		9.5%	$672.68	
4		10.0%	$702.06	
5		10.5%	$731.79	
6		11.0%	$761.86	— Results
7		11.5%	$792.23	
8		12.0%	$822.89	

The next illustration shows how the table looks when you're using two formulas.

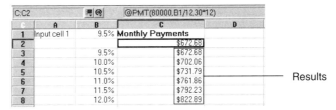

	A	B	C	D	E
1	Input cell 1	9.5%	Monthly Payments	Monthly Rate	
2			$672.68	0.7917%	
3		9.5%	$672.68	0.7917%	
4		10.0%	$702.06	0.8333%	
5		10.5%	$731.79	0.8750%	
6		11.0%	$761.86	0.9167%	— Results
7		11.5%	$792.23	0.9583%	
8		12.0%	$822.89	1.0000%	

Solving a problem by changing two variables

A **2-variable what-if table** calculates a formula by changing values for two variables in the formula. 1-2-3 substitutes different values for each variable and displays the results. For example, you can use a 2-variable table to calculate monthly payments for mortgages of $80,000, $90,000, and $100,000 using various interest rates. The variables are interest rate and total mortgage amount.

You set up this problem with a table range and two input cells outside of the table range. For a 2-variable table, the table range includes a single formula, two sets of input values, and space below the input values for 1-2-3 to display the results. The illustration below shows the set-up of the table range and the two input cells for a 2-variable table.

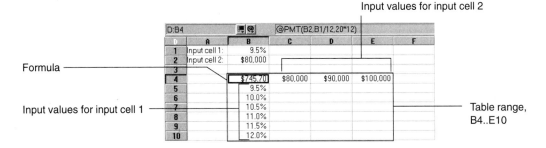

To set up a 2-variable what-if table

1. Decide where you want the table range. Make sure you leave enough room for the formula, the two sets of input values, and the results.

    Caution   1-2-3 writes over existing data in the results area.

2. Place the two input cells outside the table range. To make the input cells easy to locate, label them by putting text such as "Input cell 1" and "Input cell 2" in adjacent cells the left. If you want, enter a sample variable in each input cell to verify that the formula is correct.

3. Enter the formula in the top left cell of the table range. The formula must refer to both input cells.

4. In the first column of the table range, starting with the cell under the formula, enter the input values for input cell 1.

5. In the cells to the right of the formula, enter the input values for input cell 2.

To calculate a 2-variable what-if table

1. Select the table range.

    Include only the formulas and input values in the table range. Don't include the input cells.

2. Choose Range Analyze What-if Table.

3. Select 2 from the Number of variables drop-down box.

4. Specify input cell 1 in the Input cell 1 text box.

    Input cell 1 always represents the input values you enter in the first column of the table range.

5. Specify input cell 2 in the Input cell 2 text box.

    Input cell 2 always represents the input values you enter in the first row of the table range.

6. Choose OK.

    1-2-3 substitutes values for the two variables in the formula and displays the results as shown in the next illustration.

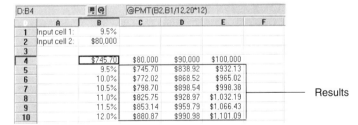

Solving a problem by changing three variables

A **3-variable what-if table** calculates a formula by changing values for three variables. 1-2-3 substitutes different values for each variable. For example, you can use a 3-variable table to calculate monthly payments for mortgages of $80,000, $90,000, and $100,000 using various interest rates, and a number of different terms, such as 10, 15, 20, and 30 years. The variables are interest rate, mortgage amount, and term. The illustration below shows the set-up for a 3-variable table using a 3D range across four worksheets.

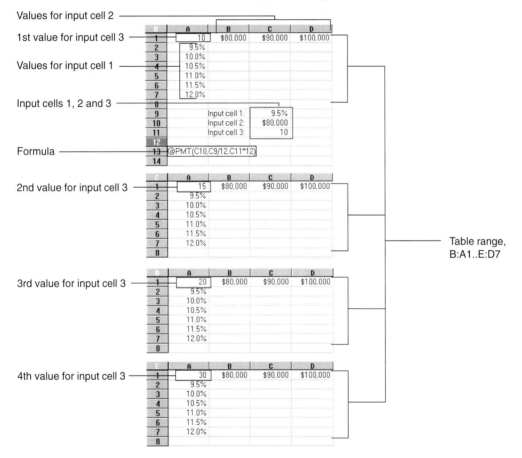

The set-up of a 3-variable table is similar to the 2-variable table, but the table range is 3D, and the third variable, the term, is different in each worksheet. You put the formula and the three input cells outside the table range. The formula and input cells appear only in the first worksheet, outside the table range. In all other ways, the set-up in each worksheet is the same.

**To set up a
3-variable
what-if table**

1. Insert as many worksheets as you need to equal the number of values for input cell 3.

2. Decide where you want the 3D table range. It must be in the same location in contiguous worksheets. Make sure you leave enough room for the formula, the input values, and the results. The table range spans two or more worksheets depending on the number of input values you use for the third variable.

   Caution   1-2-3 writes over existing data in the results area.

3. Place the input cells outside the table range and label them by typing text such as "Input cell 1," "Input cell 2" and "Input cell 3" in the cells to their left. If you want, enter sample variables in the input cells to verify the formulas.

4. In a cell outside of the table range, enter the formula you want to calculate. The formula must refer to all three input cells.

5. In the first column of the table range in the first worksheet, enter the values for input cell 1, and copy these values to all worksheets in the 3D table range.

6. In the first row of the table range in the first worksheet, enter the values for input cell 2, and copy these values to all worksheets in the 3D table range.

7. In each worksheet, enter one input value for input cell 3 in the top left cell of the table range.

   Note   You can tell which input values go with which input cells if you remember that the first input values are in a *column*, the second input values are in a *row*, and the third input values span two or more *worksheets*.

**To calculate a
3-variable
what-if table**

1. Select the 3D table range.

   Don't include the formula or input cells in the table range. If you're not sure how to select a 3D range, see page 61.

2. Choose Range Analyze What-if Table.

3. Select 3 from the Number of variables drop-down box.

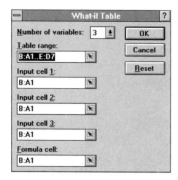

4. Specify input cell 1 in the Input cell 1 text box.

   Input cell 1 always represents the input values you enter in the first column of the table range, starting in the second row.

5. Specify input cell 2 in the Input cell 2 text box.

   Input cell 2 always represents the input values you enter in the first row of the table range, starting in the second column.

6. Specify input cell 3 in the Input cell 3 text box.

   Input cell 3 always represents the input values you enter in the top left corner of the table range.

7. Specify the cell that contains the formula in the Formula cell text box.

8. Choose OK.

   1-2-3 calculates the 3-variable what-if problem and displays the results, as shown in the next illustration.

Results

B	A	B	C	D
1	10	$80,000	$90,000	$100,000
2	9.5%	$1,035	$1,165	$1,294
3	10.0%	$1,057	$1,189	$1,322
4	10.5%	$1,079	$1,214	$1,349
5	11.0%	$1,102	$1,240	$1,378
6	11.5%	$1,125	$1,265	$1,406
7	12.0%	$1,148	$1,291	$1,435
8				
9		Input cell 1:	9.5%	
10		Input cell 2:	$80,000	
11		Input cell 3:	10	
12				
13	@PMT(C10,C9/12,C11*12)			
14				

C	A	B	C	D
1	15	$80,000	$90,000	$100,000
2	9.5%	$835	$940	$1,044
3	10.0%	$860	$967	$1,075
4	10.5%	$884	$995	$1,105
5	11.0%	$909	$1,023	$1,137
6	11.5%	$935	$1,051	$1,168
7	12.0%	$960	$1,080	$1,200
8				

Results

Results

D	A	B	C	D
1	20	$80,000	$90,000	$100,000
2	9.5%	$746	$839	$932
3	10.0%	$772	$869	$965
4	10.5%	$799	$899	$998
5	11.0%	$826	$929	$1,032
6	11.5%	$853	$960	$1,066
7	12.0%	$881	$991	$1,101
8				

Results

E	A	B	C	D
1	30	$80,000	$90,000	$100,000
2	9.5%	$673	$757	$841
3	10.0%	$702	$790	$878
4	10.5%	$732	$823	$915
5	11.0%	$762	$857	$952
6	11.5%	$792	$891	$990
7	12.0%	$823	$926	$1,029
8				

Charting what-if tables

Creating a chart is a good way to analyze the results of a what-if table. For example, if you decide you can afford a monthly payment between $800 and $900, you can see quickly from the chart below that you have six options. For more information about creating charts, see Chapter 14.

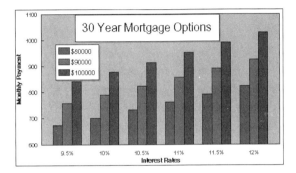

21

Using Solver

Solver is a tool for solving and analyzing mathematical problems in a worksheet. You express a Solver problem by building a model in your worksheet using the formulas already there, not by using complex modeling languages or unfamiliar metaphors. This chapter describes how to use Solver and provides examples. You can find more examples in the sample solutions file SOLVER.WK4, in the SAMPLE subdirectory of your 1-2-3 directory.

What can Solver do?

Solver can solve almost any problem that you can describe with algebraic and logical relationships (formulas) in a worksheet. Regardless of the complexity of the problem, most of your work is done before you start Solver, since Solver uses the formulas that already exist in your worksheet.

For example, suppose you use a worksheet to analyze the profits and losses of your hat manufacturing business. Solver can help you determine how to maximize profits by varying the number and mix of hats produced. This problem is in the worksheet titled PL in the Solver sample file.

The formulas in the worksheet define the problem in terms of algebraic and logical relationships that Solver understands. After you start Solver by selecting Range Analyze Solver, you identify these relationships for Solver by specifying ranges in the Solver Definition dialog box.

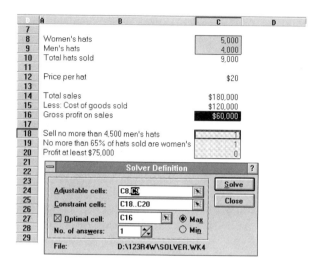

Solver can provide several answers to a problem, including the optimal answer. By finding multiple answers and presenting the values of all the variables for each answer, Solver can provide you with a wider range of possibilities, one of which might be more useful than the mathematically optimal answer. Because Solver also works with Version Manager, you can preserve any answer as part of a scenario.

You can use Solver when your worksheet model has one or more of the following characteristics:

- Uses numbers and formulas
- Can have more than one meaningful answer
- Iteration (guessing) is the only method of solving
- Contains several variables or formulas that must stay within constraints

   Note   If your problem requires that only one variable reach a single fixed value, without constraints on other variables, try using Backsolver first. For more information, see "Using Backsolver" on page 215.

The following are examples of problems that work well with Solver:

- Planning the most profitable combination of production levels at your company, given the constraints of available resources
- Analyzing a budget to find the best combination of sales increases and cost reductions
- Planning staffing levels to maximize profit without overburdening any one project
- Structuring an investment portfolio for best total return, using information on predicted income, appreciation, and diversification

Once you've found the solution you want, Solver can prepare reports that explain in detail how it approached the problem and how it reached a solution. Solver can report its results in a worksheet file so that you can save, print, or chart the results, or do further calculations.

How Solver works

Solver uses a combination of symbolic (algebraic) and numeric techniques (or "rules") to find answers. First, Solver tries to solve each problem using symbolic techniques. Then, if it can't find an answer using symbolic techniques, it turns to numeric techniques.

Symbolic and numeric solving techniques

Symbolic solving techniques use the rules of algebra. For example, suppose A2 contains the formula +A1+5.

Solver and the worksheet know that +A2=A1+5. Unlike the worksheet, however, Solver also knows that A1=A2–5. Solver uses hundreds of these rules to solve problems that you can't solve with normal worksheet recalculation.

Numeric solving techniques are essentially trial and error, based on guessing or **iteration**. When it uses numeric solving techniques, Solver starts by using the values in the adjustable cells as guesses, then repetitively adjusts these guesses until it finds an answer. Solver uses numeric techniques only if it can't solve the problem using symbolic techniques.

For example, the following formula is too complicated for symbolic techniques, so Solver would try to solve it using numeric techniques.

$A1^7+3*(B1)^7+A1*B1-120=-25$

Solver determines when to apply symbolic or numeric solving techniques to solve a problem; you don't need to tell Solver which technique to use.

For certain types of problems, Solver knows that numeric solving techniques won't yield a solution. Instead, Solver uses iteration for these problems. When using iteration, Solver may try several different starting values until it either finds an answer or gives up.

Sometimes Solver can't find an answer through iteration starting from the initial values in the adjustable cells. If this happens, Solver asks you to guess the value for some of the adjustable cells to point it in the right direction.

Multiple worksheets and files

Solver can use cells in any active worksheet or file. You can have many active files in 1-2-3, thus cells in your Solver problem can span more than one active file. However, if you make changes to any of these files that cause 1-2-3 to recalculate after Solver solves the problem, Solver discards all the answers it found.

To avoid losing your answers, create a report in a worksheet (a Solver table report) before changing anything in the active files. Remember to save the report if you want to preserve the answers. For more information, see "To save answers" on page 239.

Using Solver

Because Solver uses the relationships you created when you built your worksheet, most of the work in using Solver involves defining the constraints and the objectives of the problem.

Setting up the constraints

Constraints are logical formulas in the worksheet that specify conditions you want each answer to satisfy. A **logical formula** returns either 1 (true) or 0 (false) depending on whether a condition is satisfied and uses logical operators such as < , >, <=, >=, or = to define the condition.

In the hat manufacturer example shown below, the constraint to sell no more than 4,500 men's hats is expressed in cell C18 as the logical formula +C9<=4500.

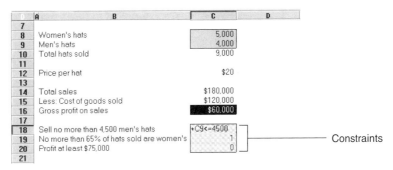

Determining adjustable cells

Adjustable cells contain the values that Solver can change when attempting to satisfy the constraints. You must provide one adjustable cell for each variable you want Solver to change. Adjustable cells can't contain formulas or text. In the example above, the adjustable cells are C8 and C9.

Determining an optimal cell

An **optimal cell** contains a value or formula that you want Solver to maximize or minimize within the constraints of the current problem. The optimal cell can be an adjustable cell but it can't be a constraint cell.

If it can use algebraic techniques to solve the problem, Solver can find an **optimal answer**. This is the answer that maximizes or minimizes the optimal cell. Otherwise, it finds a best answer. For more information, see "Optimal and best answers" on page 241. In the example, the value to maximize is gross profit on sales, so cell C16 is the optimal cell.

Viewing answers

When Solver finishes solving the problem, it places the optimal or best answer in the worksheet. The example shows that Solver found $89,357 to be the optimal answer.

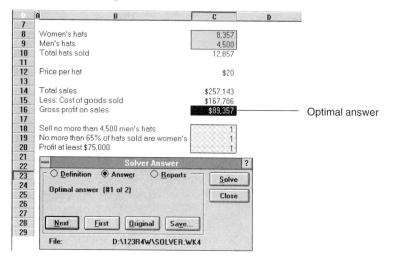

Optimal answer

The dialog box stays open to let you display other answers and create reports.

Solver example

Since Solver first tries to use the rules of algebra when it solves a problem, a simple algebraic example effectively shows how Solver works. The example here is a familiar one, finding the roots of the equation $y=ax^2-b$.

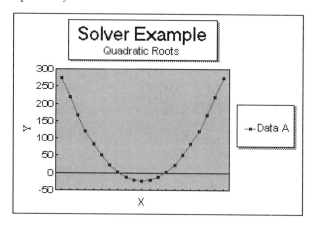

To find quadratic roots

You want to find the roots of the equation $y=3x^2-25$; that is, to find the value(s) of x where $y=0$. The value to adjust is x and the constraint is $y=0$.

1. Set up the problem in the worksheet, as shown below, using 1 as the value for x.

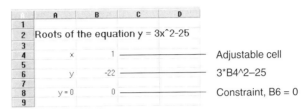

2. Choose Range Analyze Solver.

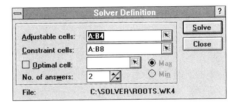

3. In the Adjustable cells text box, specify the adjustable cell (B4).

4. In the Constraint cells text box, specify the constraint cell (B8).

5. In the No. of answers text box, enter the approximate number of answers you want Solver to find. For this example, specify a number 2 or greater.

6. Choose Solve.

    1-2-3 displays the Solver Progress dialog box while Solver is working on your problem.

When Solver finds a solution, it places the answer in the worksheet and displays the Solver Answer dialog box.

Adjustable cell with
answer #1

Constraint cell
showing 1 (true)

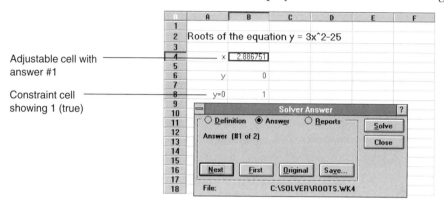

7.   To see the next answer, choose Next.

Adjustable cell with
answer #2

Constraint cell
showing 1 (true)

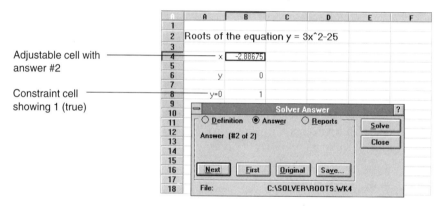

You can drag the dialog box out of the way if it covers data you need to see.

Note   If you close the Solver Answer dialog box, you can bring it back unchanged, with all answers intact, as long as you don't change anything in the worksheet that forces a recalculation. To redisplay the dialog box, choose Range Analyze Solver.

8.   Select Reports.

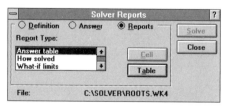

9. Select Answer table from the Report Type text box, then choose Table.

   Solver creates a new file containing information about the answers it found.

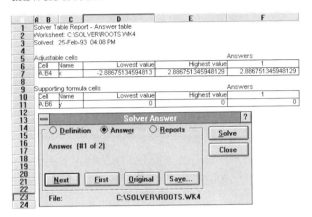

10. Choose Close.

You can create six other types of reports. See "Solver reports" on page 243 for a list of Solver reports.

To see more examples

When you're ready for more Solver examples, you can use the sample solutions file, SOLVER.WK4. The Install program copied SOLVER.WK4 to the subdirectory SAMPLE in your 1-2-3 directory. (If you're using the network version of 1-2-3, SAMPLE is a subdirectory in your personal directory.)

SOLVER.WK4 file contains 11 examples of varying complexity, ranging from simple mortgage problems to complex budgeting problems. Each example occupies a worksheet in the file. The first worksheet, shown below, is an introduction, which includes the conventions used in the sample file. A table of contents appears at the bottom of the introduction sheet. To see a specific example, look it up in the table of contents and select the appropriate worksheet tab.

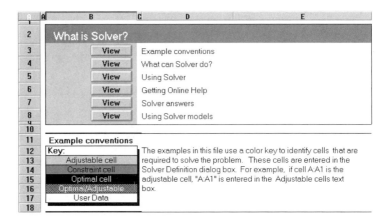

Each example in SOLVER.WK4 has the adjustable cells, constraint cells, and the optimal cell identified and ready for Solver to use. You can solve each example by using the Range Analyze Solver command or by pressing the macro button titled "Example."

To solve an example problem with the command

1. Choose Range Analyze Solver.

2. In the Solver Definition dialog box, specify the adjustable, constraint, and optimal cells, as shown in the example file.

3. Choose Solve.

To solve an example problem using the "Example" button

1. Click the "Example" button at the top of the example worksheet.

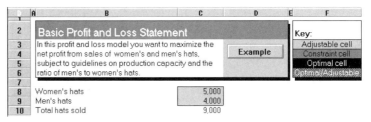

1-2-3 opens the Solver Definition dialog box with the correct values for the example already filled in.

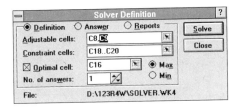

2.   Choose Solve.

Solver answers

This section describes how to save Solver answers and gives you information about how to interpret answers.

To save answers

Once you solve a problem, you can save the problem statement — the adjustable, constraint, and optimal cells — by saving the file that contains the problem. Then the next time you open the file you can choose Range Analyze Solver and solve for the answers again.

1-2-3 also provides ways to save the answers themselves. You can save a single answer with your original problem statement, or you can save a list of all answers by producing and saving an Answer table report. You can also save an answer as a scenario, which allows you to view and share the answer using Version Manager.

To save a single answer

1.   Select First or Next in the Solver Answer dialog box to display the answer you want to save.

2.   Choose Close.

3.   Make the worksheet containing the answer current, and choose File Save or File Save As to save the file.

To save a list of all answers

1.   Select Reports in the Solver Answer dialog box.

2.   Select Answer table from the Report Type list box.

3.   Choose Table.

     1-2-3 creates the report in a new file.

4.   Choose Close.

5.   Make the file containing the Answer table report current, and choose File Save or File Save As to save the file.

To save an answer as a scenario

1. Select First or Next in the Solver Answer dialog box to display the answer you want to save.

2. Choose Save.

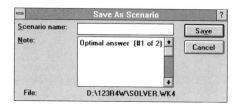

3. Enter a name in the Scenario name text box.

4. Choose Save.

You return to the Solver Answer dialog box.

5. Choose Close.

1-2-3 creates a named range for each range that you specified in the Adjustable cells text box when you defined the problem. Next, 1-2-3 creates a version for each named range using the values of the answer you chose. 1-2-3 then creates a scenario consisting of all the newly created versions. For more information on using Version Manager, see Chapter 22.

Answers and attempts

An **answer** is a result that satisfies all the constraints you specified in the problem. A result that doesn't satisfy one or more of the constraints is called an **attempt**.

The number of attempts Solver makes varies with the number of constraints you specify for the problem and the type of model you created. Solver tries many different combinations of values to try to satisfy all the constraints. If it still hasn't found an answer when these combinations are exhausted, Solver selects a few representative attempts for you to review.

Binding and nonbinding constraints

When Solver finds an answer, each constraint becomes either binding or nonbinding. A **binding constraint** is one that reached at least one of its limits during the current solution (or attempt), while a **nonbinding constraint** is one that did not.

Assume, for example, that you create a problem in which two of the constraints are INTEREST <= 13% and LOAN <= $150,000. If Solver finds an answer with an interest rate of 13% and a loan amount of $125,000, the INTEREST constraint is binding and the LOAN constraint is nonbinding.

Note that you can define a constraint as binding or nonbinding only after Solver finds an answer, and only for that answer. A binding constraint for one answer may be a nonbinding constraint for another.

Optimal and best answers

If you ask Solver to find the optimal answer, Solver attempts to do so using algebraic techniques to solve the problem.

If Solver must use iterative techniques, it has no way to determine if the maximum or minimum it found is the highest or lowest possible answer. The same iterative calculation with a different starting value might produce a different answer. In this case, Solver calls the answer it found the **best answer.** You can help Solver find other best answers by giving it different starting values.

Number of answers

Solver doesn't always find the number of answers you specify when you set up a problem. If there are fewer possible answers than you specified, Solver finds only that number of answers.

Sometimes Solver finds more answers than you specified. For example, if an equation has more roots than the number of answers you specified, Solver finds all of them. Solver also finds one more answer than specified when the original values you supplied constitute a valid answer. You can choose Solve in the Solver Answer dialog box to find out if Solver found more answers.

Avoiding negative answers

Solver sometimes returns negative numbers when you try to minimize the optimal cell. If you want the values of your adjustable cells and the optimal cell to be always positive, enter a new constraint for each adjustable cell and for the optimal cell to specify that the cells must be greater than or equal to 0.

For example, if A1 is an adjustable cell for which you want to see only positive values, include +A1>=0 as a new constraint. Make sure you specify the new constraint cells in the Solver Definition dialog box.

Avoiding roundoff errors

When Solver finds an answer, it places that answer in the adjustable cells and lets the worksheet calculate the result. In some cases, the worksheet, which sometimes uses different calculation methods from Solver, calculates a result that doesn't satisfy one or more constraints. This is called a **roundoff error**.

Roundoff errors occur most often when Solver works with very small or very large numbers. An answer with a roundoff error is still a valid answer. In most cases, roundoff errors shouldn't affect how you use the answer.

Solver displays the message "Roundoff error" in the Solver Answer dialog box if one or more constraint cells return 0 (false) due to discrepancies of 5 or fewer decimal places of precision. Solver displays the message "Minor roundoff" if one or more constraints returns 0 (false) due to discrepancies of between 6 to 16 decimal places of precision.

Other Roundoff errors can occur when

- A mathematically valid Solver answer recalculates to ERR when 1-2-3 displays it in the worksheet.

  For example, Solver can find both negative and positive values that satisfy odd-numbered roots, but the worksheet only recognizes the positive values and displays ERR when the negative value is displayed in the worksheet.

- You set 1-2-3 to recalculate either by columns or by rows.

  In this case, choose Tools User Setup Recalculation and set the recalculation order to Natural. Then solve the problem again.

To avoid a roundoff error, revise your formulas to limit operations that can cause roundoff errors, such as square roots and exponentiation. Then solve the problem again.

When the message "Roundoff error" or "Minor roundoff" appears in the Solver Answer dialog box, you can select Report, and then select Inconsistent constraints to locate the constraint cells affected by roundoff errors.

Solver reports

Solver reports help you understand how Solver determined answers, how one answer compares to other answers, and how much flexibility you have in changing an answer. This information can help you select the answer that's most appropriate for you. Because reports can be separate worksheet files, they also preserve the answers, allowing you to change the original files without losing the answers. Solver provides the following reports:

- **Answer table** lists all the answers Solver found. This report is useful if you want to list, print, or save all Solver's answers. Since 1-2-3 displays the answers in tabular form, you can also use the Range commands or run macros to compare answers. To create a chart of the answers, select the adjustable cells or optimal cell section of the report and then choose Tools Chart.

- **Cells used** shows the cells that Solver used to solve the problem. This report is useful to confirm that Solver used the cells you wanted it to use.

- **Differences** compares two answers. This report is helpful when Solver returns several answers and you want to know the difference between two answers. The Differences report highlights the cells that differ by the amount, or tolerance, you specify.

- **How solved** summarizes what Solver did to find the current answer or attempt. This report gives you information about the optimal cell, the adjustable cells, binding constraints, nonbinding constraints, inconsistent constraints, and any cells for which Solver needs you to supply guess values.

- **Inconsistent constraints** lists the constraint cells that weren't satisfied and shows you how you can adjust their formulas to get a valid answer. For example, if the report shows that you must rewrite a constraint formula, such as +A1>=B1*5, as +A1>=B1*5+1000, you know you must add 1,000 to the formula to satisfy that constraint. This may not be the only change you must make to get a valid answer.

- **Nonbinding constraints** identifies constraints that were satisfied by the current answer but didn't have an impact on the value of any adjustable cell; that is, didn't reach any limit. When a constraint is nonbinding, the constraint isn't necessarily irrelevant to the problem. It can become binding in a later variation. However, it's a good idea to check the problem definition to see if the nonbinding constraint duplicates or is superceded by another constraint.

- **What-if limits** is useful if you want to change an answer. The "Range of values found for all answers" section of the report lists the lowest and highest values you'll find for each adjustable cell if you browse through all Solver's answers.

  The "What-if limits for answer #" section contains an estimate of the minimum and maximum values you can assign to each adjustable cell in the current answer and still satisfy all constraints. This range assumes that the values of all other adjustable cells remain constant.

  For example, suppose an answer has a value of 3 and 7 for adjustable cells A1 and B1, respectively. If the what-if limits for A1 are from 2 to 4 and the what-if limits for B1 are from 5 to 10, you can vary A1 within the range of 2 to 4 and still satisfy all constraints as long as B1 is left at its current value of 7. Similarly, you can vary the value in B1 within the range of 5 to 10 as long as A1 remains at 3.

Tips on using Solver

This section provides information that can help you set up problems for Solver.

Using @functions in Solver problems

Since Solver problems are based on ordinary worksheets, @functions that are useful in a worksheet are equally useful in Solver problems based on that worksheet. Here are some things to remember when using @functions:

- Make sure the formulas in your model contain @functions that Solver supports.

- **?** **Help**   For a list of the @functions Solver supports, search on "@Functions in Solver problems" in Help.

- Adding and multiplying @functions together, or using large ranges in @HLOOKUP, @VLOOKUP, or statistical @functions, may make a problem difficult to solve.

- Limit the use of @CHOOSE, @HLOOKUP, @IF, @INDEX, @INT, @MOD, @ROUND, and @VLOOKUP. Also, don't combine these @functions in a formula. Although Solver supports these @functions, they can make a problem difficult to solve.

- Limit the use of nested @functions, especially @IF. If Solver can't solve a problem that has many nested @functions, rewrite the @functions across several cells.

- If Solver has solved a problem and you want to save the answers, don't make changes that cause a recalculation in any active file containing the following @functions: @@, @CELL, @CELLPOINTER, @INFO, @ISNAME, @ISRANGE, @NOW, @RAND, @TODAY, and any database @function that refers to an external table.

  Such changes not only recalculate the file containing the @function, but also recalculate every other active file, including the file(s) containing the Solver problem. Solver interprets the recalculation as a change to the problem and discards any answers it found.

Maximum problem size

Solver can't solve large problems that require more memory than your computer can provide. Both the number of cells involved and the complexity of the model affect Solver's ability to solve a problem. In particular, the number of cells containing formulas affecting the optimal cell can have a significant effect.

Here are some guidelines for designing a problem that Solver can solve quickly and efficiently:

- Solver uses the combined total of adjustable cells, constraint cells, the optimal cell, and any other cells it needs to compute the answer. Try to keep this combined total to fewer than 1,000 cells.

- Use Tools Audit to determine the number of formulas affecting the optimal cell. If a formula isn't connected directly or indirectly to an adjustable cell you can convert it to a constant to simplify the problem. You can do this by converting formulas to their values using Edit Paste Special, or by using the {RANGE-VALUE} macro command.

- The number of formulas and the number of relationships between formulas in the model can sometimes have more impact than size.

- Increasing the number of adjustable cells and constraint cells usually increases the time required to find all the answers.

- Using @functions other than @SUM and @AVG increases the chance that Solver needs you to supply guess values before it can find an answer.

- Increasing the number of adjustable cells and @functions increases the chance that 1-2-3 won't have enough memory to solve the problem.

[?] Related Help topics

You can use macros to perform most of the functions that you perform with Solver menu commands. For more information, search on "Macros" in Help, select the topic "Macro command categories" and select "Solver" as the category.

22

Using Version Manager

You can use Version Manager to perform advanced what-if analysis. For example, you can create and test financial scenarios, or analyze business assumptions to discover financial possibilities. You can use Version Manager by yourself, or you can share files and create versions and scenarios in a workgroup. This chapter describes how to use Version Manager to create and share versions and scenarios.

What are versions?

Versions are sets of different data for the same named range. Each version has a name, a date and time stamp, the name of the person who created or modified the version, and optional styles and comment. You use Version Manager to create and manage versions.

For example, suppose you enter the values 520, 435, 315, and 225 in the range A:B2..A:E2. You then use Version Manager to name this range Income and to create a version called High Income, as shown below.

High Income version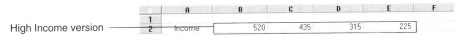

You then enter the values 440, 360, 220, and 125 in Income and create a second version named Level Income, as shown below.

Level Income version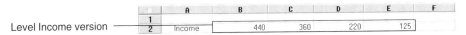

Finally, you create a third version using the values of 315, 270, 165, and 78 named Low Income.

Low Income version

1-2-3 saves all three versions of Income along with other information including your name as creator of the version, the date and time you created the version and, optionally, any styles you applied to the version's range, and a comment.

You can create versions of any named range in a file. For example, as well as creating versions of Income, you can name another range Expenses and create versions named High Expenses, Level Expenses, and Low Expenses.

What are scenarios?

A **scenario** is a named group of versions. For example, you can create scenarios by grouping different versions of the ranges Income and Expenses. You can group the High Income version of Income with the Low Expenses version of Expenses to create a scenario named Best Case.

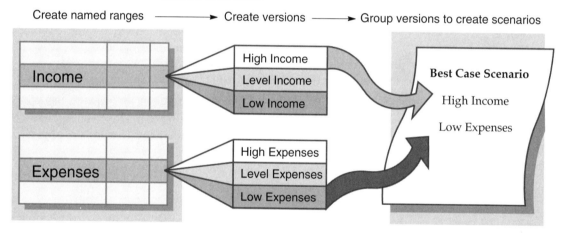

You can also create a scenario named Worst Case by grouping the Low Income version of Income with the High Expenses version of Expenses, as shown on the next page.

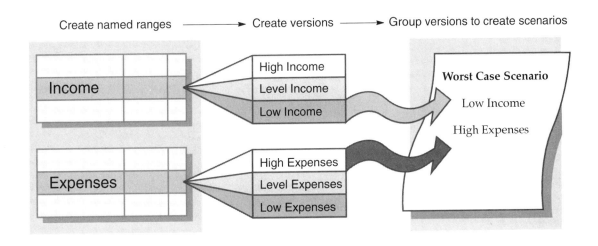

Create named ranges ────▶ Create versions ────▶ Group versions to create scenarios

High Income
Level Income
Low Income

Income

Worst Case Scenario

Low Income

High Expenses

High Expenses
Level Expenses
Low Expenses

Expenses

Working with Version Manager

When you choose Range Version, 1-2-3 displays the Version Manager window, containing the Version Manager or the Version Manager Index. You use the Manager and Index to create versions and scenarios for the current file. You can move back and forth between the Manager, the Index, and the worksheet.

You use the **Manager** to work with one version at a time. You can use the Manager to create, delete, and update versions; display a version in the worksheet; and change version information, such as a version comment.

Use these buttons to manage versions

Click to list named ranges

Click to list versions; click a version to display it in the worksheet

Click to switch to the Index

? Help For information about the function of each Manager button, search on "Versions" in Help and choose the topic "Range Version Manager." The Help topic contains a picture of the Manager. To pop up a description of any Manager button, point to the button in the picture and click it.

You use the **Index** to work with more than one version or scenario at a time and track changes. For example, you can use it to group versions into a scenario and to modify a scenario. You can also use the Index, like the Manager, to work with one version at a time.

Using the Index, you can see information about many versions simultaneously; sort the versions by range name, version name, scenario name, date, or creator; and create or modify a scenario by grouping versions.

Click to sort versions
and scenarios

Click to collapse or
expand the list of
versions

Click these buttons
to manage versions
and scenarios

Click to display
comments

Scroll through the list
of named ranges and
versions

Click to switch to
the Manager

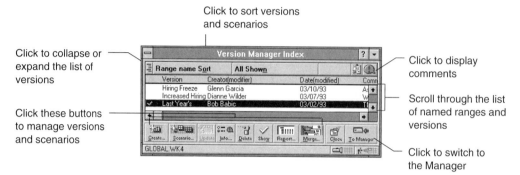

? **Help**   For information about the function of each Index button, search on "Scenarios" in Help and select the topic "Range Version Manager Index." The Help topic contains a picture of the Index. To pop up a description of any Index button, point to the button in the picture and click it.

You can leave the Version Manager window open while you work, shrink it to an icon, move it, and size it. Increasing the size of the window vertically when you're working with the Manager is a way to display comments about versions.

To move between the worksheet, Manager, and Index

You often move back and forth between the worksheet, the Manager, and the Index. For example, you can enter data in a range, then use the Manager to name the range and create a version. Next you can move back to the worksheet to enter new data in the range and return to the Manager to create a new version. Then you can switch from the Manager to the Index and group one of these versions with versions of other named ranges to create a scenario.

1.   To move back and forth between the Manager and Index, choose To Index or To Manager, or press ALT+T.

2.   To move back and forth between the Version Manager window and the worksheet, click the worksheet, click the Version Manager window, or press ALT+F6.

Using versions

You can use Version Manager to create, delete, and update versions. You can also change information saved with a version, such as a comment, and you can display different versions of named ranges in the worksheet.

To create a version

You can create versions of a range only if it is named. You can use Version Manager to name a range and create versions of that range. You can also use Version Manager to create versions of ranges you previously named using the Range Name command. For rules about naming ranges and information about using Range Name, see Chapter 8.

1. Enter data for the version into the range.

2. If you already named the range, make sure the cell pointer is in the range. If the range is unnamed, select the entire range.

3. Choose Range Version.

4. Choose Create.

5. If you haven't already named the range, you can accept the default range name or enter a different name in the Range name text box.

6. Accept the default version name or enter a name in the Version name text box.

7. To add a comment about the version, enter it in the Comment text box.

8. Under Sharing options, select an option: Unprotected, Protected, or Protected & hidden. Unprotected is the default.

9. To save any styles you applied to the version, select the Retain styles check box.

    Note   When you share a file on a Lotus Notes® server, the file is sealed. If you protect a version, you can't unprotect it unless you know the password for unsealing the file and have access to the Notes server.

10. Choose OK.

To display a version in the worksheet

1. Choose Range Version.
2. In the Manager, in the Named range drop-down box, select the range for which you want to display a version.
3. Select the version from the "With version(s)" drop-down box.

You can also display a version in the worksheet by double-clicking it in the Index.

To display more than one version

If you created versions for several named ranges, you can select a version for each range and display these versions in the worksheet.

1. Choose Range Version.
2. In the Index, hold down CTRL and click the versions you want to display in the worksheet.
3. Choose Show.

To modify the version settings

You can change the comment, the style setting, and the sharing setting for a version. You can also rename the range.

1. Choose Range Version.
2. In the Manager, select the version from the "With version(s)" drop-down box; or in the Index, select the version from the list.

    If the version you want to modify is hidden, you must use the Index. Select "Hidden only" from the Shown drop-down box, then select the version you want to modify.
3. Choose Info.

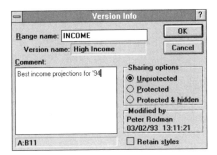

4. To rename the range, enter a new name in the Range name text box.

5. To modify the comment, edit it in the Comment text box.

6. To save the range's styles with the version when you update the version data, select the Retain styles check box.

    The next time you update this version, 1-2-3 updates the styles as well as the data for the version.

7. To modify the sharing setting, select a sharing option: Unprotected, Protected, or Protected & hidden.

    Note   When you share a file on a Lotus Notes server, the file is sealed. If you protect a version, you can't unprotect it unless you know the password for unsealing the file and have access to the Notes server.

8. Choose OK.

To update a version   Any time you modify the data or styles in a version, you must update the version if you want to save your changes.

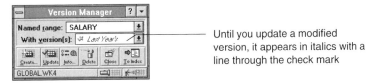

Until you update a modified version, it appears in italics with a line through the check mark

1. Choose Range Version.

2. In the Manager, select the version from the "With version(s)" drop-down box.

You can use the Index to update more than one version at a time.

3. In the worksheet, enter the new data and styles for the version.

4. In the Manager, choose Update.

   1-2-3 asks you to confirm the update.

5. Choose OK.

? **Help**   For information about how to modify a protected version or a protected and hidden version, search on "Modifying versions" in Help and select the topic "Version Info."

To delete a version

1. Choose Range Version.

2. In the Manager, select the version from the "With version(s)" drop-down box; or in the Index, select one or more versions.

   Note   You can only delete unprotected versions. To delete a protected version, select the version, choose Info, and change the sharing option to Unprotected.

3. Choose Delete.

   1-2-3 asks you to confirm the deletion.

4. Choose OK.

To create a version report

You can create reports about versions. A report can list the versions for a selected named range. It can also show the version data, the effect of selected versions on formulas in the worksheet, and audit information, such as who last modified a version.

1. Choose Range Version.

2. In the Index, choose Report.

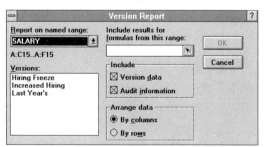

3. In the "Report on named range" drop-down box, select a range.

4. In the Versions list box, select the version or versions you want 1-2-3 to report on.

5. To see how the selected versions affect the results of formulas in the worksheet, specify the address or name of the range containing the formulas in the "Include results for formulas from this range" text box.

6. To include the data for the selected versions, select the Version data check box.

7. To include the names of users who created and last modified the version, with the date and time the version was created or last modified, select the Audit information check box.

8. Under Arrange data, select By columns or By rows.

9. Choose OK.

1-2-3 creates the report in a new file and gives the file a unique name beginning with REPORT; for example, REPORT03.WK4, as shown below. You can print and save a version report just like any other file.

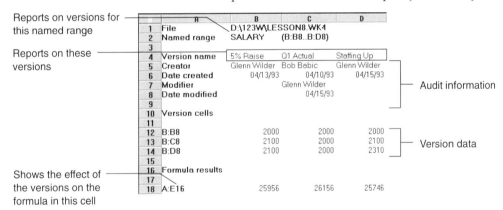

Reports on versions for this named range

Reports on these versions

Shows the effect of the versions on the formula in this cell

Audit information

Version data

To sort versions

In the Index, you can sort versions so that you see only the versions you want to work with. Often, you sort versions before grouping them to create a scenario. Sorting also helps you track changes to versions and scenarios.

You can sort versions by range name, version name, creator or modifier, and date created or modified. You can also sort by scenario to see which versions comprise a scenario.

1.   Choose Range Version.

2.   In the Index, select a sorting option from the Sort drop-down box.

The illustration below shows versions sorted by range name.

Click to see sorting
options

Use this view to
select versions
for a scenario

The next illustration shows versions sorted by date created.

Versions sorted by
date

Using scenarios

You can group selected versions for different named ranges to create scenarios. This section describes how to create, display, modify, and delete scenarios.

To create a scenario

1. Choose Range Version.
2. In the Index, hold down CTRL and click the versions you want to group into a scenario.

   Select only one version from each range. The version name appears in the Selected versions list box.
3. Choose Scenario.

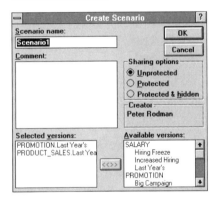

4. Accept the default scenario name or enter a different name in the Scenario name text box.
5. To add a comment about the scenario, enter it in the Comment text box.
6. Under Sharing options, select an option: Unprotected, Protected, or Protected & hidden.

   Note   When you share a file on a Lotus Notes server, the file is sealed. If you protect a version, you can't unprotect it unless you know the password for unsealing the file and have access to the Notes server.
7. To add a version to the scenario, select the version in the Available versions list box, and choose << or double-click the version.

8. To remove a version from the scenario, select the version in the Selected versions list box, and choose >> or double-click the version.

   1-2-3 removes the version name from the Selected versions list box.

9. Choose OK.

1-2-3 creates a scenario with the name you specified, comprised of the versions you grouped. The Index displays your new scenario with any other scenarios, sorted by name.

To display a scenario

To display one scenario in the worksheet, double-click it.

1. Choose Range Version.
2. Select Scenario name from the Sort drop-down box.
3. Select the scenario you want to display in the worksheet.
4. Choose Show.

To modify a scenario

You can change the group of versions that comprise a scenario. You can also modify the comment and the sharing setting.

1. Choose Range Version.
2. In the Index, select Scenario name from the Sort drop-down box.

   If the scenario you want to modify is hidden, select "Hidden only" from the Shown drop-down box.
3. Select the scenario.
4. Choose Info.

You can modify the sharing options for more than one scenario at a time. Select the scenarios and choose Info.

5. To modify the comment, edit it in the Comment text box.

6. To add a version to the scenario, select the version in the Available versions list box, and choose << or double-click the version.

    The version name appears in the Selected versions list box.

7. To remove a version from the scenario, select the version in the Selected versions list box, and choose >> or double-click the version.

    1-2-3 removes the version name from the Selected versions list box.

8. To modify the sharing setting, select a sharing option: Unprotected, Protected, or Protected & hidden.

9. Choose OK.

    ? **Help**   For information about how to modify a protected scenario or a protected and hidden scenario, search on "Modifying scenarios" in Help and select the topic "Scenario Info."

To delete a scenario

1. Choose Range Version.

2. In the Index, select Scenario name from the Sort drop-down box.

3. Select one or more scenarios.

4. Choose Delete.

    1-2-3 asks you to confirm the deletion.

5. Choose OK.

    Note   When you delete a scenario, you delete a grouping of versions, not the versions themselves.

Sharing versions and scenarios

You can share versions and scenarios in a workgroup. For example, you can share an income statement projection worksheet with your co-workers, letting them enter their projections for income and expenses as versions of named ranges. Then you can group different versions to create scenarios. You can share files containing versions and scenarios in three ways: using Lotus Notes, using a network, and without a network.

Sharing files using Lotus Notes

To share files using Lotus Notes, you create a **shared file**, a sealed 1-2-3 file saved on a Notes server. Then everyone in the workgroup can create, delete, modify and display versions and scenarios in the shared file. Workgroup members can simultaneously work with versions and scenarios without writing over each other's work. You can use Lotus Notes to replicate shared files among Notes servers.

To create a shared file

1. Open the file you want to share.

2. Use Version Manager to create named ranges and give each at least one version.

   A named range must already have at least one version in order for workgroup members to be able to create versions.

3. Use Style Protection to allow changes to cell contents in the named ranges.

   For information about unprotecting ranges, see "To seal a file and leave specified ranges unprotected" on page 146.

4. Choose File Save As.

5. Select the shared file type, .NS4, in the File type drop-down box.

6. In the Notes servers drop-down box, select the name of a Notes server accessible to everyone you want to share the file with, and, if necessary, select the directory in the Directory list box.

   If you want to test the file before putting it on the Notes server, you can select your local Notes directory in the Notes servers drop-down box. Then, after you finish testing, you can copy it to the Notes server.

7. Enter a file name in the File name text box, and choose OK.

   1-2-3 displays the Set Password dialog box.

8. In the Password text box, enter a password to seal the shared file.

A password can include 15 characters or less. 1-2-3 displays an
* (asterisk) for each character as you enter the password. 1-2-3 is
case-sensitive for passwords, so you must remember the exact
combination of uppercase or lowercase letters you use when you
create the password.

9. In the Verify text box, enter the same password, and choose OK.

1-2-3 saves the file as a shared file with the extension .NS4 and seals
the file with the password you entered, protecting all cells except the
ranges you marked as unprotected.

To use a shared file

1. Choose File Open.

2. Select the shared file type, .NS4, from the File type drop-down
   box.

3. Select the name of a Notes server from the Notes servers
   drop-down box.

4. Select the file name in the File name list box.

5. Choose OK.

6. Use Version Manager to create, modify, delete, or display
   versions and scenarios in the shared file.

   Note You can create and display versions of unprotected
   named ranges only.

7. Choose File Save Versions to save the new versions and
   scenarios you created.

If another user creates versions or scenarios in a shared file and
saves the file while you're using it, 1-2-3 beeps and displays the
message "New versions have been posted" in the title bar. To display
newly created versions or scenarios, refresh the file.

To refresh a shared file

1. Choose Range Version.

2. In the Index, choose the Refresh button, shown at left.

1-2-3 makes available all newly created versions and scenarios. A dot
appears next to all newly created versions and scenarios until you
display them in the worksheet or choose the Mark All Unread
button, shown at left.

Note   The Refresh button appears only if Lotus Notes is installed on your computer. Refresh is dimmed when the shared file has no new versions or scenarios or when the current file isn't a shared file.

Sharing files using a network

To share files using a network, you create a file on a network file server that all members of your workgroup can access. Your co-workers can create, modify, delete and display versions and scenarios in the file. You can save changes to a file shared over a network only if you have the file reservation.

To share a file on a network file server

1. Open the file you want to share.
2. Use Range Name to name the ranges for which you want your co-workers to create versions.
3. To unprotect the named ranges, use Style Protection.

   For information, see "To seal a file and leave specified ranges unprotected" on page 146.
4. To seal the file with a password, use File Protect.

   Sealing a file prevents changes to the file except in the unprotected ranges. For more information, see "Sealing a file" on page 145.
5. Choose File Save As.
6. Select a network file server from the Drives drop-down box.
7. Enter a file name in the File name text box.
8. Choose OK.

To use a file shared on a file server

1. Choose File Open.
2. In the Drives drop-down box, select the network file server where the file is stored.
3. Select the file name in the File name list box.
4. Choose OK.

   If another user has the file reservation, 1-2-3 displays a message, and you can't save changes to the file. You can open the file for reading only, and you can try to get the reservation later.

To save changes to the file, you can also use File Save As to save the file with a different name. Later when the file reservation is available, you can merge your versions and scenarios into the shared file. For information about merging versions and scenarios, see page 264.

5. Use Version Manager to create, modify, delete, or display versions and scenarios in the shared file.

    Note   You can create versions of unprotected named ranges only.

6. Choose File Save to save the new versions and scenarios you created.

 ? **Help**   For more information about file reservations, search on "reservation" in Help.

Sharing files without a network

To share files without a network, create a file and send copies of it to everyone in your workgroup. You can maintain a master copy of the file; your co-workers enter versions and scenarios in their own separate copies of the file. After they return their copies, you can merge everyone's versions and scenarios into the master copy of the file.

Note   When you merge versions and scenarios, make sure the **destination file**, the one you're copying to, contains ranges with the same names and dimensions as the named ranges in the **source file**, the one you're copying from. 1-2-3 copies the new versions from the source file into the destination file.

To share a file without a network

1. Open the file you want to share.

2. Use Range Name to name the ranges for which you want your co-workers to create versions.

3. Use Style Protection to unprotect the named ranges.

    For information, see "To seal a file and leave specified ranges unprotected" on page 146.

4. Use File Protect to seal the file with a password.

    Sealing a file prevents changes to the file except in the unprotected ranges. For more information, see "Sealing a file" on page 145.

5. Use File Save As to save the file.

To merge versions and scenarios

1. Make sure the source file and the destination file are both active.

To display a list of merged versions, save the destination file immediately before merging. Then merge the files, and in the Index, select New only from the Shown drop-down box.

2. Make the destination file the current file.

3. Choose Range Version.

4. In the Index, choose Merge.

5. In the "From file" drop-down box, select the name of the source file.

6. To merge only versions and scenarios created on or after a particular date, enter the date in the "Modified on or after date" text box.

   Enter the date in day-month-year, day-month, or long international format.

7. To merge only versions and scenarios created or last modified by a particular user, select the user's name in the "Last modified by" drop-down box.

8. Choose OK.

1-2-3 displays a message with the results of the merge. For a detailed explanation of this message, press **F1 (HELP)** or click the ? button in the message box. After you merge the new versions into your master copy, you can again share copies of the file with everyone in the workgroup.

? Related Help topics

For information about Version Manager @functions, search on "Information @Functions." For information about Version Manager macros, search on "Version Manager macros."

Tutorial lesson 8 gives you hands-on practice creating versions and scenarios. Choose Help Tutorial to start the Tutorial.

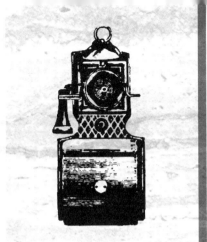

Part VI
Working with Databases

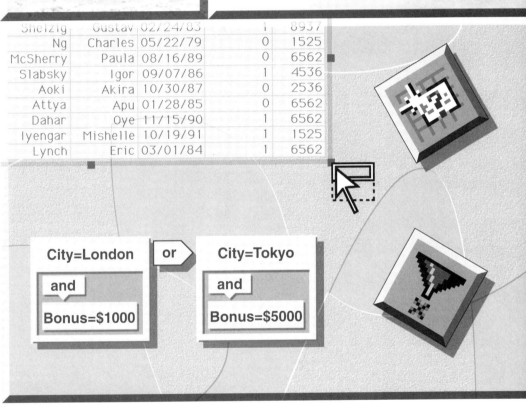

Shelzig	Gustav	02/24/83	1	8937
Ng	Charles	05/22/79	0	1525
McSherry	Paula	08/16/89	0	6562
Slabsky	Igor	09/07/86	1	4536
Aoki	Akira	10/30/87	0	2536
Attya	Apu	01/28/85	0	6562
Dahar	Oye	11/15/90	1	6562
Iyengar	Mishelle	10/19/91	1	1525
Lynch	Eric	03/01/84	1	6562

City=London or **City=Tokyo**

and

Bonus=$1000

and

Bonus=$5000

23

Working with 1-2-3 Databases

1-2-3 makes using database tables easy because you work entirely with menu commands, the mouse, and SmartIcons. You never have to memorize or type field names, criteria ranges, values, or logical operators. This chapter describes how to create and query 1-2-3 database tables and external tables that you connect to. For information about connecting to external database tables, see Chapter 24.

What is a 1-2-3 database table?

A **1-2-3 database table** is a worksheet range containing data organized as fields and records. A **field** is a column that contains a single category of data, such as telephone numbers. A **record** is a row containing data for each field, such as one person's name, ID number, department, and telephone number. The top cell in each column must contain a **field name**, a label that identifies the category of data in the column.

	A	B	C	D	E	F	G
1	LAST	FIRST	ID	EXT	DEPT	CITY	
2	Amadeus	Jordan	3307	4260	Sales	Los Angeles	
3	Anthony	Ruth	978	1851	Marketing	Boston	
4	Janelle	Rapsody	9372	1876	Manufacturing	Baltimore	
5	Cooke	Mattie	970	1915	Sales	Birmingham	
6	Jean	Betty	9057	1899	Executive	Cambridge	
7	Alexey	Elijah	86	3500	Sales	New York	
8	Leaya	Bashe	231	2262	Sales	Paris	
9	Moriah	Joshua	734	8975	Research	Boston	
10	Shing	Victor	4481	0752	Sales	London	
11	Antoinette	Erika	1426	968	Research	Tokyo	

A field — (points to column)

Field names — (points to row 1)

A record — (points to row 7)

You set up a 1-2-3 database table with field names, fields, and records so you can manipulate large amounts of data and get precisely the information you need. Once you set up a 1-2-3 database table, you can perform queries by creating query tables; and you can find, add, and delete records. You can also use database @functions.

Creating a 1-2-3 database table

A 1-2-3 database table must fit on a single worksheet and can contain up to 256 fields and 8,191 records.

To create a 1-2-3 database table

1. Enter field names in adjacent cells in an empty row. Field names must be in one row only; this is the first row of your table.

Field names ———

Use the following guidelines when naming fields:

- Use a label for each field name, rather than a number or formula. If you use numbers and formulas as field names, you can get unexpected results.

- To enter a field name that begins with a number or other non-alphabetic character, precede the name with a label-prefix character.

- Don't use the same field name for more than one field in the same table.

- Don't use , (comma), . (period), : (colon), ; (semicolon), - (hyphen), # (number sign), ~ (tilde), ! (exclamation point), spaces, or arithmetic operators in a field name.

- Don't use field names that look like cell addresses, such as P12, X24, or EX100.

2. Enter the data for the first record in the row immediately below the field names. Don't leave an empty row.

- You can enter text, numbers, @functions, or formulas. You get more reliable results when you query a database table if your @functions and formulas contain absolute rather than relative references.

First record ———

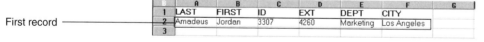

- Don't use a repeating character, such as a hyphen, to separate the row containing field names from the data.

- You get more reliable results when you query a table if all entries in the same field contain the same type of data. It's better, for example, if a field for street addresses contains all labels rather than a mixture of labels and values.

3. Enter the other records without leaving empty rows between them.

   1-2-3 lets you enter duplicate records, but a database table is more convenient to use if each record has at least one unique field entry. For example, include a field containing unique ID numbers when you create a table.

4. If you want, you can name your 1-2-3 database table using the Range Name command.

   Assigning a range name to a database table makes it easier to specify the table for Tools Database commands and @functions. Also, you must name your tables if you want to join them. For more information about naming a range, see Chapter 8.

   Use the following rules when you name tables:

   • The row containing the field names must be the first row of the named range.

   • To avoid confusion, don't use a range name that matches a field name in the same table or any other table you want to query.

5. If you want, you can add styles, such as text attributes, number formats and alignments, to the data in a database table. For information about changing the appearance of data in a worksheet, see Chapter 11.

Using Criteria

You use criteria when you work with query tables, join database tables, and when you find, append, and delete records. **Criteria** tell 1-2-3 which records you want to work with. Rather than entering criteria in a range, you specify and manipulate them directly in a dialog box. The database dialog boxes display criteria and the relationships between multiple criteria graphically. This makes criteria easy to understand and use.

In all the dialog boxes where you build criteria, you can specify numbers, labels, formulas, @functions, and logical operators. You build a criterion in a dialog box by selecting a field, a logical operator, and a value. 1-2-3 provides field names and values for each field in the table; you don't have to write them down or memorize them.

Select a field; for example, DEPT

Select a logical operator; for example, =

Select a value; for example, Sales

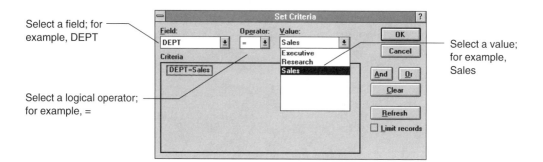

Using @functions and formulas in criteria

You can enter an @function or a formula as the value in a criterion. For example, to find students whose grades are below the class average, you can enter an @function as shown below.

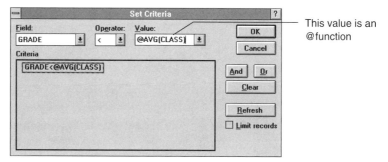

This value is an @function

To find anyone whose profit-sharing bonus wasn't equal to .1 percent of the net profits, you can enter a formula as the value of the criterion as shown below.

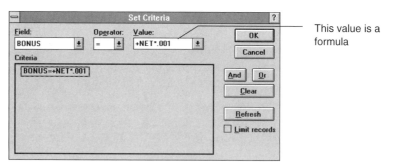

This value is a formula

Using multiple criteria

You can specify more than one criterion by using the logical operators And and Or. When you use And with multiple criteria, you narrow the search. When you use Or, you expand the search.

For example, suppose you want records of employees who work in the Sales department in Boston. First, you specify the criterion CITY=Boston. Next, to narrow the search, you choose the logical operator And. Then, you specify a second criterion, DEPT=Sales. The illustration below shows how 1-2-3 graphically represents the And relationship between multiple criteria.

Specify the first criterion

... then choose And

... then specify the next criterion

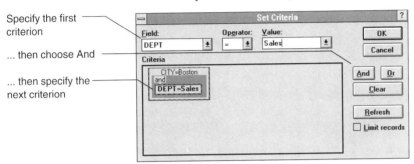

You can use Or to display records of employees who work in either Boston or Paris. First, you specify the criterion CITY=Boston. Next, to expand the search, you choose Or as the logical operator. Then, you specify the second criterion, CITY=Paris. The illustration below shows how 1-2-3 graphically represents the Or relationship.

Specify the first criterion

... then choose Or

... then specify the next criterion

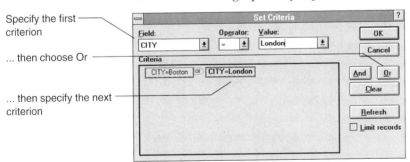

You can also specify multiple criteria with combinations of And and Or relationships. For example, suppose you want to display the records of employees in the Sales department who work in either Boston or London. All records must meet the criteria DEPT=Sales, And CITY=Boston Or CITY=London. The next illustration shows how 1-2-3 graphically represents the logical relationship between these criteria.

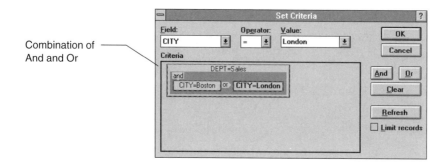

Combination of — And and Or

Changing relationships between criteria

You can change the logical relationship between one criterion and another by dragging a criterion to a different position. For example, the illustrations below show how you can drag the box containing the criterion DEPT=Research to the right to change CITY=Boston And DEPT=Research to CITY=Boston Or DEPT=Research.

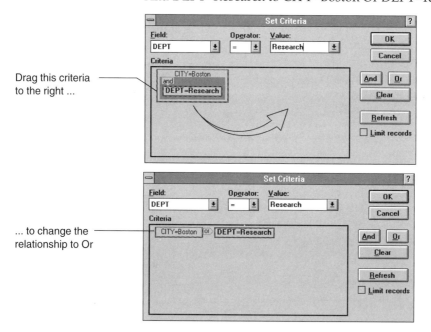

Drag this criteria to the right ...

... to change the relationship to Or

You can move and copy a box containing more than one criterion. Select the box and SHIFT+drag to move it or CTRL+drag to copy it.

Using wildcard characters in criteria

You can also specify **wildcard characters** in the value of a criterion to search for records that match certain characters in a field. To match any single character, use a ? (question mark) where you want the match. For example, if you specify Jo?n as the value, as shown below, 1-2-3 displays last names such as John, Joln, Jonn, Jorn and so on.

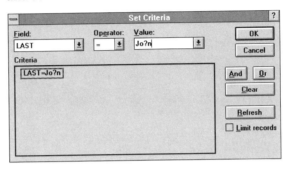

The * (asterisk) matches all characters from * to the end of the label (up to, and including, the 512-character maximum). For example, if you specify Jo*, as shown below, 1-2-3 displays all last names that begin with Jo, such as Joanas, Joannas, Johnson, Jones and so on.

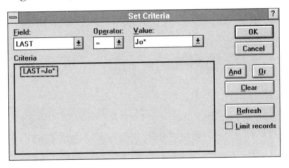

Using query tables

A **query table** is a workspace where you can work with data from a 1-2-3 database table or an external table. It's set up like a database table with fields, field names, and records. You can specify criteria and choose which fields to display, so the query table contains only the database records you want. In the query table, you can display data to use in reports and models without changing any data in the source database table.

The source database table

A query table

You can name a query table, style it, and sort the records in it. After working with data in a query table, you can leave the data in the source database table intact or update the table to reflect your changes. You can also refresh the data in a query table to reflect changes in the source database table.

To create a query table

1. Choose Tools Database New Query.

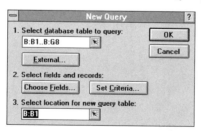

2. Specify the range containing the database table; or, if the table you want to query is an external table or a named table, select the table name from the drop-down list.

   To query an external table you're not connected to, choose External and connect to the table.

You can also choose which fields to display and set criteria after you create the query table.

3. To specify which fields you want to appear in the query table, and the order of these fields, choose Choose Fields and follow the procedure for choosing fields described on page 278.

4. To specify which records appear in the query table, choose Set Criteria and follow the procedure for setting criteria described on page 276.

When you query an external table, by default 1-2-3 limits the number of records in the query table to the first 25 that meet the criteria; use Set Criteria to change this limit.

5. Specify a location for the query table. Make sure the query table doesn't overlap the database table.

Caution   1-2-3 writes over existing data in the query table range.

If you specify the top left cell of a range, the query table contains as many of the fields and records as fit within the boundaries of the worksheet.

If you specify a multiple-cell range, 1-2-3 displays only the fields and records that fit in that range. For example, if you specify a range of 5 columns and 10 rows, 1-2-3 displays a query table that contains the first 5 fields and the first 10 records in the order in which they appear in the database table. If you subsequently size the query table larger, 1-2-3 displays the additional fields and records.

6. Choose OK.

 1-2-3 displays the query table. A dashed border around the query table indicates that you can size it to display more data. You can use the icon at left to expand the table to show all additional fields and records that fit within the worksheet boundaries.

To select an entire query table, click the border of the table. To select an entire field, click the cell containing the field name. You can also size, move, copy and delete a query table as you do a drawn object. For more information, see "Working with drawn objects" on page 182.

To style a query table

When you create a query table, it inherits the styles and formats from the source database table. You can style the fields in a query table and change the appearance of data. For example, you can change the number format or the text color in a field.

1. To style the data in a field, select the first cell in the column below the field name.

2. Apply styles using Style Lines & Colors, Style Font & Attributes, and Style Number Format.

   For more information about changing the appearance of data, see Chapter 11.

3. Choose Query Refresh Now to apply the styles or formats to all the other cells in the field.

To set criteria for a query table

When you set criteria for a new or existing query table, only data matching the criteria appears in the query table. For more information about using criteria, see page 269.

1. Do one of the following:

   - To set criteria for a new query table, select the range containing the database table, choose Tools Database New Query, then choose Set Criteria.

   - To set criteria for an existing query table, click the border of the query table to select it, then choose Query Set Criteria.

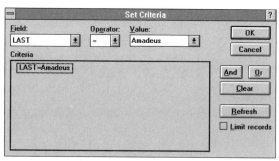

2. Specify a criterion by doing the following:
   - Select the field from the Field drop-down box.
   - Select the logical operator from the Operator drop-down box.
   - Specify the value in the Value drop-down box.

   For example, if you want the records of everyone in the Sales department, the criterion is DEPT=Sales; where DEPT is the field, = is the logical operator, and Sales is the value.

3. To narrow the search, choose And and repeat Step 2.

4. To expand the search, choose Or and repeat Step 2.

5. To remove a criterion, click the box that contains the criterion and choose Clear.

6. To apply new or changed criteria to the query table without closing the Set Criteria dialog box, choose Refresh.

7. To specify the number of records you want to appear in the query table, select the Limit records check box and enter a number.

8. Choose OK.

For example, to display in your query table only records for people in the Sales department in London and Paris, you set the criteria DEPT=Sales, And CITY=London Or CITY=Paris, as shown in the dialog box below.

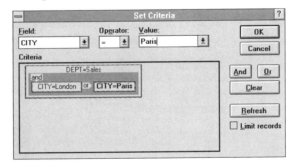

The next illustration shows the query table before and after using Query Set Criteria to set these criteria.

Before

C	A	B	C	D	E	F	G	H
1								
2		LAST	FIRST	ID	EXT	DEPT	CITY	
3		Amadeus	Jordan	3307	4260	Sales	Los Angeles	
4		Cooke	Mattie	970	1915	Sales	Birmingham	
5		Jean	Betty	9057	1899	Executive	Cambridge	
6		Alexey	Elijah	86	3500	Sales	New York	
7		Leaya	Bashe	231	2262	Sales	Paris	
8		Moriah	Joshua	734	8975	Research	Boston	
9		Shing	Victor	4481	0752	Sales	London	
10								

After

C	A	B	C	D	E	F	G	H
1								
2		LAST	FIRST	ID	EXT	DEPT	CITY	
3		Leaya	Bashe	231	2262	Sales	Paris	
4		Shing	Victor	4481	0752	Sales	London	
5								

To choose fields in a query table

You can specify what fields you want to appear in a new or existing query table. You can also specify the order in which you want the fields to appear.

1. Do one of the following:

   • To choose fields for a new query table, select the range containing the database table, choose Tools Database New Query, then choose Choose Fields.

   • To choose fields for an existing query table, select the query table, and then choose Query Choose Fields.

   The Selected fields list box displays all the fields in the query table.

2. To remove fields from the query table, select them from the Selected Fields list box and choose Clear.

3. To add a field that appears in the database table but not in the query table, choose Add. Then select the field name, select an option under Insert, and choose OK.

4. To change the order of the fields in the query table, select a field in the Selected Fields list box and click the up or down arrow until the field is in the position you want.

5. Choose OK.

? **Help**   In the Choose Fields dialog box, you can also create a computed column by choosing Formula. For example, you can create a column that calculates a 5% bonus based on the value in the SALES column. For information about computed columns and how to create them, search on "Computed columns" in Help.

To rename a query table

When you create a query table, 1-2-3 assigns a default name to the table, starting with Query 1. You can use the Query Name command to assign a more descriptive name to the table. You can use a query table name in formulas, and you can also go to and select a named query table by using Edit Go To.

1. Select the query table.

2. Choose Query Name.

    The default name of the query table appears in the Query name text box.

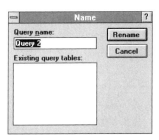

3. Enter the new name in the Query name text box.

    The name can be up to 15 characters long. You can't name a query table with the same name as another query table in the current file.

4. Choose Rename.

To sort records

You can change the order of the records in a 1-2-3 database table or query table by sorting them.

1. Select a cell in the query table, or select the range containing the database table.

    Don't include the field names in the range containing the database table.

2. Choose Query Sort to sort a query table or Range Sort to sort a database table.

    If you're sorting a query table, the "Sort by" drop-down box displays the names of the fields in the query table. If you're sorting a database table, "Sort by" is a text box where you specify a cell in the field you want to sort by.

Before sorting a database table, add a new column and use Range Fill to fill it with a sequence of numbers. This column defines the pre-sorted order of records. When you sort the table, include this column in the sort range. You can restore the original order by sorting on this column.

3. Under "Sort by," select the name of the field in the query table you want to sort by, or select a cell in the field of the database table.

    The field you sort by is your **sort key**. You can use up to 255 sort keys.

4. Select an option.

    *   Ascending sorts A – Z, and smallest number to largest number.

    *   Descending sorts Z – A, and largest number to smallest number.

    For example, you can sort in order of highest to lowest sales totals.

5. To specify additional sort keys, choose Add Key and repeat steps 3 and 4.

    For example, if the Last_Name field is sort key 1, select the First_Name field as sort key 2.

6. Choose OK.

1-2-3 sorts data according to the sort order specified during installation. The **sort order** is the order 1-2-3 uses for letters, numbers, blank cells, and symbols when you sort. The default sort order, Numbers first, sorts in the following order:

- Blank cells
- Labels beginning with a space
- Labels beginning with numbers in numerical order
- Labels beginning with letters in alphabetical order, with lowercase letters preceding uppercase letters; for example, a before A, b before B, and so forth
- Labels beginning with other characters in the Lotus Multibyte Character Set (LMBCS) code order

  Note For more information about LMBCS code order, see Appendix A.

- Values in numerical order

To change the default sort order, use the 1-2-3 Install program.

? **Help** For more information about different sort orders, search on "sort order" in Help. For information about deleting sort keys, search on "Clearing sort ranges and keys" in Help.

To refresh a query table

You can refresh a query table to reflect changes in the source database table.

1. Select the query table.
2. Choose Query Refresh Now.

? **Help** You can also use Query Refresh Now to update any settings you specified with Query Set Options. For more information, search on "Query options" in Help.

To update a database table

You can update records in the source database table to reflect changes in a query table. For example, suppose you're consolidating the London and Paris sales offices to Barcelona. First you create a query table and set criteria so that only members of the London and Paris Sales departments appear in the table. You edit all these records to make the location Barcelona. Then you update the source database table with the modified records.

1.   Choose Query Set Options.

2.   Select "Allow updates to source table."

3.   Choose OK.

4.   Edit the query table.

5.   Choose Query Update Database Table.

Note   Since you can't update more than one database table at a time, you can't update joined tables. You also can't update computed columns or aggregate fields.

Finding records

You can use Tools Database Find Records to highlight database table records that you want to modify or review. Also, when you specify multiple criteria, it's a good idea to check that the criteria select the correct records. Tools Database Find Records highlights all the records in a 1-2-3 database table that meet the criteria you specify.

To find records

1.   Select the range containing the database table.

2.   Choose Tools Database Find Records.

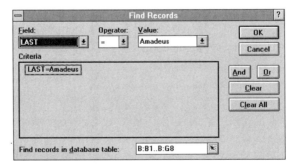

3. Specify a criterion by doing the following:
   - Select the field from the Field drop-down box.
   - Select the logical operator from the Operator drop-down box.
   - Specify the value in the Value drop-down box.

   For example, to find the records of everyone in the Sales department, the criterion is DEPT=Sales; where DEPT is the field, = is the logical operator, and Sales is the value.

4. To narrow the search, choose And and repeat step 3.

   For example, to find everyone in the Sales Department whose salary is greater than $40,000, choose And, then specify SALARY>40,000; where SALARY is the field, > is the logical operator, and 40,000 is the value.

5. To expand the search, choose Or and repeat step 3.

   For example, to find everyone in the Sales Department or in the Finance Department, choose Or, then specify DEPARTMENT=Finance; where DEPARTMENT is the field, = is the logical operator, and Finance is the value.

6. Choose OK.

If you want to distinguish the records you found from other data in the table, use Style Lines & Color to give a background color to the collection of found records.

1-2-3 highlights a collection of all records that meet your criteria. You can move around and edit the highlighted records as described below.

To	Press
Go to the next record	**CTRL+ENTER**
Go to the previous record	**CTRL+SHIFT+ENTER**
Go to the next cell in a record	**ENTER**
Go to the previous cell in a record	**SHIFT+ENTER**
Edit data in a record	**F2 (EDIT)**, make your edits, and press **ENTER** to go to the next cell
Deselect the collection of highlighted records	**ESC**, or click any cell

Appending records to a database table

The best way to add records to the bottom of a 1-2-3 database table is to use Tools Database Append. When you use this command, 1-2-3 expands the named range of the table to include the appended records. Also, you can use this command to append records to an external table.

You can also append new records to a 1-2-3 database table by entering data for each field in the row immediately below the last record in the table. If the appended records are outside of the original named range of the table, however, you must use the Range Name command to redefine the range so it includes the new records.

To append records

1. Select the range containing the records you want to append to the database table.

   Make sure to include the field names as the first row of the range. All the field names in the range you're appending must match the field names in the table to which you're appending records.

2. Choose Tools Database Append Records.

3. In the "To database table" text box, specify the table to which you're appending the records.

4. Choose OK.

1-2-3 appends the records to the bottom of the database table and expands the table range. After appending, you can sort records in the table. For more information about sorting records, see page 280.

Deleting records from a database table

You can delete records from one database table at a time. 1-2-3 deletes all records that meet the criteria you specify. Before deleting records, you may want to use Tools Database Find Records to check that the criteria select the correct records. For more information about using Tools Database Find Records, see page 282.

To delete records

1. Select the range containing the 1-2-3 database table.
2. Choose Tools Database Delete Records.
3. Specify a criterion by doing the following:
   - Select the field from the Field drop-down box.
   - Select the logical operator from the Operator drop-down box.
   - Specify the value in the Value drop-down box.

   For example, if you want to delete the records of everyone in the Sales department, the criterion is DEPT=Sales, where DEPT is the field, = is the logical operator, and Sales is the value.
4. To narrow the search, choose And and repeat step 3.
5. To expand the search, choose Or and repeat step 3.
6. Choose OK.

1-2-3 deletes the records that match the criteria you specified. If you delete the wrong records, you can restore them by immediately choosing Edit Undo.

? Related Help topics

You can use Tools Database Crosstab to create a crosstab table summarizing data from a 1-2-3 database table. For information about crosstab tables and an example, search on "Cross-tabulation" in Help.

You can query multiple database tables simultaneously. For information about joining two or more tables, search on " Joining database tables" in Help.

In a query table you can create an alias for a field name by entering the new field name in place of the original. You can also use Query Show Field As to specify an alias field name for 1-2-3 to display in place of a current field name in a query table. Using either method changes only the field name in the query table, not the field name in the database table. For more information, search on "Field name alias" in Help.

You can use Query Aggregate to perform calculations on groups of data from a query table. For example, you can calculate sales by salesperson, by month of sale, or by account. For more information, search on "Aggregate columns" in Help.

You can use Query Show SQL to display the SQL command equivalent for creating the current query table. You can copy this SQL statement to the Clipboard to use, for example, in macros. For more information, search on "SQL" in Help.

Tutorial lesson 7 gives you hands-on practice working with a 1-2-3 database. Choose Help Tutorial to start the Tutorial.

24

Working with External Databases

You can connect to a database table outside 1-2-3 and work with it the same as you work with a 1-2-3 database table. This chapter describes how to connect to an external database table, create an external table, send commands to an external database, and disconnect from an external table. Chapter 23 describes how to work with the data once you've brought it into 1-2-3.

What's an external database table?

An **external database table** is a group of related records stored in a file other than a .WK4 file, such as a dBASE IV .DBF file. An external table can be on a personal computer, a network server, a mainframe, or a CD-ROM.

Connecting to an external database table

To use 1-2-3 commands on data in an external database table, you must first connect to the table. You connect to an external database table by using Tools Database Connect to External and a DataLens driver. A **DataLens driver** is a program that 1-2-3 uses to access data in external database tables. To connect to an external database table, you must know the name of the appropriate DataLens driver and the name of the table.

> **Note** 1-2-3 includes DataLens drivers for Paradox, dBASE IV, SQL Server, Informix, and IBM Database Manager. You use the 1-2-3 Install program to install the DataLens drivers that come with 1-2-3. For information about these drivers, see *DataLens Drivers for 1-2-3*.

Depending on the DataLens driver you select and how it's configured, 1-2-3 may prompt you for a user ID and password. If so, enter the user ID and password in the appropriate text boxes and select OK. If 1-2-3 prompts you for a user ID and password but you don't need them to connect to the driver, just select OK.

To connect to an external database table

1. Choose Tools Database Connect to External.

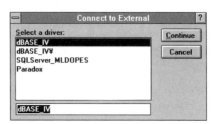

   If you know the name of the driver, the external database, and the external table, you can combine steps 2 through 4 by entering the names, separated by a space, in the text box. For example, enter DBASE_IV D:\123R4W\SAMPLE EMPLOYEE where DBASE_IV is the driver name; D:\123R4W\SAMPLE is the database name; and EMPLOYEE is the table name.

2. Specify the driver and choose Continue.

   If necessary, enter a user ID and password.

To display database names automatically, add a database record to the registration file, LOTUS.BCF. For more information, see DataLens Drivers for 1-2-3.

3. Specify the external database or directory and choose Continue.

   If 1-2-3 can locate the external databases, it displays the names in the list box. If 1-2-3 doesn't display the name of the external database you want to use, type it in the text box.

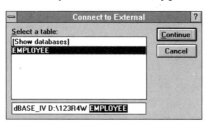

4. Specify the external database table and choose Continue.

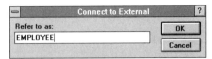

5. Accept the default range name for the table or enter a different name in the "Refer to as" text box, and choose OK.

The range name is the name you use in 1-2-3 to refer to the external table. If you change the default name, the name of the table in the database stays the same. You use the range name, for example, in queries, database @functions, and when disconnecting from the table.

By default 1-2-3 displays the name of the external table as the range name, unless you already have a range with this name in the file. If you already used the range name in the current file, the "Refer to as" text box is blank. If this happens, enter a name of up to 15 characters in the text box.

After connecting to the external table, you can use the Tools Database and Query commands to work with the external table the same way you work with a 1-2-3 database table. See Chapter 23 for information about using these commands.

? **Help**   After connecting to an external table, you can also use database @functions and macros to analyze the data. For more information, search on "Database @functions" and "Database macro commands" in Help.

Creating an external database table

You can use 1-2-3 to create a table in an external database. To create a new external table, you model it on an existing 1-2-3 database table.

> **Note**   When you create a new external table from a model table, make sure the 1-2-3 file containing the model table is active.

To create an external database table

1. Choose Tools Database Create Table.
2. Connect to the external table as described in steps 2 through 5 on page 288.
3. Specify the range that contains the model table in the Model table range text box.

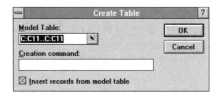

4. If your DataLens driver requires or supports a table creation command, specify one in the Creation command text box.

    A table creation command specifies additional information about the table. For example, the Paradox driver lets you use a table creation command to specify a sort order for the table. See the chapter about your driver in *DataLens Drivers for 1-2-3* for information about the creation commands you can use.

5. To copy the records from the model table, select the "Insert records from model table" check box.

6. Choose OK.

    1-2-3 creates a new table in the external database. To add records to the new table, use Tools Database Append Records. For more information, see "Appending records to a database table" on page 284.

Sending commands to an external database

When you want to perform a task specific to a particular database, you can use Tools Database Send Command. For example, you may want to encrypt an external database table or set an index in a multiple-index file. Depending on the driver you're using, you can send driver-specific commands directly to the DataLens driver or external database.

When sending a command to an external database, you must use the syntax required by the database management system that maintains the database. 1-2-3 doesn't validate your command syntax. For specific information about the commands you can send, see *DataLens Drivers for 1-2-3* or check with your database administrator.

To send a command to an external database

1. Choose Tools Database Send Command.

2. Specify a driver and choose Continue.

   If the drop-down box doesn't display the driver you want, use the Install program to install the driver.

3. Specify the directory or external database and choose Continue.

   If necessary, specify a user ID and password. If 1-2-3 doesn't display the name of the external database you want, type it in the text box.

To display database names automatically, add a database record to the registration file, LOTUS.BCF. For more information, see DataLens Drivers for 1-2-3.

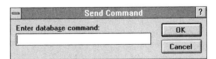

4. Enter the command.

   You can enter up to 512 characters.

5. Choose OK.

? **Help** You can also use the {SEND-SQL} macro command to send SQL commands to a database. For more information, search on "Database macro commands" in Help.

Disconnecting from an external database table

Disconnecting from an external database table ends all data exchange between 1-2-3 and the external table. After you disconnect, any queries, database @functions, or macros that refer to the table will result in ERR. 1-2-3 doesn't update these queries or @functions until you reconnect to the external table. 1-2-3 reconnects when you select a cell in a query table that queries an external table and choose Query Refresh Now.

To disconnect from an external database table

1. Choose Tools Database Disconnect.

2. Select the range name of the external database table from which you want to disconnect.

3. Choose OK.

1-2-3 disconnects from the database table you specified.

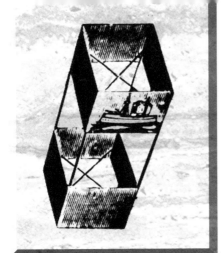

Part VII
Automating and Customizing 1-2-3

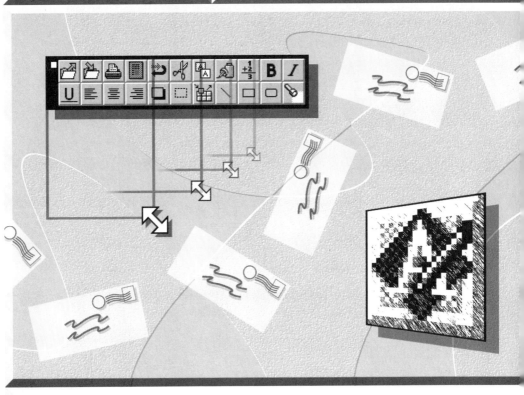

25

Customizing SmartIcons

SmartIcons provide a quick, simple way to do many 1-2-3 tasks. This chapter describes how to work with sets of SmartIcons, create customized icon sets, assign a macro to an icon, and change the appearance of an icon. For an overview of SmartIcons and a description of how to use them, see page 12.

? **Help**   For a SmartIcons reference organized by function, with a picture and description of each icon, search on "SmartIcons" in Help.

Working with sets of SmartIcons

In addition to the default sets, 1-2-3 provides several specialized sets of SmartIcons, such as sets for editing and sets for working with macros. You can select which set you want to display; hide or show the set of SmartIcons; move the set or the SmartIcons in it; and change the display size of SmartIcons.

To select which set of SmartIcons to display

To select the set you want to display, you can use the status bar or choose Tools SmartIcons. Use the status bar when you want to switch quickly between sets. Use Tools SmartIcons when you want to see a description of each icon in each set.

1.   Do one of the following:

   • Click the SmartIcons selector on the status bar and select the icon set.

Select a set from this list

Default Sheet
Editing
Formatting
Goodies
Macro Building
Printing
Sheet Auditing
WorkingTogether
Hide SmartIcons

| Automatic | | Arial MT | 12 | 03/06/93 4:59 PM | ▭ | Ready |

   • Choose Tools SmartIcons, select the icon set from the drop-down list, and choose OK.

To hide or show a set of SmartIcons

1. Do one of the following:
   - Click the SmartIcons button on the status bar and choose Hide SmartIcons or Show SmartIcons.
   - Choose View Set View Preferences; and under Show in 1-2-3, select or deselect the SmartIcons check box. Then choose OK.

To move the set of SmartIcons

1. Choose Tools SmartIcons.
2. In the Position drop-down box, select Floating, Left, Top, Right, or Bottom.
3. Choose OK.

Selecting Left, Top, Right, or Bottom displays the SmartIcons set within the 1-2-3 window in the position you specified. If you select Floating, you can drag the SmartIcons set to any position inside or outside the 1-2-3 window, and you can manipulate the set as shown below.

Click here to hide the set of SmartIcons

Drag the title bar to move the set

Drag a border to size the set

To move SmartIcons in a displayed set

You can use the mouse to rearrange the SmartIcons in a displayed set.

1. Point to the icon you want to move.
2. Hold down CTRL and drag the icon where you want it in the set.

   To move an icon to the end of the set, press CTRL and drag the icon outside the set.
3. Release the mouse button.

To size SmartIcons

You can change the display size of SmartIcons.

1. Choose Tools SmartIcons.
2. Choose Icon Size.
3. Select Medium or Large.
4. Choose OK.

Medium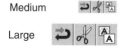

Large

Creating and modifying sets of SmartIcons

You can modify any set of SmartIcons, your own sets or the default sets. The set that 1-2-3 displays by default depends on the current selection. You can modify sets of SmartIcons by moving, adding, removing, and grouping icons. You can also customize and name your own icon sets. For example, you can create a set called SpecialSet that contains only the icons you use most frequently.

To create or modify sets of SmartIcons

1. Choose Tools SmartIcons.
2. Select the SmartIcons set you want to modify or use as the basis for a new set.

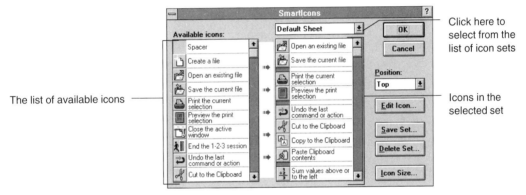

The list of available icons

Click here to select from the list of icon sets

Icons in the selected set

3. To modify the selected icon set, do one or more of the following:
   - To add an icon to the selected icon set, drag it from the Available icons list box to the position you want in the selected set and release the mouse button.
   - To remove an icon from the selected set, drag it outside the list box and release the mouse button.
   - To move an icon in the selected set, drag the icon to the position you want and release the mouse button.
   - To group icons in the selected set, move them into the order you want. Then drag a spacer icon from the Available icons list box to the position you want in the selected set and release the mouse button. Repeat this as many times as you want to separate groups of icons.

4. To save your changes as a new icon set, choose Save Set; enter a name in the Name of set text box; accept the default file name or enter a new file name in the File name text box; choose OK.

    1-2-3 saves the new set and adds it to the list of sets. 1-2-3 stores the new set in a file using the file name you specified and the extension .SMI.

5. Choose OK.

    1-2-3 also saves changes you made to any existing sets.

To delete a set of SmartIcons

1. Choose Tools SmartIcons.

2. Choose Delete Set.

3. Select the set or sets you want to delete.

4. Choose OK.

    1-2-3 deletes the selected sets and redisplays the SmartIcons dialog box.

5. Choose OK.

Customizing icons

You can assign a macro to an icon and create your own bitmap for the icon. For example, you can create a macro that enters your company name in a special style in the worksheet. Then you can create an icon with your company logo on it and assign the macro to this new icon. For information about creating a macro, see Chapter 26.

To create the bitmap for your icon, you can

- Copy the bitmap of an existing icon and edit it
- Start with a blank button and paint your own bitmap
- Copy a bitmap to the Clipboard from another application, such as Paintbrush, and paste it into a blank icon

  Note   You must use the mouse to change the appearance of an icon.

To change the appearance of an icon

1. If you plan to paste a bitmap into a blank button, copy the bitmap to the Clipboard.

2. Choose Tools SmartIcons.

3. Choose Edit Icon.

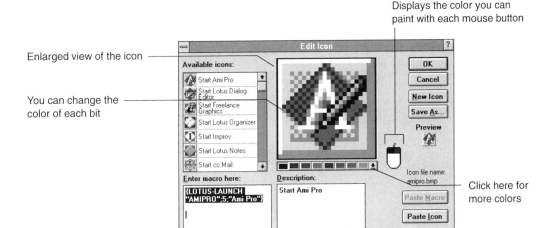

Displays the color you can paint with each mouse button

Enlarged view of the icon

You can change the color of each bit

Click here for more colors

4. To start with a blank icon, choose New Icon.

1-2-3 prompts you to enter a file name for your custom icon and, after you choose OK, displays an enlarged view of a blank icon.

5. To paste a bitmap from the Clipboard, choose Paste Icon.

6. To copy an existing icon so you can edit the bitmap, select the existing icon from the Available icons list box and choose Save As.

1-2-3 prompts you to enter a file name for your custom icon and, after you choose OK, displays an enlarged view of a copy of the existing icon.

Caution If you edit the original bitmap of a custom icon, you change the icon's appearance permanently.

7. To paint a blank icon or modify a copy of the bitmap for an existing icon, click a color in the color bar with either mouse button, and then click the bits you want to paint in the enlarged view.

1-2-3 changes the color of the bits and updates the Preview icon.

8. Choose OK.

   1-2-3 displays the new icon at the bottom of the Available icons list in the SmartIcons dialog box. You can add the new icon to any icon set, as described in "To create or modify sets of SmartIcons" on page 297.

9. Choose OK.

   1-2-3 saves your icon as a .BMP file.

To assign a macro to an icon

1. If you plan to assign an existing macro to your custom icon, copy the macro to the Clipboard.

   You can copy a macro to the Clipboard from the Transcript window or from the worksheet.

2. Choose Tools SmartIcons.

3. Choose Edit Icon.

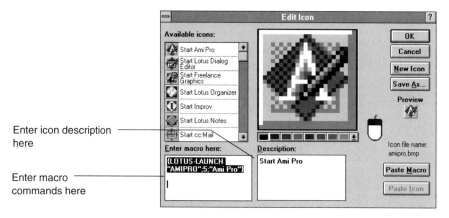

Enter icon description here

Enter macro commands here

4. From the Available icons list box, select the icon to which you want to assign the macro.

5. Assign the macro to the icon in any of the following ways:
   - Choose Paste Macro to paste a macro from the Clipboard into the "Enter macro here" text box.
   - Type the macro in the "Enter macro here" text box.
   - Enter {BRANCH *macroname*} in the "Enter macro here" text box.

     Use this method to assign a longer macro to an icon, where *macroname* is the name of a macro in a worksheet. In order for this macro to run when you click the icon, the file containing the macro must be active.

6. If you want a description to appear next to the icon in the dialog box, enter it in the Description text box.

   This description also appears in the title bar of the 1-2-3 window when you point to an icon in a displayed set and hold down the right mouse button.

7. Choose OK.

   1-2-3 displays the new icon at the bottom of the Available icons list in the SmartIcons dialog box. You can add the new icon to any icon set, as described in "To create or modify sets of SmartIcons" on page 297.

8. Choose OK.

26

Using Macros to Automate Your Work

You can create macros to do 1-2-3 tasks automatically. The 1-2-3 macro language has more than 200 macro commands. Many of these commands automate menu choices and mouse or keyboard actions. Other macro commands perform programming functions such as branching and calling subroutines. This chapter describes how to plan, create, name, run, debug and save a macro.

> **? Help**   Help provides detailed information about each macro command. To browse through macro commands by category, search on "macros" in Help, and select the topic "Macro Command Categories."

What is a macro?

A **macro** is a series of commands that automates a 1-2-3 task. You can use macros to automate repetitive tasks, streamline complex procedures, and create applications based on 1-2-3.

Suppose you often have to enter your company name and style it as shown below.

Instead of repeating this task, you can do it once and record it as a series of macro commands. Then you can create a macro from the recorded commands. Whenever you want to enter the company name, you run the macro.

The macro below, named Company, automates the task of entering and styling the company name. It was created from recorded macro commands.

Macro

Summary of how to create a macro

This section summarizes the steps for creating and running a macro. The sections that follow describe each step in detail.

1. Plan the macro.

   You can save time and prevent errors by planning what you want a macro to do and knowing all the steps needed to accomplish the task.

2. Decide where to enter the macro.

   You can enter a macro in a worksheet file with other data or in a **macro library**, a worksheet file that contains only macros.

3. Create the macro commands.

   You can record macro commands or write them yourself. You can also edit recorded macro commands and combine them with commands you write yourself.

4. Name the macro.

   You name a macro by giving it a range name.

5. Run the macro.

   You can run a macro using menu commands, keyboard shortcuts, a macro button, SmartIcons, or the macro transcript.

6. Debug the macro.

   You debug a macro if it doesn't do what you expected. **Debugging** is the process of finding and correcting errors in macro syntax and logic.

7. Document the macro.

   You document a macro so that you and others can remember the macro name and what the macro does.

8. Save the macro.

   You save a macro by saving the file that contains the macro.

Planning a macro

The first step in planning a macro is to determine what you want the macro to do. Before recording a macro, jot down all the menu commands and other mouse and keyboard actions you need to perform.

If you're writing a macro yourself, or combining recorded commands with commands you write yourself, consider creating a flow chart to map out the order and logic of the steps in the task. A flow chart can help you determine which steps to record and which to write yourself.

Deciding where to enter a macro

You can enter a macro in a worksheet file with other data or in a **macro library**, a worksheet file containing only macros.

Entering a macro with other data

If you use a macro with only one file, it's simplest to enter the macro in that file. When you enter macros, avoid writing over other data in the file. When you insert or delete rows and columns of data in the file, avoid writing over your macros. To keep your data and your macros intact, follow these guidelines:

- Put macros in a separate worksheet rather than in a worksheet containing other data. You can name the worksheet to make it easy to find.
- If you want to put macros and other data in the same worksheet, put the macros below and to the right of the data area.

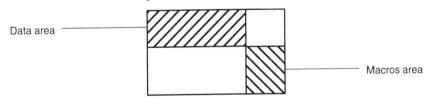

Data area

Macros area

If you put macros and other data in the same worksheet, name a cell at the beginning of the macros area with a range name such as Macros. This makes it easy to move between the macros area and the data area.

> **Caution** If you put macros and data in the same worksheet, inserting rows or columns in the data area moves the macros in the macros area. This changes addresses in the macros, and references in the macro won't work. In a macro, it's always best to refer to named ranges rather than addresses.

Entering a macro in a macro library

If you use a macro with several files, you can store the macro in a macro library. You can organize a macro library by using a separate worksheet for each group of related macros.

The macro library file must be active when you run a macro stored there. For example, suppose that the Company macro is stored in a macro library named MACROLIB.WK4. To enter the company name in a file called SALESREPS, MACROLIB must be active and SALESREPS must be the current file.

Creating macro commands

To create the commands in a macro, you can write them from scratch or use recorded commands. You can record keystrokes, menu choices, and mouse actions as a series of macro commands in the **Transcript window**.

Some macro commands have no equivalent menu choices or mouse actions. Since you can't record these commands, you must write them yourself. For example, you'll often write {*subroutine*}, {IF}, and {BRANCH} commands to direct the flow of control in a macro.

Often the most efficient way to create macro commands is to edit recorded commands and combine them with commands you write yourself. All 1-2-3 macro commands have a structure, or **syntax**. When you write a macro yourself or edit recorded commands, you must use the correct syntax, or the command won't work. This section describes the syntax and rules for creating macro commands.

Macro command syntax

The illustration below shows the syntax for a macro command with no arguments.

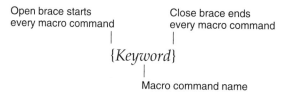

Open brace starts every macro command

Close brace ends every macro command

{*Keyword*}

Macro command name

The next illustration shows the syntax of a macro command with arguments.

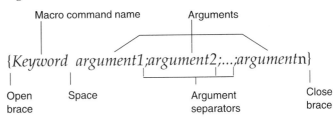

Macro command name   Arguments

{*Keyword argument1;argument2;...;argument*n}

Open   Space   Argument   Close
brace   separators   brace

The first word in a macro command is the **keyword**, the macro command name. The keyword tells 1-2-3 what action to perform.

argument1, *argument2*, and *argument*n represent required and optional arguments. You must include required arguments; you can omit optional arguments. **Arguments** supply information that 1-2-3 needs to complete the command. In the documentation, optional arguments are enclosed in [ ] (brackets).

When you use more than one argument with a command, you separate the arguments with an **argument separator**, such as ; (semicolon), the default argument separator. You leave no spaces between arguments.

1-2-3 doesn't check the syntax of a macro command until you run the macro containing the command. When you run a macro containing incorrect syntax, 1-2-3 displays a message with the name and location of the incorrect command. You can use this information to debug the macro. For more information, see "Debugging a macro" on page 322.

Arguments

Macro commands use four types of arguments: values, text, locations, and conditions.

A **value argument** is a number, a numeric formula, or the range name or address of a cell that contains a number or numeric formula. The following command uses the value argument 24 to assign a point size of 24 to cell A5.

{STYLE-FONT-SIZE 24;A5}

A **text argument** is any sequence of characters including letters, numbers, and symbols, enclosed in " " (quotation marks); a text formula; or the range name or address of a cell that contains a label or text formula.

For some macro commands that use a text argument, you can specify any text. When you enclose this text in quotation marks, 1-2-3 uses the text exactly as you specified it. For example, the following command enters HI, THERE in the current cell.

{CELL-ENTER " HI, THERE"}

For other commands that use a text argument, you must use specific text. For example, the {STYLE-ALIGN-VERTICAL} command aligns data vertically in a range. For the *alignment-style* argument, you can specify the text "TOP", "CENTER", or "BOTTOM", but no other text. The following command top-aligns data vertically in the range A5..B10.

{STYLE-ALIGN-VERTICAL " TOP" ;A5..B10}

A **location argument** is a range name or address, or any formula that evaluates to a range name or address. Usually, these locations are in the current file or in another active file. Some commands can also use a location that refers to a range in a file on disk.

The command below uses two location arguments. This command copies the contents of the range DEBTS from the BUDGET file on disk to the rows immediately below the range TARGET in the current file. It expands Target to include the copied data.

{APPENDBELOW TARGET;<<BUDGET>>DEBTS}

For location arguments, it's best to use range names rather than addresses. This ensures that the locations are correct even if you insert or delete rows, columns, or worksheets in the file.

Often you use location arguments in macro commands that redirect the flow of control, such as {BRANCH}. In these commands, 1-2-3 interprets the locations to be in the worksheet or file that contains the macro, unless you specify the name of another file. For all other macro commands, 1-2-3 interprets locations to be in the current worksheet in the current file.

To refer to another worksheet in a location argument, you must precede the address or range name with a worksheet letter or worksheet name. To refer to another file, you must precede the address or range name with a **file reference**, the name of the file enclosed in << >> (two left angle brackets and two right angle brackets).

For example:

- {BRANCH A21} redirects the flow of control to cell A21 in the worksheet containing the macro.
- {BRANCH Chicago:A21} redirects the flow of control to cell A21 in the worksheet named Chicago in the file containing the macro.
- {BRANCH <<BUDGET>>C:A21} redirects the flow of control to cell A21 in worksheet C in the file BUDGET.
- {CELL-ENTER " Hello" ;A21} enters the text Hello in cell A21 in the current worksheet in the current file.
- {CELL-ENTER " Hello" ;B:A21} enters the text Hello in cell A21 in worksheet B in the current file.
- {CELL-ENTER " Hello" ;<<BUDGET>>B:A21} enters the text Hello in cell A21 in worksheet B in the file BUDGET.

[?] **Help**   For more information about the flow-of-control macro commands, search on "Macros," select the topic "Macro Categories" and select the category "Flow-of-control."

A **condition argument** is an expression that 1-2-3 evaluates as true or false. A condition argument can be

- A logical formula using one of the logical operators $<, >, =, < =, > =, < >$, #AND#, #NOT#, and #OR#
- One of the @functions @TRUE, @FALSE, @ISERR, @ISNA, @ISNUMBER, @ISRANGE, or @ISSTRING
- Any number or numeric formula; text or text formula; an address or range name; a blank cell; or a cell containing the value NA or ERR

For example, the command below uses the logical formula VAL<100 as a condition argument. This command continuously recalculates each cell in the range PAYMENT, column by column, until the value in cell VAL falls below 100 or the number of recalculations equals 50.

{RECALCCOL PAYMENT,VAL<100,50}

The command below uses cell A1 as a condition argument. If this cell contains either a logical formula that results in true, or any other entry that 1-2-3 evaluates to true, 1-2-3 performs the commands in the same cell as the {IF} command. Otherwise, 1-2-3 skips the {BEEP} and {QUIT} commands and performs the {LET} command in the next cell down the column. This command puts the text YOU'RE CORRECT in cell A5.

```
{IF A1}{BEEP}{QUIT}
{LET A5:"YOU'RE CORRECT"}
```

Argument separators

When a macro command has two or more arguments, you use argument separators to separate each argument from the one that follows. The ; (semicolon) is always a valid argument separator. Using semicolon as your argument separator ensures that your macros are portable and will work in any country. In addition, you can choose Tools User Setup International Style and specify , (comma) or . (period) as a valid argument separator.

Rules for writing macro commands

Follow these rules when you edit recorded macro commands or write macro commands yourself.

- When you enter macro commands in a worksheet, enter them as text in consecutive cells in a column.

  You can enter more than one command in a cell, up to 512 characters. In most cases, however, it's better to enter one command per cell. This makes the macro easier to read and debug. Some commands, such as the {IF} command, must be followed by at least one more command in the same cell.

Macro commands entered one per cell

```
{SELECT A:B2}
{INSERT-SHEETS "AFTER";1}
{COLUMN-WIDTH 30}
{QUIT}
```

The same macro commands entered all in one cell

```
{SELECT A:B2}{INSERT-SHEETS "AFTER";1}{COLUMN-WIDTH 30}{QUIT}
```

- Start and end a macro command in the same cell.

Correct

{CONTENTS REPORT;INCOME;12;117}

Incorrect

{CONTENTS REPORT;
INCOME;12;117}

- Start a macro command with an { (open brace), and end it with a } (close brace).
- Type the keyword immediately after the open brace, leaving no spaces before the keyword or in the keyword.

Many macro commands have a hyphenated multi-word keyword. Don't put any spaces between the hyphenated words, and don't use underscores instead of hyphens. You can type the keyword in any combination of uppercase and lowercase letters.

- If you include arguments in the command, separate the keyword from the first argument with one space. If you include no arguments in a command, include no spaces.
- Don't include any spaces in the command, other than the space between the keyword and the first argument and spaces that are part of text enclosed in " " (quotation marks).

This command has a text argument with spaces as part of the argument

{GET-LABEL "Type your first name, please: ",FIRST}
{QUIT}

This command has no arguments; thus, no spaces

- If a command includes two or more arguments, use an argument separator to separate each argument from the one that follows.
- If you omit an optional argument between two other arguments, enter an argument separator as a placeholder.

For example, the {CONTENTS} command shown below takes four arguments. The first two arguments are required, and the last two are optional.

Both optional arguments omitted at the end of the command; no argument separators needed

{CONTENTS REPORT;INCOME}

Argument separator takes the place of the omitted optional argument; 117 is the fourth argument

{CONTENTS REPORT;INCOME;;117}

- In text arguments enclose literal text in quotation marks.

1-2-3 assumes that text not enclosed in quotation marks is a range name used as a location argument, rather than literal text.

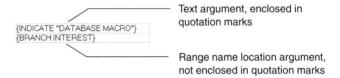

Text argument, enclosed in quotation marks

Range name location argument, not enclosed in quotation marks

To enter a quotation mark within text already enclosed in quotation marks, type *two* quotation marks. For example, to make a macro display the text Now using a " Database" Macro, use the following command:

{INDICATE "Now using a "" Database"" Macro" }

- End a macro with a blank cell or a {QUIT} command.

1-2-3 stops performing this macro at the {QUIT} command

1-2-3 stops performing this macro at a blank cell

To write a macro command yourself

1. Select a cell.

2. Type {

3. Type the macro keyword; or press **F3 (NAME)**, select a keyword from the list, and choose OK.

4. Enter the required arguments, and any optional arguments you want.

5. Type }

6. Press **ENTER**.

Recording a macro

You can create many useful macros by recording macro commands in the Transcript window and copying them into a worksheet, a macro button, or an icon. This section describes how to record a macro, edit macro commands in the Transcript window, and copy a recorded macro.

When you record a macro, each command appears on a single line in the Transcript window. Your most recent actions appear as macro commands at the bottom of the window. Commands for less recent actions appear at the top. When the transcript is full, 1-2-3 discards the commands at the top, your least recent actions.

When you quit 1-2-3, all macro commands in the transcript are lost. To save recorded macro commands, you must copy them from the Transcript window and paste them into a worksheet, a macro button, or an icon.

To clear the Transcript window

Before recording macro commands, it's a good idea to clear the Transcript window of any previous commands. This makes it easy to find the commands you want.

1. Choose Tools Macro Show Transcript.

2. Make the Transcript window active.

3. Choose Edit Clear All.

To record a macro

Macro recording is off by default. Once you turn on recording, it stays on in the current 1-2-3 session and future sessions until you turn it off.

1. Choose Tools Macro Record.

2. Perform the task you want to record.

   For example, choose commands, enter data, and move around in the worksheet, the file, or between files and other open windows.

To edit commands in the Transcript window

You can also edit recorded macro commands after you've copied them into a worksheet, a macro button, or an icon.

1. Make the Transcript window active.

2. Edit the macro commands by using the Edit commands and typing directly into the Transcript window.

You often have to edit a macro command to make it work on the current selection rather than on the particular range that 1-2-3 recorded. For example, when you widen column B to 25 characters, 1-2-3 records this action as the following macro command:

{COLUMN-WIDTH 25;B:A1}

You can edit this recorded command to make it widen the column containing the current cell. Just remove the optional location argument, B:A1, as shown below.

{COLUMN-WIDTH 25}

To copy a recorded macro

1. Choose Tools Macro Show Transcript.

2. Select the macro commands you want to copy.

3. Choose Edit Copy.

4. Do any of the following:

   • To paste the macro into a worksheet, click a cell, and choose Edit Paste.

   • To paste the macro into a button, choose Tools Macro Assign to Button, select the "Enter macro here" text box, and press **CTRL+V**.

   • To paste the macro into an icon, choose Tools SmartIcons, choose Edit Icon, and choose Paste Macro. For more information, see page 300.

If you paste a recorded macro into a worksheet, name the range that contains the macro, as described in "Naming a macro" on the next page. For information about creating a macro button, see "Working with a macro button" on the next page.

Naming a macro

1-2-3 accepts the following types of macro names:

- A **backslash name** consists of a \ (backslash) followed by a single letter; for example, \d. To run a macro with this type of name, you press CTRL+ the letter. Naming a macro \0 (zero) creates an autoexecute macro that runs automatically every time you open or retrieve the file. For more information, see "Using autoexecute macros" on page 321.

- A **multiple-character name** is an ordinary range name. This type of name is convenient for indicating what the macro does. It also makes it easy to avoid duplicating macro names because you can't use the same range name in a file more than once. If you try to run a range-name macro and two or more active files contain a macro with the same name, 1-2-3 runs the macro in the current file. You run a range-name macro with ALT+F3 (RUN) or Tools Macro Run.

Note   If you use CTRL+ *a letter* to run a macro and this combination is the same as a keyboard shortcut using CTRL+ *a letter*, the macro overrides the keyboard shortcut. For example, if you run a macro named \e by pressing CTRL+E, this macro overrides the keyboard shortcut for center-aligning the current selection, CTRL+E.

To name a macro, name the first cell of the macro using the Range Name command. You name macro subroutines, branch locations, and data used by macro arguments the same way that you name a macro. Macro names follow all the rules for range names. For more information, see "Naming ranges" on page 85.

Working with a macro button

You can draw a macro button on a worksheet and assign a macro to run when you click the button. You can store the assigned macro in the button or in a range. Storing the macro in the button is convenient for running short recorded macros or simple macros that you write yourself. Referring to a macro range name or address in the button is convenient for running longer, more complex macros that use subroutines, loops, and branches.

Note   You can also assign a macro to an icon and run the macro by clicking an icon. For more information about assigning a macro to an icon, see page 300.

To create a macro button

To run a macro with a button, you must first create the button in the worksheet where you want to run the macro.

1. Choose Tools Draw Button.

2. Move the mouse pointer where you want the macro button to appear.

3. Do one of the following:

    *   Click to create the macro button in the default size.

    *   Drag across the worksheet and release the mouse button when the macro button is the size you want.

    1-2-3 places the button on the worksheet and then opens the Assign to Button dialog box.

4. To replace the default label "Button" with a more descriptive name, enter the label in the "Button text" text box.

    It's a good idea to name the button with a name that reminds you of what the macro does.

5. Do one of the following:

    *   To assign a macro to the button now, go to step 3 of the next procedure.

    *   To assign a macro to the button later, choose OK.

You see the button in the worksheet.

**To assign a macro
to a button**

You can put a simple macro in the button, or use a button to run a macro that's in a range in the current file.

1. Select the button by SHIFT+clicking it or by using the lasso icon.

2. Choose Tools Macro Assign to Button.

3. To assign a macro to run from a range in the current file, do the following:

    • Select Range in the "Assign macro from" drop-down box.

    • Select the macro name in the Existing named ranges list box, or specify the macro address or name in the Range text box.

4. To assign a macro to run from macro commands in the button, do the following:

    • Select Button in the "Assign macro from" drop-down box.

    • Enter the macro in the "Enter macro here" text box.

    You can type the macro commands, or press CTRL+V to paste commands copied from the worksheet or from the Transcript window. For information about copying a macro from the Transcript window, see "To copy a recorded macro" on page 314.

5. To change the label on the button, enter the label in the "Button text" text box.

6. Choose OK.

The macro button with a macro assigned to it appears where you drew it on the worksheet. You can click the button to run the macro, as described on the next page.

	A	B	C	D	E	F
2	Toronto	$47	$426.00			
3	Ottawa	$36	$97.00			
4	Montreal	$52	$302.00		Saver	
5	Winnipeg	$27	$362.00			
6						

To modify the button, select it and choose Tools Macro Assign to Button again. For example, to change the button label, assign a different macro to the button, or edit the macro commands in the button.

Running a macro

When you run a macro, 1-2-3 performs the task that the macro automates. You can run a macro when the file containing the macro is active and 1-2-3 is in Ready mode. If you try to run a range-name macro and two or more active files contain a macro with the same name, 1-2-3 runs the macro in the current file.

To run an unnamed macro

1. Select the first cell of the macro.

2. Press ALT+F3 (RUN) or choose Tools Macro Run.

3. Choose OK.

To run a backslash macro

1. Press CTRL and the single-letter name simultaneously.

For example, to run a macro named \a, press CTRL+a. 1-2-3 runs the macro.

Note You can also run a backslash macro with ALT+F3 (RUN). See "To run a range-name macro" below.

To run a range-name macro

1. Move the cell pointer to the worksheet area that you want the macro to act on.

2. Press **ALT+F3 (RUN)** or choose Tools Macro Run.

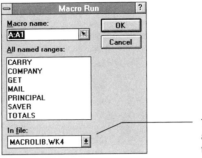

To see range names in another active file, select the file from this drop-down list

3. Select the macro name from the All named ranges list box or enter the macro name or address in the Macro name text box.

4. Choose OK.

To run a macro with a button

1. Make sure the worksheet containing the button is the current worksheet.

2. If necessary, move the cell pointer to the worksheet area that you want the macro to act on.

3. Click the button.

To run macro commands from the Transcript window

You can run macro commands directly from the Transcript window. Playing back macro commands from the Transcript window is useful when you want to repeat something you just did, but don't want to save the macro commands. It's also a way to test macro commands before copying them into a worksheet.

1. Move the cell pointer to the worksheet area that you want the macro to act on.

2. Choose Tools Macro Show Transcript.

3. Select the block of macro commands that you want to run.

4. Choose Transcript Playback.

Stopping a macro

Most macros run for a few seconds and then end. Large macro applications, however, can run much longer. While a macro is running, you can't do anything else in 1-2-3. For this reason, you may sometimes want to stop a macro while it's running.

> **Note**   You can't stop a macro that contains a {BREAKOFF} command. The {BREAKOFF} command prevents users from stopping a macro; the {BREAKON} command restores the ability to stop a macro. These commands are useful when you're creating an interactive macro for other users and don't want them to be able to stop the macro.

To stop a macro

1. Press CTRL+BREAK while the macro is running.

    Unless the macro contains a {BREAKOFF} command, 1-2-3 stops the macro after it completes the current command, and displays a message.

2. Press ESC or choose OK to clear the message and return to Ready mode.

After you stop the macro, you can resume working with 1-2-3.

Recalculating during a macro

Whether or not 1-2-3 recalculates data while a macro is running depends on the recalculation setting in the most recently-opened file.

- When you run a macro with recalculation set to Manual, 1-2-3 recalculates formulas only when it encounters a {CALC}, {RECALC}, or {RECALCCOL} command in the macro; or when you press F9 (CALC) during an interactive macro.

- When you run a macro with recalculation set to Automatic, 1-2-3 recalculates formulas automatically whenever a command in the macro changes data in the file.

In general, macros run faster with recalculation set to Manual. When recalculation is set to Manual, however, a macro may produce inaccurate results if the macro changes data and then uses the result of a formula that depends on that data. You can avoid inaccurate results by putting a {CALC}, {RECALC}, or {RECALCCOL} command in the macro at any point where data is likely to change.

The following macro commands change data but don't cause an automatic recalculation, even with recalculation set to Automatic: {CONTENTS}, {DEFINE}, {FILESIZE}, {FOR}, {GET}, {GET-FORMULA}, {GET-LABEL}, {GET-NUMBER}, {GET-RANGE}, {GETPOS}, {LET}, {LOOK}, {PUT}, {READ}, {READLN}, {SET}.

Instead of recalculating data immediately after performing one of these commands, 1-2-3 defers recalculation until any of the following happens:

- You press ENTER or a pointer-movement key
- A macro command equivalent to ENTER or a pointer-movement key occurs in the macro
- A {CALC}, {RECALC}, or {RECALCCOL} occurs in the macro

To set recalculation

1. Choose Tools User Setup.
2. Choose Recalculation.
3. Under Recalculation, select Automatic or Manual.
4. Choose OK.
5. Choose OK again to close the User Setup dialog box.

Using autoexecute macros

An **autoexecute macro** is a macro that runs automatically when you open the worksheet file that contains the macro. You create an autoexecute macro by naming it \0 (backslash zero). 1-2-3 runs autoexecute macros when the "Run autoexecute macros" check box in the User Setup dialog box is checked.

The result of certain macros depends on the autoexecute setting. For example, suppose a macro contains a {FILE-OPEN} command that opens a file containing an autoexecute macro.

- If "Run autoexecute macros" is checked, 1-2-3 opens the file and runs the autoexecute macro, but doesn't resume running the original macro.
- If "Run autoexecute macros" isn't checked, 1-2-3 opens the file and continues running the original macro, but doesn't run the autoexecute macro.

Debugging a macro

Sometimes, when you first run a macro, it doesn't do what you expect, or 1-2-3 displays a message. When a macro doesn't run correctly, you have to debug it.

You can correct obvious errors of spelling or typing by editing the macro commands just as you edit any cell entry. When a macro results in a message, it's usually because of incorrect syntax. The message tells you the name and location of the incorrect command.

When debugging a macro, check for the following common errors:

- Spelling errors, including incorrect spelling of keywords, such as {WINDOWOFF} instead of {WINDOWSOFF}; or misspellings of range names, such as Proft instead of Profit

- Omitting a hyphen in a hyphenated macro keyword, or putting in an extra hyphen in a hyphenated keyword

- Using an underscore instead of a hyphen in a macro keyword

- Missing braces around a command

- Enclosing a command in parentheses or square brackets instead of braces

- Spaces where there shouldn't be any, such as between the { (open brace) and the keyword in a macro command; between arguments; in an @function within a command; in a range name; or before or after a hyphen in a hyphenated keyword

- Missing required arguments

- Missing or misplaced argument separators, when you intentionally omitted an optional argument between two other arguments

- Using an invalid argument separator

- Arguments of the wrong type; for example, a text argument where 1-2-3 expects a number

- Incorrect cell or range references; for example, a reference to a nonexistent range or to a range name that's no longer associated with a range

- Range names or addresses without worksheet letters or file references, when you need these to specify a location argument

- Macro names or subroutine names that duplicate macro keywords, such as Quit, Return, or Query

- Missing quotation marks around text arguments that must be enclosed in quotation marks; for example, {EDIT-GOTO Rates} instead of {EDIT-GOTO "Rates"}
- Omitting a {CALC} command after a macro command that changes data; this can cause formulas to have unreliable results
- A blank cell or a cell containing a value, which ends the macro before you meant it to end

To use Step mode and Trace

When you can't find any obvious errors of typing, spelling, or syntax, you can debug the macro using Step mode and Trace. These are debugging tools that are most effective when you use them together to examine a macro as it runs.

Using Step mode, you can run a macro one command at a time. Trace opens the Macro Trace window which displays the macro command that 1-2-3 is about to perform. As you run the macro step by step, if there's an error, the Macro Trace window shows the command that caused the error.

1. Move the cell pointer to the first cell of the macro you want to debug.

2. Choose Tools Macro Single Step or press **ALT+F2 (STEP)**.

   1-2-3 displays the Step indicator in the status bar.

3. Choose Tools Macro Trace.

   1-2-3 displays the Macro Trace window, shown below.

The address of the current macro command

The current macro command

4. Run the macro.

   For more information about running a macro, see page 318.

5. Press any key to execute one command at a time until you find the command that caused the error.

   The Macro Trace window shows you the current location and the macro command that 1-2-3 is currently performing.

When you find the error, end the macro by pressing **CTRL+BREAK** and then **ESC** or **ENTER**. Step mode and Trace are still on, and 1-2-3 still displays the Step indicator and the Macro Trace window. You don't need to turn Step or Trace off before editing the macro to correct it.

Edit the command where the error occurred. After you edit the macro, run through it again step by step to check that there are no other problems.

When you finish debugging and editing the macro, press **ALT+F2** (**STEP**) or choose Tools Macro Single Step to turn Step mode off. To close the Macro Trace window, choose Tools Macro Trace again.

Documenting a macro

After a macro runs correctly, it's a good idea to document it. Documenting a macro is helpful when you or someone else is revising the macro, or when you're trying to remember what it does long after you last used it. The illustration below shows a fully documented macro.

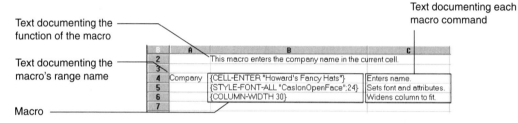

Text documenting each macro command

Text documenting the function of the macro

Text documenting the macro's range name

Macro

When entering a backslash name, type a label-prefix character (', ", or ^) before entering the name so 1-2-3 won't interpret the backslash as the repeating text label-prefix character.

Document the macro name by entering a label in the cell to the immediate left of the macro's first cell. If you use a multiple-character label, choose one that describes the macro's function. You can also document the function of the macro by typing a brief description in the rows above the macro. To document macro commands or subroutines, type a description in the cells to the immediate right of the commands.

Saving a macro

You save a macro the same way you save any other worksheet data: save the file containing the macro. You can save a file by choosing File Save or File Save As. For more information, see "Saving a file" on page 56.

Learning about each macro

Help provides detailed information about each of the more than 200 macro commands. The *User's Guide* doesn't list individual macro commands.

To find information about a macro

1. In an empty cell, type {

2. Press **F3 (NAME)**.

    The Macro Keywords dialog box appears, containing an alphabetical list of all macro keywords.

3. Find the macro you want either by typing in the list box or scrolling through the list.

4. Select the macro you want to learn about and press **F1 (HELP)**.

1-2-3 displays a Help topic with detailed information about the macro including syntax, arguments, notes, and examples. To print the Help topic, choose File Print Topic in the Help window.

You can also search on individual macro commands in Macro Help. To open Macro Help, choose Help Contents, select "Macros," then select "Individual Macro Commands."

? Related Help topics

You can use the Lotus Dialog Editor to create and edit custom dialog boxes, and you can use the {DIALOG} macro to display these dialog boxes in 1-2-3. For more information, open the Dialog Editor application and choose Help Contents.

Info components contain information about the current 1-2-3 session. Each info component contains the current value of a setting that controls the appearance or behavior of 1-2-3. When you omit an optional argument in a macro command, 1-2-3 often uses the current value of an info component in place of the omitted argument. For a description of every info component, search on "Info components" in Help.

27

Using 1-2-3 with Other Applications

You can transfer data between 1-2-3 and other Windows applications by sending mail, creating DDE and OLE links, and performing OLE embedding. This chapter describes how you can use 1-2-3 to work with other Lotus and Windows applications.

Using mail

Mail is an easy way to send data for use in 1-2-3 and other applications. You can use File Send Mail to send a range, chart, drawn object, or an entire file as an electronic mail message. To do this, you need Lotus Notes Release 2.1 for Windows or later or Lotus cc:Mail™ Release 1.11 for Windows or later.

You can also use File Send Mail with other mail applications that use the Vendor-Independent Messaging Interface (VIM®), and with Microsoft Mail running under Windows for Workgroups Version 3.1.

If you use Lotus Notes or cc:Mail and the mail application is open, 1-2-3 notifies you when you get new mail by beeping and displaying an envelope in the status bar. Click the envelope to go to your mail application.

To send mail from within 1-2-3

1. Choose File Send Mail.

2. Choose OK.

A dialog box for sending mail from your mail application appears. After you use the dialog box to send a mail message, you return to 1-2-3.

> **Note** If you're using Lotus Notes or cc:Mail, 1-2-3 opens your mail application if it's not already open.

To attach a file to a mail message

1. Make the file you want to attach the current file.

2. Choose File Send Mail.

   The dialog box that appears depends on whether you changed the file since you last saved it or never saved it.

If the file is unmodified:	If the file is modified or unsaved:

3. Select the Attach or Save and attach check box.

4. Choose OK.

If you haven't modified the file, the dialog box from your mail application appears. If you have modified the file, 1-2-3 automatically saves it, and then the dialog box from your mail application appears. If you never saved the file, the File Save As dialog box appears so you can name the file; then the dialog box from your mail application appears.

To insert a selection in a mail message

1. Select the range, chart, or drawn object you want to include in the mail message.

2. Choose File Send Mail.

   Depending on what you selected to send, 1-2-3 displays a dialog box like the one below.

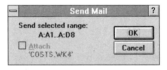

3. Choose OK.

A dialog box for sending mail from your mail application appears. After you use the dialog box to send a mail message, you return to 1-2-3.

Linking 1-2-3 with other applications

In the Microsoft Windows environment, you can share information across applications using links based on Dynamic Data Exchange (DDE) and Object Linking and Embedding (OLE). A **link** is a dynamic connection between a file in one Windows application and a file in another Windows application. Depending on the type of link, your linked data looks like ordinary worksheet data, or like a drawn object.

Using links to share data between applications is useful when you expect the data to change. For example, if you keep financial information in a 1-2-3 worksheet and use the same information in an Ami Pro® for Windows document, you can keep the data in the document up-to-date by linking it to the worksheet.

Every link involves a server and a client. The **server** contains the original data; the **client** uses that data. For example, when you create a link from a 1-2-3 worksheet to an Ami Pro document, 1-2-3 is the server because it provides data to Ami Pro. Ami Pro is the client because it uses the data from 1-2-3.

The server and client files can be any files created in Windows applications that support DDE or OLE, except the Untitled file in some applications. 1-2-3 supports OLE and DDE as both a client and a server.

A server can provide data to several clients, and a client can get data from several servers. In addition, a 1-2-3 file can be both a server and a client simultaneously.

> **Note**   You can't create a DDE or OLE link between two 1-2-3 worksheets or files. You use formulas to link worksheets. For more information, see "Referring to other files in formulas" on page 98.

Links can be automatic or manual. An **automatic link** updates the client application automatically when you change the data in the server application. A **manual link** updates only when you choose Edit Links Update.

Creating links

1-2-3 provides several ways to create links. You choose a method based on how much you want to control the link process. You can copy and paste the link from a server application, or you can create the link from within 1-2-3. When you paste a link, you can let 1-2-3 choose the link format, or you can choose a format yourself.

[?] **Help**   You can also use macros or the @DDELINK @function to create links. For information about using macros to create links, search on "Macros" in Help, select the topic "Macro Command Categories" and select "DDE and OLE." For more information about @DDELINK, search on "Information @functions."

To link to another application from a 1-2-3 file

When you link to another application from 1-2-3, the other application is the server, and 1-2-3 is the client. The simplest way to create a link is to copy and paste it, using Edit Copy and Edit Paste Link. In this case, 1-2-3 selects an appropriate format for the link. If you want more control over the appearance of the link, you can use Edit Paste Special and select the format yourself.

[?] **Help**   You can also use Edit Links Create to create the link without using the Clipboard and without leaving 1-2-3. For more information, search on "links" in Help and select the topic "Edit Links Create."

To let 1-2-3 choose the link format

1. Start the application and open the file that contains the original data.

   For example, to link to an Ami Pro document from a 1-2-3 worksheet, start Ami Pro and open or create the document that contains the data. The document must be named; it can't be Untitled.

2. Select the data you want to include in the 1-2-3 file.

   For example, in the Ami Pro document, select the text you want to include.

3. Choose Edit Copy to copy the data to the Clipboard.

   Leave the application open. If you want, you can minimize the application's window to an icon.

4. Start or return to 1-2-3 and open the file where you want the data.

5. Select the location in the worksheet where you want the data to appear.

If you're pasting text or cell data, select a range or the top left cell of a range. If you're pasting a chart, drawn object, bitmap, or picture, select a range or a drawn object.

Caution 1-2-3 writes over any existing data in the range if you paste text or cell data.

 6. Choose Edit Paste Link.

1-2-3 selects an appropriate format and creates the link.

To select the link format yourself

1. Repeat steps 1 through 5 of "To let 1-2-3 choose the link format" above.

2. Choose Edit Paste Special.

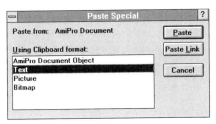

The list box displays the formats that are shared between the server application and 1-2-3, the client.

3. In the "Using Clipboard format" list box, select a format.

The following are examples of common formats:

- **Picture** (sometimes referred to as Windows Metafile) scales well.
- **Bitmap or DIB** provide better representations of a graphic than Picture, but don't scale well.
- **Text** maintains characters but not attributes.

4. Choose Paste Link.

The data from the server application appears in the 1-2-3 worksheet. Because you selected Paste Link, the data you pasted is linked to the data in the server application. If the linked data in the server application changes, the data in your 1-2-3 worksheet updates.

To link to a 1-2-3 file from another application

When you link to 1-2-3 from another application, 1-2-3 is the server and the other application is the client.

1. Make the 1-2-3 file that contains the original data the current file.

   For example, to link to a 1-2-3 worksheet from a Freelance Graphics® presentation, start 1-2-3 and open or create a file that contains the data. The file must be a named file; it can't be Untitled.

2. Select the range, chart, or drawn object you want to use in the other application.

3. Choose Edit Copy.

   Leave 1-2-3 open. If you want, you can minimize the 1-2-3 window to an icon.

4. Start the other application and open the file you want to contain the data.

5. If necessary, indicate the position where you want the data to appear.

6. Paste the link.

   The command is usually Edit Paste Link or Edit Paste Special, but is different depending on the application.

The data from 1-2-3 appears in the client file.

Getting information about links

You can see information about all client links in the current 1-2-3 file without having to switch to other applications. This is useful when you have several links and you want to review them.

To get information about DDE or OLE links

1. Choose Edit Links.

2. Select DDE/OLE Links from the Link type drop-down box.

3. Select a link from the list of link names.

The illustration below shows an example of the Links dialog box when a link from Ami Pro to 1-2-3 is selected.

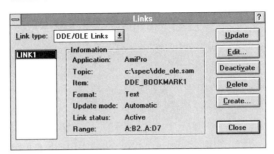

- **Application** is usually the name of the application that contains the original data. For DDE, this is the application name and path. For OLE, this is the object type created by the application.

- **Topic** is usually the drive, directory, and name for the file that contains the original data.

- **Item** is the location or name of the original data, such as a spreadsheet range or a bookmark.

- **Format** is the data format for the link.

- **Update mode** indicates whether the link is set to update automatically or manually. To update a manual link, choose Update.

- **Link status** indicates whether the link is active or inactive. An active link either updates automatically or is ready to be updated manually, depending on the current update mode. An inactive link is not up-to-date. You can choose Update to reactivate the link.

- **Range** is the range of cells that contains the linked data.

4. Choose Close.

To get information about DDE links

When you create a DDE link, 1-2-3 places the @function @DDELINK in the top left corner of the link's destination range. You can look at this @function for information about the link. The illustration below shows a DDE link to Ami Pro in a 1-2-3 file.

1-2-3 displays @DDELINK in the edit line ...

... when you select the top left cell of the link

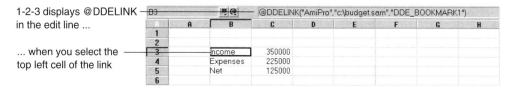

The arguments for @DDELINK contain information about the link, as shown below.

@DDELINK("AmiPro","c:\budget.sam","DDE_BOOKMARK1")

- *app* is the DDE server application name
- *topic* is the file name, including path of the DDE server
- *item* is the DDE data item to link to

? Help   For more information about @DDELINK, search on "Information @functions" in Help.

Modifying links

You can change the set-up of a link without leaving 1-2-3. This is useful, for example, if you want to change the link format. You can also update, delete, and deactivate links.

To edit a link

You can also edit a link by editing its @DDELINK @function.

1. Choose Edit Links.
2. Select DDE/OLE links from the Link type drop-down box.
3. Select the link from the list.
4. Choose Edit.

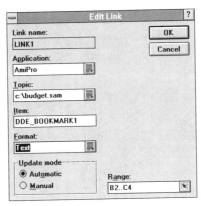

5. Change the application, topic, item, and format as necessary.

6. Under Update mode, select an option.

- Automatic updates the link automatically when the link is active.

- Manual updates the link only when you choose Update in the Edit Links dialog box.

7. To change the range, in the range text box, specify the range where you want to place the link data.

8. Choose OK to edit the link and return to the Links dialog box.

9. Choose Close to return to the file.

To update, delete, or deactivate a link

1. Choose Edit Links.

2. Select DDE/OLE links from the Link type drop-down box.

3. Select the link from the list.

4. Do one of the following:

- To get a new copy of the data from the server application, choose Update.

- To delete the link permanently from the file, choose Delete.

  1-2-3 deletes the link and stops updating the linked data. Changes to source data no longer appear in the 1-2-3 file, and you can't update the link.

- To stop updating the link temporarily, choose Deactivate.

  1-2-3 stops updating the linked data, but doesn't delete the link. Changes in the source data don't appear in the 1-2-3 file until you update the link. You can choose Update when you want to make the link active again.

You can also delete a link by deleting its @DDELINK @function.

5. Choose Close.

? Help For detailed information on using macros with links, search on "Link macros" in Help.

Embedding objects

Without exiting 1-2-3, you can create text or a picture in another Windows application and embed that data as an object in the current 1-2-3 file. When you embed an object from another application into a 1-2-3 file, the object and its data are stored in the .WK4 file, but you use the other application to create and edit the object.

Suppose, for example, that you want to create a graphic and add it to your worksheet. You can launch Freelance Graphics from within 1-2-3, create the graphic, then embed it in your worksheet. You can also copy existing information from another application to embed in your worksheet.

To embed a new object

1. Make the 1-2-3 file into which you want to embed new data the current file and select where you want the embedded object to appear.

   You can select a cell or a drawn object.

 2. Choose Edit Insert Object.

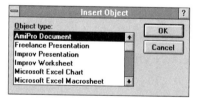

   The Object type list box displays all available applications that support OLE and the types of objects the applications create.

3. In the Object type list box, select the type of object you want to create.

   For example, to create a Freelance Graphics picture, select Freelance Presentation.

4. Choose OK.

   1-2-3 opens the application or makes it active if it's already open.

5. Create the object in the application you opened.

6. Choose File Update in the application to save the object.

7. Choose File Exit or File Exit & Return to exit the application and return to 1-2-3.

The data appears as an embedded object in the 1-2-3 file. You can double-click the object to restart the other application and edit the original data.

To embed an existing object

1. Select the object and copy it to the Clipboard.

2. Make the 1-2-3 file into which you want to embed the object the current file.

3. Select the location in the worksheet where you want the data to appear.

   You can select a range, chart, or drawn object. 1-2-3 places the embedded object slightly to the right and below the range or drawn object you select.

4. Choose Edit Paste Special.

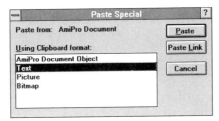

   The list box displays the formats that are shared between the server application and 1-2-3.

5. Select the object format from the "Using Clipboard format" list box.

6. Choose Paste.

The data appears as an embedded object in the 1-2-3 file. You can double-click the object to restart the other application and edit the original data.

Part VIII
Appendixes

A

Using the Lotus Multibyte Character Set (LMBCS)

1-2-3 for Windows uses the American National Standards Institute (ANSI) character set to display and print characters, and the Lotus Multibyte Character Set (LMBCS) to store characters. This appendix describes how to use LMBCS codes to enter characters that aren't on your keyboard. The tables in this appendix list all the LMBCS codes you can use.

Entering LMBCS characters

You can enter any LMBCS character by using the @CHAR @function or an **extended compose sequence**, a series of keystrokes. You can also enter some LMBCS characters by using a **compose sequence**, another series of keystrokes. The tables in this appendix list a compose sequence for all characters that have a compose sequence.

LMBCS codes are divided into two different groups, Group 0 and Group 1. In this appendix, there is a separate table for each group.

To enter a character by using @CHAR

1. Enter @CHAR in your worksheet.

   You can use the @Function menu, or you can type it.

2. Specify, as the @function argument, the LMBCS code number for the character you want to enter.

   For example, the LMBCS code for the section symbol (§) is 277. To enter §, enter @CHAR(277) in your worksheet.

 3. Confirm the entry by clicking the Confirm button or by pressing ENTER or ↑, ↓, →, ←.

To enter a character by using extended compose

The keystrokes you use for extended compose depend on whether the character is in Group 0 or Group 1. For Group 0, you use a 0 and the LMBCS code; for Group 1, you use a 1 and the key code.

1. Press **ALT+F1** (**COMPOSE**) twice.

2. Press 0 or 1 according to which group the LMBCS character is in.

3. Press - (hyphen).

4. Do one of the following:

    - If the character is in Group 0, type the LMBCS code listed in the first column of the LMBCS tables. If the LMBCS code has only two digits, precede it with a 0 (zero).

      For example, the ! (exclamation point) is in Group 0 and has a LMBCS code of 33. To enter it, press **ALT+F1** (**COMPOSE**) twice and type 0-033.

    - If the character is in Group 1, type the three-digit key code listed in the second column of the LMBCS tables.

      For example, the § (section symbol) is in Group 1 and has a key code of 021. To enter it, press **ALT+F1** (**COMPOSE**) twice and type 1-021.

 5. Confirm the entry by clicking the Confirm button or by pressing **ENTER** or ↑, ↓, →, ←.

Note   If Windows can't display a LMBCS character, a fallback character appears. Windows supports the ANSI character set. To enter ANSI codes in 1-2-3, press **ALT+** a number from the number keypad. See your Windows documentation for information about what numbers to use and what characters Windows can display.

To enter a character by using a compose sequence

1. Press **ALT+F1** (**COMPOSE**) and type the characters listed in the second column of the LMBCS tables.

    For example, to enter the character £, press **ALT+F1** (**COMPOSE**) and type L=.

 2. Confirm the entry by clicking the Confirm button or by pressing **ENTER** or ↑, ↓, →, ←.

Note   In the LMBCS tables, if a compose sequence is in bold, you must type the characters in the order they appear in the table. All other compose sequences are not order-sensitive.

LMBCS tables

The tables that follow list the LMBCS codes for 1-2-3 and the characters they produce.

LMBCS codes 32 through 255 comprise Group 0. These characters represent Code Page 850 characters 32 to 255. The first table lists these LMBCS codes.

LMBCS codes 256 through 511 comprise Group 1. These codes produce characters previously available in the Lotus International Character Set (LICS), as well as other characters available in the IBM code page supported by the country driver. The second table lists the first 127 of these codes; the remaining Group 1 LMBCS codes duplicate Group 0 codes.

LMBCS codes 512 and above comprise other groups of characters that 1-2-3 can store in a file as LMBCS codes, but can't display or print.

Group 0

This section describes the Group 0 LMBCS characters.

Note   Codes 1 through 31 aren't LMBCS codes. Using @CHAR with the numbers 1 through 31 produces the characters for LMBCS codes 257 through 287, listed in the Group 1 table.

LMBCS code	Compose sequence	Description	Character
32		Space	Space
33		Exclamation point	!
34		Double quotes	"
35	+ +	Pound sign	#
36		Dollar sign	$
37		Percent	%
38		Ampersand	&
39		Close single quote	'
40		Open parenthesis	(
41		Close parenthesis	)
42		Asterisk	*
43		Plus sign	+
44		Comma	,
45		Minus sign	−
46		Period	.
47		Slash	/

Continued

LMBCS code	Compose sequence	Description	Character
48		Zero	0
49		One	1
50		Two	2
51		Three	3
52		Four	4
53		Five	5
54		Six	6
55		Seven	7
56		Eight	8
57		Nine	9
58		Colon	:
59		Semicolon	;
60		Less than	<
61		Equal sign	=
62		Greater than	>
63		Question mark	?
64	a a or A A	At sign	@
65		A, uppercase	A
66		B, uppercase	B
67		C, uppercase	C
68		D, uppercase	D
69		E, uppercase	E
70		F, uppercase	F
71		G, uppercase	G
72		H, uppercase	H
73		I, uppercase	I
74		J, uppercase	J
75		K, uppercase	K
76		L, uppercase	L
77		M, uppercase	M
78		N, uppercase	N
79		O, uppercase	O
80		P, uppercase	P
81		Q, uppercase	Q
82		R, uppercase	R
83		S, uppercase	S
84		T, uppercase	T
85		U, uppercase	U
86		V, uppercase	V

Continued

LMBCS code	Compose sequence	Description	Character
87		W, uppercase	W
88		X, uppercase	X
89		Y, uppercase	Y
90		Z, uppercase	Z
91	((	Open bracket	[
92	/ /	Backslash	\
93	))	Close bracket	]
94	v v	Caret	^
95		Underscore	_
96		Open single quote	'
97		a, lowercase	a
98		b, lowercase	b
99		c, lowercase	c
100		d, lowercase	d
101		e, lowercase	e
102		f, lowercase	f
103		g, lowercase	g
104		h, lowercase	h
105		i, lowercase	i
106		j, lowercase	j
107		k, lowercase	k
108		l, lowercase	l
109		m, lowercase	m
110		n, lowercase	n
111		o, lowercase	o
112		p, lowercase	p
113		q, lowercase	q
114		r, lowercase	r
115		s, lowercase	s
116		t, lowercase	t
117		u, lowercase	u
118		v, lowercase	v
119		w, lowercase	w
120		x, lowercase	x
121		y, lowercase	y
122		z, lowercase	z
123	(-	Open brace	{
124	^ /	Bar	|
125	) -	Close brace	}

Continued

LMBCS code	Compose sequence	Description	Character
126	- -	Tilde	~
127		Delete	⌂
128	C ,	C cedilla, uppercase	Ç
129	u "	u umlaut, lowercase	ü
130	e '	e acute, lowercase	é
131	a ^	a circumflex, lowercase	â
132	a "	a umlaut, lowercase	ä
133	a `	a grave, lowercase	à
134	a *	a ring, lowercase	å
135	c ,	c cedilla, lowercase	ç
136	e ^	e circumflex, lowercase	ê
137	e "	e umlaut, lowercase	ë
138	e `	e grave, lowercase	è
139	i "	i umlaut, lowercase	ï
140	i ^	i circumflex, lowercase	î
141	i `	i grave, lowercase	ì
142	A "	A umlaut, uppercase	Ä
143	A *	A ring, uppercase	Å
144	E '	E acute, uppercase	É
145	**a e**	ae diphthong, lowercase	æ
146	**A E**	AE diphthong, uppercase	Æ
147	o ^	o circumflex, lowercase	ô
148	o "	o umlaut, lowercase	ö
149	o `	o grave, lowercase	ò
150	u ^	u circumflex, lowercase	û
151	u `	u grave, lowercase	ù
152	y "	y umlaut, lowercase	ÿ
153	O "	O umlaut, uppercase	Ö
154	U "	U umlaut, uppercase	Ü
155	o /	o slash, lowercase	ø
156	**L = l = L– or l–**	British pound sterling symbol	£
157	O /	O slash, uppercase	Ø
158	x x or X X	Multiplication sign	×
159	f f	Guilder	ƒ
160	a '	a acute, lowercase	á
161	i '	i acute, lowercase	í
162	o '	o acute, lowercase	ó
163	u '	u acute, lowercase	ú
164	n ~	n tilde, lowercase	ñ

Continued

LMBCS code	Compose sequence	Description	Character
165	N ~	N tilde, uppercase	Ñ
166	a _ or A _	Feminine ordinal indicator	ª
167	O _ or o _	Masculine ordinal indicator	º
168	? ?	Question mark, inverted	¿
169	RO ro R0 or r0	Registered trademark symbol	®
170	-]	End of line symbol/Logical NOT	¬
171	**1 2**	One half	$^1/_2$
172	**1 4**	One quarter	$^1/_4$
173	! !	Exclamation point, inverted	¡
174	< <	Left angle quotes	«
175	> >	Right angle quotes	»
176		Solid fill character, light	
177		Solid fill character, medium	▓
178		Solid fill character, heavy	█
179		Center vertical box bar	│
180		Right box side	┤
181	**A '**	A acute, uppercase	Á
182	**A ^**	A circumflex, uppercase	Â
183	**A '**	A grave, uppercase	À
184	CO co C0 or c0	Copyright symbol	©
185		Right box side, double	╡
186		Center vertical box bar, double	║
187		Top right box corner, double	╗
188		Bottom right box corner, double	╝
189	c | c / C | or c /	Cent sign	¢
190	Y = y = Y - or y -	Yen sign	¥
191		Top right box corner	┐
192		Bottom left box corner	└
193		Bottom box side	┴
194		Top box side	┬
195		Left box side	├
196		Center horizontal box bar	─
197		Center box intersection	┼
198	a ~	a tilde, lowercase	ã
199	A ~	A tilde, uppercase	Ã

Continued

LMBCS code	Compose sequence	Description	Character
200		Bottom left box corner, double	╚
201		Top left box corner, double	╔
202		Bottom box side, double	╩
203		Top box side, double	╦
204		Left box side, double	╠
205		Center horizontal box bar, double	═
206		Center box intersection, double	╬
207	XO xo X0 or x0	International currency sign	¤
208	d -	Icelandic eth, lowercase	ð
209	D -	Icelandic eth, uppercase	Ð
210	E ^	E circumflex, uppercase	Ê
211	E "	E umlaut, uppercase	Ë
212	E '	E grave, uppercase	È
213	i <space>	i without dot (lowercase)	ı
214	I '	I acute, uppercase	Í
215	I ^	I circumflex, uppercase	Î
216	I "	I umlaut, uppercase	Ï
217		Bottom right box corner	┘
218		Top left box corner	┌
219		Solid fill character	█
220		Solid fill character, lower half	▄
221	/ <space>	Vertical line, broken	¦
222	I '	I grave, uppercase	Ì
223		Solid fill character, upper half	▀
224	O '	O acute, uppercase	Ó
225	s s	German sharp (lowercase)	ß
226	O ^	O circumflex, uppercase	Ô
227	O '	O grave, uppercase	Ò
228	o ~	o tilde, lowercase	õ
229	O ~	O tilde, uppercase	Õ
230	/ u	Greek mu, lowercase	μ
231	p -	Icelandic thorn, lowercase	þ
232	P -	Icelandic thorn, uppercase	Þ
233	U '	U acute, uppercase	Ú
234	U ^	U circumflex, uppercase	Û
235	U '	U grave, uppercase	Ù

Continued

LMBCS code	Compose sequence	Description	Character
236	y '	y acute, lowercase	́y
237	Y '	Y acute, uppercase	́Y
238	^ –	Overline character	–
239		Acute accent	´
240	- =	Hyphenation symbol	-
241	+ –	Plus or minus sign	±
242	- - or = =	Double underscore	=
243	**3 4**	Three quarters sign	$^3/_4$
244		Paragraph symbol	¶
245		Section symbol	§
246	: -	Division sign	÷
247	, ,	Cedilla accent	̧
248	^ 0	Degree symbol	°
249		Umlaut accent	··
250	^ .	Center dot	·
251	^ 1	One superscript	^{1}
252	^ 3	Three superscript	^{3}
253	^ 2	Two superscript	^{2}
254		Square bullet	■
255		Null	

Group 1

This section describes the Group 1 LMBCS characters.

LMBCS code	Key code	Compose sequence	Description	Character
256	(000)		Null	
257	(001)		Smiling face	☺
258	(002)		Smiling face, reversed	☻
259	(003)		Heart suit symbol	♥
260	(004)		Diamond suit symbol	♦
261	(005)		Club suit symbol	♣
262	(006)		Spade suit symbol	♠
263	(007)		Bullet	●
264	(008)		Bullet, reversed	◘
265	(009)		Open circle	○
266	(010)		Open circle, reversed	◙
267	(011)		Male symbol	♂
268	(012)		Female symbol	♀
269	(013)		Musical note	♪
270	(014)		Double musical note	♫
271	(015)		Sun symbol	☼
272	(016)		Forward arrow indicator	►
273	(017)		Back arrow indicator	◄
274	(018)		Up-down arrow	↕
275	(019)		Double exclamation points	‼
276	(020)	!p or !P	Paragraph symbol	¶
277	(021)	SO so S0 or s0	Section symbol	§
278	(022)		Solid horizontal rectangle	—
279	(023)		Up-down arrow, perpendicular	↨
280	(024)		Up arrow	↑
281	(025)		Down arrow	↓
282	(026)		Right arrow	→
283	(027)	m g	Left arrow	←
284	(028)		Right angle symbol	∟
285	(029)		Left-right symbol	↔
286	(030)	b a	Solid triangle	▲
287	(031)	e a	Solid triangle inverted	▼
288	(032)	" <space>	Umlaut accent, uppercase	¨
289	(033)	~ <space>	Tilde accent, uppercase	~

Continued

LMBCS code	Key code	Compose sequence	Description	Character
290	(034)		Ring accent, uppercase	°
291	(035)	^ \<space\>	Circumflex accent, uppercase	^
292	(036)	' \<space\>	Grave accent, uppercase	'
293	(037)	' \<space\>	Acute accent, uppercase	'
294	(038)	„ ^	High double quotes, opening	„
295	(039)		High single quote, straight	'
296	(040)		Ellipsis	...
297	(041)		En mark	–
298	(042)		Em mark	—
299	(043)		Null	
300	(044)		Null	
301	(045)		Null	
302	(046)		Left angle parenthesis	<
303	(047)		Right angle parenthesis	>
304	(048)	\<space\> ”	Umlaut accent, lowercase	..
305	(049)	\<space\> ~	Tilde accent, lowercase	~
306	(050)		Ring accent, lowercase	°
307	(051)	\<space\> ^	Circumflex accent, lowercase	^
308	(052)	\<space\> '	Grave accent, lowercase	'
309	(053)	\<space\> '	Acute accent, lowercase	'
310	(054)	”v	Low double quotes, closing	„
311	(055)		Low single quote, closing	‚
312	(056)		High double quotes, closing	”
313	(057)	_ \<space\>	Underscore, heavy	—
314	(058)		Null	
315	(059)		Null	
316	(060)		Null	
317	(061)		Null	
318	(062)		Null	
319	(063)		Null	
320	(064)	O E	OE ligature, uppercase	Œ
321	(065)	o e	oe ligature, lowercase	œ
322	(066)	Y ”	Y umlaut, uppercase	Ÿ
323	(067)		Null	
324	(068)		Null	
325	(069)		Null	
326	(070)		Left box side, double joins single	╞
327	(071)		Left box side, single joins double	╟

Continued

LMBCS code	Key code	Compose sequence	Description	Character
328	(072)		Solid fill character, left half	▌
329	(073)		Solid fill character, right half	▐
330	(074)		Null	
331	(075)		Null	
332	(076)		Null	
333	(077)		Null	
334	(078)		Null	
335	(079)		Null	
336	(080)		Bottom box side, double joins single	╨
337	(081)		Top box side, single joins double	╤
338	(082)		Top box side, double joins single	╥
339	(083)		Bottom single left double box corner	╙
340	(084)		Bottom double left single box corner	╘
341	(085)		Top double left single box corner	╒
342	(086)		Top single left double box corner	╓
343	(087)		Center box intersection, vertical double	╫
344	(088)		Center box intersection, horizontal double	╪
345	(089)		Right box side, double joins single	╡
346	(090)		Right box side, single joins double	╢
347	(091)		Top single right double box corner	╖
348	(092)		Top double right single box corner	╕
349	(093)		Bottom single right double box corner	╜
350	(094)		Bottom double right single box corner	╛
351	(095)		Bottom box side, single joins double	╧
352	(096)	i j	ij ligature, lowercase	ij
353	(097)	I J	IJ ligature, uppercase	IJ
354	(098)	f i	fi ligature, lowercase	fi
355	(099)	f l	Fl ligature, lowercase	fl
356	(100)	' n	n comma, lowercase	'n
357	(101)	l .	l bullet, lowercase	l·
358	(102)	L .	L bullet, uppercase	L·
359	(103)		Null	
360	(104)		Null	
361	(105)		Null	
362	(106)		Null	
363	(107)		Null	

Continued

LMBCS code	Key code	Compose sequence	Description	Character
364	(108)		Null	
365	(109)		Null	
366	(110)		Null	
367	(111)		Null	
368	(112)		Single dagger symbol	†
369	(113)		Double dagger symbol	‡
370	(114)		Null	
371	(115)		Null	
372	(116)		Null	
373	(117)		Null	
374	(118)	**T M T m** or **t m**	Trademark symbol	™
375	(119)	**l r**	Liter symbol	ℓ
376	(120)		Null	
377	(121)		Null	
378	(122)		Null	
379	(123)		Null	
380	(124)	**K R K r** or **k r**	Krone sign	Kr
381	(125)	**- [**	Start of line symbol	⁻
382	(126)	**L I L i** or **l i**	Lira sign	₤
383	(127)	**P T P t** or **p t**	Peseta sign	Pt

Note　LMBCS codes 384 through 511 duplicate LMBCS codes 128 through 255, for use with code groups of other countries. Refer to LMBCS codes 128 through 255 in the Group 0 table starting on page 343 for a list of these characters.

B

Using Memory Efficiently

Many factors affect the amount of memory available to 1-2-3 and the amount of memory 1-2-3 uses. Some important factors are the type and amount of memory on your system, how you configure your system's memory for Windows, other programs in memory, and how you structure your files. This appendix describes how 1-2-3 uses memory and ways you can conserve memory.

Note For information about how to configure your system's memory for Windows, see your Windows documentation.

How 1-2-3 allocates memory

Knowing how 1-2-3 allocates memory helps you conserve memory when setting up files and entering data. When you enter data in a file, 1-2-3 uses memory to track information about the file. For example, 1-2-3 keeps track of all cells containing data.

To make processing faster and more efficient, 1-2-3 divides each column into groups of 8 cells. When you enter data in any of the 8 cells in a group, 1-2-3 prepares each cell in the group to receive data. This is called **opening** a cell.

1-2-3 also divides columns into larger sections of 512 cells each. Within each section, 1-2-3 opens the cells between the top and bottom entries. For example, if you enter data in A1 and A512, 1-2-3 opens A1..A512. However, if you make entries in A1 and A513, 1-2-3 opens only A1..A8 and A513..A520, not the cells in between, because A1 and A513 are in different 512-cell sections.

Note In some cases, opening cells takes more memory than stated above. For instance, the first entry you make in a worksheet takes approximately 30 extra bytes because 1-2-3 creates a table to track your future entries.

Regaining memory

When you start to run out of memory on your computer, processing slows down noticeably. To speed up processing and avoid running out of memory, you can do the following:

- Structure your files for efficient memory use.
- Eliminate blocks of unusable memory.
- Remove unneeded worksheet entries and settings.
- Consolidate worksheets and files.
- Remove unneeded formulas.
- Turn off Undo.

If you run out of memory, you may not be able to complete your last command or entry. If there are active files you want to save, close other open windows, and then try to save the files. You can also gain memory by removing other programs from memory, and by closing any files you're not working in.

Structuring files efficiently

The easiest way to use memory efficiently in 1-2-3 is to keep data areas as close together as possible. Enter your data in focused areas of the worksheet rather than scattering it all over the worksheet and the file.

For example, entering data in cells A1 and A513 uses more memory than entering the same data in cells A1 and A2 because 1-2-3 allocates memory in sections of 512 cells.

In addition, to structure your files efficiently, you can:

- Insert additional rows of data rather than additional columns.

  1-2-3 allocates additional memory in vertical blocks.

- Use fewer worksheets.

  Entering data in additional worksheets uses more memory. It's more efficient to enter data in blank areas of existing worksheets rather than adding new worksheets.

Eliminating blocks of unusable memory

As you build files, memory can fragment into small blocks of unused memory surrounded by large blocks of used memory. Sometimes the blocks of unused memory are too small for 1-2-3 to use. This can happen when you're first building a spreadsheet and making many changes, such as adding different styles and fonts.

The surest way to regain fragmented memory is to save and close your files, exit 1-2-3, then restart 1-2-3, and open your files again. Saving the file you're working on, closing it, and reopening it without exiting 1-2-3 can also eliminate fragmented memory. When you read a file back into memory, 1-2-3 places the entire file in one large block of memory, if possible, consolidating the small blocks of unusable memory.

Removing unneeded data and settings

Cells that contain unnecessary data or settings waste memory. You can restore this memory by finding and removing the unneeded data or settings.

To find unneeded data or settings, first find the active area of each worksheet (the rectangular area between the top left entry and the bottom right entry) by pressing END HOME. If the active area is bigger than you expected, it probably contains unneeded data or settings. You can use END CTRL+HOME to find the active area of a multiple-sheet file.

To remove unneeded data and settings:

- Select only the data you need, choose File Save As and use the "Selected range only" option to save this data to a new file. Then delete the old file.

- Select unneeded data, styles, charts, and other drawn objects, and choose Edit Clear to delete them.

- Select entire columns, rows, and worksheets containing unneeded data or settings, and choose Edit Delete to delete them.

Consolidating worksheets and files

Every worksheet and file containing data requires memory. If you need more memory, consolidate your data into fewer worksheets and fewer files. Then delete the unneeded worksheets and files.

Open windows also use substantial amounts of memory, even if you reduce the windows to icons. To conserve memory, close any windows you're not using.

Removing unneeded formulas

Formulas use more memory than their results. If your file includes formulas and you need only the results, you can save memory by converting the formulas to values.

Use Tools Audit to find all formulas in the current file or in all active files. For more information, see page 196.

To convert formulas to values

1. Select the range containing the formulas.
2. Choose Edit Cut.
3. Choose Edit Paste Special.
4. Select Formulas as values.
5. Choose OK.

Turning off Undo

When Undo is turned on, the amount of memory available can vary significantly after each command. If you erase a large range, for example, 1-2-3 uses lots of memory to store the range for Undo. If you're running out of memory, choose Tools User Setup and deselect Undo.

Hard disk storage

Another memory constraint is the amount of hard disk space available to 1-2-3. Windows uses space on the hard disk for a **swap file**. This is a hidden file that reserves hard disk space for Windows to use when it gets low on memory. You can configure the swap file to give 1-2-3 more space on your hard disk. For information about configuring the Windows swap file, see your Windows documentation.

Insufficient space problems can also occur when you put too many files on your hard disk. If you try to write data to a filled hard disk, Windows returns a message saying the disk is full and asking you to choose another drive for the file, either a disk drive or another hard disk partition.

To avoid running out of hard disk space, use the Windows File Manager to delete files you no longer need. Obsolete files on the hard disk take up space that you can use to store current files. If you want to keep obsolete files, copy them to floppy disks before deleting them from the hard disk.

C

Formulas for @Functions

This appendix lists the formulas that 1-2-3 uses to calculate some statistical and financial @functions.

? Help For complete information about each @function, including calculation methods and examples, refer to @Function Help. Search on "@Functions" in Help, and select the topic "@Functions."

@Function and Formula		*Variables*
@ACCRUED	Standard and short coupon formula: $$ai = p * \frac{r}{m} * \frac{a}{nl}$$ Long coupon formula: $$ai = p * \frac{r}{m} * \sum_{i=1}^{nc} \frac{a_i}{nl_i}$$	p = par value r = annual coupon rate m = coupons per year a = accrued days a_i = number of accrued days in the ith quasi-coupon period nl = number of days in quasi-coupon period nl_i = number of days in the ith quasi-coupon period nc = number of whole or partial coupons i = current iteration (1 through nc)
@CTERM	$$\frac{\ln(fv/pv)}{\ln(1 + int)}$$	fv = future value pv = present value int = interest rate $\ln$ = natural logarithm

Continued

@Function and Formula	Variables
@DB $$(1 - rate)^{(p-1)} * (rate) * c$$ where $rate = 1 - \left(\dfrac{s}{c}\right)^{\frac{1}{l}}$	c = amount paid for asset s = estimated value of asset and end of its life l = number of periods to depreciate asset to its salvage value p = time period for which you want to find depreciation
@DDB $$\dfrac{(bv * 2)}{n}$$	bv = book value in that period n = life of the asset
@DSTD $$\sqrt{\dfrac{\sum (v_i - avg)^2}{n}}$$	n = number of values in *field* v_i = the *i*th value in *field* avg = average of values in *field*
@DSTDS $$\sqrt{\dfrac{\sum (v_i - avg)^2}{n - 1}}$$	n = number of values in *field* v_i = the *i*th value in *field* avg = average of values in *field*
@DVAR $$\dfrac{\sum (v_i - avg)^2}{n}$$	n = number of values in *field* v_i = the *i*th value in *field* avg = average of values in *field*
@DVARS $$\dfrac{\sum (v_i - avg)^2}{(n - 1)}$$	n = number of values in *field* v_i = the *i*th value in *field* avg = average of values in *field*
@FV $$pmt * \dfrac{(1 + int)^n - 1}{int}$$	pmt = periodic payment int = periodic interest rate n = number of periods

Continued

@Function and Formula	Variables
@FVAL Ordinary annuity: $$fv = \left(pmt * \frac{(1 + i)^n - 1}{i} \right) + pv * (1 + i)^n$$ Annuity due: $$fv = \left(pmt * \frac{(1 + i)^n - 1}{i} \right) * (1 + i) + pv * (1 + i)^n$$	fv = future value pmt = payments i = interest n = term pv = present value
@IRATE Ordinary annuity: $$pv * (1 + i)^n + pmt * \left(\frac{(1 + i)^n - 1}{i} \right) - fv = 0$$ Annuity due: $$pv * (1 + i)^n + pmt(1 + i) * \left(\frac{(1 + i)^n - 1}{i} \right) - fv = 0$$	pmt = amount of periodic payment pv = value of the investment fv = future value of the investment i = interest
@MIRR $$\left(\frac{- @NPV(ir, ci) * (1 + ir)^n}{@NPV(if, co) * (1 + if)} \right)^{\frac{1}{n-1}} - 1$$	ir = reinvestment interest rate ci = set of cash inflows if = finance interest rate co = set of cash outflows n = total number of flows
@NPV $$\sum_{i=1}^{n} \frac{v_i}{(1 + int)^i}$$	$v_i...v_n$ = series of cash flows in range int = interest rate n = number of cash flows i = current iteration (1 through n)
@PMT $$prin * \frac{int}{1 - (int + 1)^{-n}}$$	$prin$ = principal int = periodic interest rate n = term
@PMTC $$\frac{prin}{1 - (int^{-n})} * (int - 1)$$ where $int = \left(\frac{1 + interest}{2} \right)^{\frac{1}{6}}$	$prin$ = principal n = term

Continued

@Function and Formula	Variables
@PRICE Given yield with one coupon or less to redemption: $$\left[\frac{rv + \frac{100 * r}{m}}{1 + \left(\frac{dsr}{e} * \frac{y}{m}\right)}\right] - \left[\frac{a}{e} * \frac{100 * r}{m}\right]$$ Given yield with more than one coupon to redemption: $$\left[\frac{rv}{\left(1 + \frac{y}{m}\right)^{n-1+\frac{dsc}{e}}}\right] + \left[\sum_{k=1}^{n} \frac{100 * \frac{r}{m}}{\left(1 + \frac{y}{m}\right)^{k-1+\frac{dsc}{e}}}\right] - \left[100 * \frac{r}{m} * \frac{a}{e}\right]$$	p = price per \$100 par value rv = redemption value per \$100 par value n = number of whole and partial coupons between settlement and maturity dsc = number of days of settlement to next coupon dsr = number of days from settlement to redemption e = number of days in coupon period m = number of periods per year a = number of days from coupon to settlement r = annual interest rate y = yield k = current iteration (1 through n)
@PV $$pmt * \frac{1 - (1 + int)^{-n}}{int}$$	pmt = periodic payment int = periodic interest rate n = term
@RATE $$\left(\frac{fv}{pv}\right)^{1/n} - 1$$	fv = future value pv = present value n = term
@SLN $$\frac{(c - s)}{n}$$	c = cost of the asset s = salvage value of the asset n = useful life of the asset
@STD $$\sqrt{\frac{\sum(v_i - avg)^2}{n}}$$	n = number of items in list v_i = the ith value in list avg = average of values in list

Continued

@Function and Formula	Variables
@STDS $$\sqrt{\dfrac{\sum (v_i - avg)^2}{n - 1}}$$	n = number of items in list v_i = the ith value in *list* avg = average of values in *list*
@SYD $$\dfrac{(c - s) * (n - p + 1)}{(n * (n + 1)/2)}$$	c = cost of the asset s = salvage value of the asset p = period for which depreciation is being calculated n = calculated useful life of the asset
@TERM $$\dfrac{\ln(1 + (fv * int/pmt))}{\ln(1 + int)}$$	pmt = periodic payment fv = future value int = periodic interest rate $\ln$ = natural logarithm
@VAR $$\dfrac{\sum (v_i - avg)^2}{n}$$	n = number of values in list v_i = the ith value in *list* avg = average of values in *list*
@VARS $$\dfrac{\sum (v_i - avg)^2}{(n - 1)}$$	n = number of values in list v_i = the ith value in *list* avg = average of values in *list*

Continued

@Function and Formula	Variables
@VDB Double-declining balance depreciation: $$\frac{(bv * d)}{n}$$ Straight-line depreciation: $$\frac{(bv - s)}{r}$$	bv = book value in that period d = percentage of straight-line depreciation n = useful life of the asset s = salvage value of the asset r = remaining useful life of the asset
@YIELD Given price with one coupon or less to redemption: $$\left[\frac{\left(\frac{rv}{100} * \frac{r}{m}\right) - \left(\frac{p}{100} + \left(\frac{a}{e} * \frac{r}{m}\right)\right)}{\left(\frac{p}{100} + \left(\frac{a}{e} * \frac{r}{m}\right)\right)}\right] * \left[\frac{m * e}{dsr}\right]$$	p = price per \$100 par value rv = redemption value per \$100 par value dsr = number of days from settlement to redemption e = number of days in coupon period m = number of coupons per year a = number of days from coupon to settlement r = annual interest rate

Index

Note Page numbers in **bold** refer to definitions.

Symbols

& (ampersand), 92
<< >> (angle brackets), 99, 308
' (apostrophe), 70, 137
> (arrowhead), 28
* (asterisk), 93, 125, 135, 146, 273
@ (at sign), 38, 94, 107, 136
\ (backslash), 315
{ } (braces), 38, 311
[] (brackets), 108, 307
^ (caret), 70, 93, 137
: (colon), 39, 122, 268
, (comma), 108, 268, 310
$ (dollar sign), 68, 94, 101
... (ellipsis), 28
= (equal sign), 95
! (exclamation point), 122, 268
> (greater-than symbol), 93
< (less-than symbol), 39, 93
– (minus sign), 93, 94
(number sign), 94, 268
( ) (parentheses), 94, 101, **109**
. (period), 94, 108, 122, 268, 310
+ (plus sign), 93, 94, 136
??? (question marks), 122, 273
" " (quotation marks), 70, 94, 109, 307
; (semicolon), 108, 307, 310
/ (slash), 39, 70, 93
~ (tilde), 268. *See also* **Help***
| (vertical bar), 67, 137, 180

A

Absolute references in formulas, **101**, 102–103
Accelerator keys. *See* Keyboard shortcuts
Active file, **43**
Active window, 11, 20

Add-ins. *See* **Help***
Adding
  See also Creating; Inserting
  borders and frames, 120, 186
  chart titles and notes, 166
  colors, 119, 187
  columns, 81–84
  designer frames, 120, **186**
  drawn objects, 177
  fields to query tables, 279
  @functions to @Function menu, 112
  headers and footers, 136
  page breaks, 137–139
  print titles, 139–140
  rows, 81–84
  SmartIcons to an icon set, 297
  units titles, chart, 170
  worksheets, 14, 45–46
Addresses
  cell, 14, **59**, 94
  in formulas, 97
  range, 60
Adjustable cells, Solver, **233**
Adjusting addresses, 101
Aggregate columns. *See* **Help***
Alias, field name. *See* **Help***
Aligning data, 121–123
  labels and values, 69
Alphabetizing. *See* Sorting.
Ampersand (&) in text formulas, 92
Analyzing data
  frequency distributions, **205**
  matrixes, **211**
  regressions, **207**
Analyzing formulas
  circular references, 199–201
  dependents, 198

file links, 202
  precedents, 197
Anchoring drawn objects.
    See Fastening drawn objects
#AND#, logical operator
  in criteria, 271
  in formulas, 92
  in macros, 309
Angle brackets (<< >>) in file
    references, 99, 308
Answers and attempts, Solver,
    240–243
Apostrophe ('), 70, 137
Appending records to database
    tables, 284
Applications, client and server, 329
Arcs, creating, 178
Area charts, **158**
Argument separators, **108**, 307, 310
    See also **Help***
Arguments
  enclosing in quotation marks, 109
  in @functions, **108**
  for individual @functions, 113
    See also **Help***
  in macro commands, **307**, 311
  types of, 109, 307
Arithmetic operators, **93**
Arranging drawn objects, 188–192
Arrow keys, 49
  and entering data, 67–68
  selecting ranges with, 61
Arrows, creating, 178
Assigning
  See also Adding
  macros to buttons, 317–319
  macros to SmartIcons, 300–301
Assumptions. *See* Versions.

F

---

* Choose Help Search from the 1-2-3 menu and type the index topic.

* Choose Help Search from the 1-2-3 menu and type the index topic.

Lotus 1-2-3 Release 4 for Windows
Reader Comment Form

Once you're familiar with 1-2-3 Release 4 for Windows, please fill out both sides of this form and mail it to:

Lotus Development Corporation
55 Cambridge Parkway
Cambridge, MA 02142
Attention: 1-2-3 for Windows Documentation Dept.

Your name and address:

_____

_____

_____

_____

Check the box that best describes your rating for each part of the documentation set:

Documentation	Excellent	Very good	Good	Fair	Poor	Didn't use
User's Guide						
What's New						
DataLens Drivers for 1-2-3						
Online Help						
Online Tutorial						
Guided Tour						
Network Administrator's Guide						

Are you
- ☐ A new 1-2-3 user
- ☐ Familiar with 1-2-3

Check your level of computer knowledge
- ☐ Beginner
- ☐ Intermediate
- ☐ Advanced

1. Are there sections of the documentation you especially like?
Why? _____
_____
_____
_____
_____

2. Are there topics left out or requiring more explanation?
Why? _____
_____
_____
_____
_____

3. Did you find errors in the documentation?
Where? _____
_____
_____
_____
_____

4. What part of the documentation did you use most to learn the program?
Why? _____
_____
_____
_____
_____

5. What books or online documentation would you add to the documentation set?
Why? _____
_____
_____
_____
_____

6. Other comments? _____
_____
_____
_____
_____

Thank you for completing this form. Your comments will help us improve our documentation.